Innovative Voices
in Education

Innovative Voices in Education

Engaging Diverse Communities

Eileen Gale Kugler
Executive Editor

ROWMAN & LITTLEFIELD EDUCATION

A division of

ROWMAN & LITTLEFIELD PUBLISHERS, INC.
Lanham • New York • Toronto • Plymouth, UK

Published by Rowman & Littlefield Education
A division of Rowman & Littlefield Publishers, Inc.
A wholly owned subsidiary of The Rowman & Littlefield Publishing Group, Inc.
4501 Forbes Boulevard, Suite 200, Lanham, Maryland 20706
http://www.rowmaneducation.com

Estover Road, Plymouth PL6 7PY, United Kingdom

British Library Cataloguing in Publication Information Available

Library of Congress Cataloging-in-Publication Data

Kugler, Eileen Gale, 1950-
  Innovative voices in education : engaging diverse communities / Eileen Kugler.
    p. cm.
  Summary: "Diverse schools offer enriched academic and social environments, as students and families of different backgrounds and experiences provide a vibrant mosaic of insights, perspectives, and skills. This book highlights stories from around the world, as innovative teachers, educational leaders, and community activists passionately share personal accounts of their successes, challenges, and lessons learned"— Provided by publisher.
  Includes bibliographical references and index.
  ISBN 978-1-61048-539-5 (hardback) — ISBN 978-1-61048-540-1 (paper) — ISBN 978-1-61048-541-8 (ebook)
  1. Children of minorities—Education—United States. 2. Children of immigrants—Education—United States. 3. Multicultural education—United States. I. Title.
  LC3731.K84 2012
  370.1170973—dc23
                              2011029001

∞ ™ The paper used in this publication meets the minimum requirements of American National Standard for Information Sciences—Permanence of Paper for Printed Library Materials, ANSI/NISO Z39.48-1992.

Printed in the United States of America

To Joyce Nyati, a South African grandmother
lovingly raising her grandchildren with few resources,
whose wisdom inspires me daily.

and

To my parents Edith and Milton Gale,
whose encouragement and pride were a priceless gift.

Contents

COURAGEOUS LEADERS

COMMUNITY: THE VILLAGE IT TAKES

GLOBAL PERSPECTIVES

Foreword

Edwin C. Darden

Right before our eyes, the nature of K–12 public education in the United States is experiencing a tectonic shift. Few people recognize it because, unlike an earthquake, this change is subtle and pervasive.

As someone who has written about, worked on, lived, and admired racial and ethnic diversity for more than 30 years, I see schools returning to their maiden mission of building community, citizenship, and civic harmony—in addition to building strong academic skills and imaginative minds. The reality is that public schools have always represented the crossroads of America, serving as a rallying point that crashes through income differences, language barriers, geographic perspectives, and more. Schools serve as a microcosm of society, a patriotic institution that glues our fragile democracy together.

Lately, however, schools are too often where cultural battles are waged. Organizations and individuals with sharply different visions of what the United States should be arrive at the schoolhouse gate with agenda in hand, declaring that "children are our future," and then seek to create policies, practices, and beliefs that will shape students in their image.

But there is an alternative, as this book demonstrates. *Innovative Voices in Education: Engaging Diverse Communities* is a triumph because it heralds how diverse students, educators, parents, and communities are deeply interdependent. Various authors with different perspectives suggest ways to build unity, how to understand different perspectives, and how to mine diversity as a national asset that strengthens our individuality while binding us together in a human tapestry.

The voices of the authors are clear, strong, and honest. In every chapter they remain student-focused, encouraging schools to be a place where people are more open-minded and kinder and who create a sense of connectedness that goes beyond mere words and results in students of all backgrounds who are more successful in school and in life. This eloquent rendition powerfully makes the case that we have little to fear and everything to learn from "the Other" and stresses our shared pursuit of the American dream.

It provides specific examples of how the fabulous mix of race, ethnicity, and culture create rich experiences that dramatically enhance book-learning. The compilation alternates smartly between scholarly social science research, practical classroom strategies, common-sense advice, on the one hand, and casual, everyday storytelling.

Crafting solutions that build understanding among diverse students and families will undoubtedly be one of the top issues that define an effective free, public education in this new century. The challenge is to educate kids and welcome families with extremely different backgrounds and who therefore may see the world, themselves, and their peers with dissimilar eyes. Educators, students, parents, and communities will all feel the aftershocks as they discover that what once seemed comfortable and easy is no longer satisfying. Their new normal becomes a quest for greater understanding beyond their limited personal experiences.

It does not matter where you live. A 2011 census analysis showed that 22 of the 100 largest urban regions are now "majority minority." Of those same 100, about 36 feature ethnic mosaic suburbs where at least 35% of the non-white population resides. Similarly, Hispanic/Latino immigrants are increasingly drawn to rural areas seeking job opportunities, and that influx transforms communities and creates an unprecedented and pressing need for diverse services.

Innovative Voices in Education explains the steps needed to achieve successful diversity: respectful schools, powerful and caring teachers, courageous leaders, a true community, and a multicultural and global perspective. The book acknowledges how tough it is to wrestle peaceful coexistence from the clashing cultures and values that converge in public schools. Still, the contents contain sparkling insights and practical advice. For example, two immigrant young people talk candidly about their identity development and balancing U.S. and country-of-birth cultures while attending a suburban high school. That kind of innovative voice is rarely heard. Teachers talk about strategies they developed to help students move beyond stereotypes of themselves and peers. That instructional gift is not an add-on to their teaching but rather a critical piece of their responsibilities to inspire bright minds. Principals reveal their successes—and frustrations—as they lead schools where diversity is the mainstream as well as schools where students of color have been marginalized and underserved. These voices are honest, informative, and thought-provoking

Perhaps timing is the key. The U.S. Supreme Court and federal courts are essentially closing the door to legal diversity efforts. Judges are saying that the U.S. Constitution is a barrier to official efforts to defeat the historic problem of segregated neighborhoods. But school districts are not handcuffed by courts that insist upon a crimped interpretation of the common good. Locating new school buildings so that the attendance zone pulls from different racial ethnic neighborhoods, creating magnet schools, relying on socioeconomic status for school assignments, and a roster of other techniques are all legitimate and legally approved ways for leaders to demonstrate how diversity is a priority. While the ideal student mix cannot be mandated by law, it can be implemented voluntarily. Therefore, it is all the more important for school officials, communities, and policy makers to willingly and intentionally seize the lifelong virtues of diverse classrooms.

This book strikes the right chords, telling just the right stories in a logical and compelling way. Embracing diversity requires nothing less. Now, it is up to readers to not only listen to the wisdom contained in these pages but heed the call.

Edwin C. Darden, J.D
President, Education Advocacy Firm, Inc.
Springfield, Virginia

Edwin C. Darden is President of the Education Law Association. He is director of Education Law and Policy for Appleseed, a non-profit legal justice center, where he focuses on parent involvement issues and gaining greater academic opportunities for students attending high-poverty schools. Darden is interracially married, a past President of the Interracial Family Circle of Washington, D.C., Maryland, and Virginia, and former Vice President of the National Association of Multi-Ethnic Americans. In his earlier role with the National School Boards Association he studied and wrote about the legal issues involved when schools assign students to maximize the benefits of racial and ethnic diversity. Darden's commentaries have been published in the New York Times, the Washington Post, and the NAACP magazine, Crisis. He has appeared on NPR, CNN, Fox, and national newscasts.

Preface

Eileen Gale Kugler

A child sits in class, pencil in hand. What does the teacher know about him, beyond the few words he has uttered in class? Who is this child? Is he my child, or your child, or one of "those kids" from "those families"?

Every human being wants to feel valued, to count, to matter. It is the keystone that enables them to develop their unique skills and abilities. Unfortunately, not all children are led to believe they have value, in the very place where they should be budding and blossoming. In many classrooms, the worth of some children is discounted, consciously or unconsciously. Those students aren't the ones who are preordained to be the high achievers. They live in the shadows, no one bothering to get to know who they really are.

The result is that far too many students of color, immigrants, and students in poverty are unknown quantities at school. They disconnect from their education, underachieve, and drop out of high school, let alone go on to post-secondary education. This under-performance by so many of our youth impacts not only them and their families, but all of us. In today's global community, we cannot afford to squander resources, particularly precious human resources.

To be successful in school and in life, it is vital for students to connect personally with school. They must believe that they and their families have value there. Schools leaders and faculty must gain insight into the students at every desk, recognize their strengths and the challenges they face. The educators must not only state that their goal is "achievement for all," but they must authentically believe it and take the actions that will create learning environments where students of every background can be successful and families are valued as allies in that endeavor.

The good news is that there are schools and communities that are doing just that. Many of these remain under the radar. There are hard-working teachers breaking new ground, partnering with parents, as they challenge themselves to provide each child the opportunity and the resources to succeed. There are courageous principals, forging new directions and galvanizing staffs to ensure their schools are places where children of all backgrounds are flourishing and their families are engaged. And there are community trailblazers who are collaborators in student success, empowering the entire family.

This book brings their stories into the open. In my work strengthening diverse schools over the past decade, I have worked with some extraordinary individuals doing groundbreaking work. "Have you documented what you are doing?" I often ask, asserting, "Others need to know about what is going on here." The response is usually eyes rolling, as the educator gets back to the work at hand. It is clear they feel they cannot take time away from the challenging and significant work to figure out where and how to write about it. I have to respect that.

And yet, I feel there is innovative work that needs to be documented. There are insights and lessons learned that need to be shared. I finally decided I had to play a role in this myself. I went to several colleagues around the country and asked if they would write one chapter for a book if I handle all the arrangements. The response was overwhelmingly positive. I wanted this book to resonate with their voices, to tell their stories. I said I would work with authors on refining the chapters, but it would be their tales to tell. Our collaborative vision for this book began.

That's when the book began a life of its own. Other educators shared stories about extraordinary efforts around the country that needed to be a part of this book. I met several educators through education Twitter Chats, interactive dialogues on Twitter. Colleagues and friends suggested educators in other countries with their own insights into this issue, and the book soon had an international perspective. The next thing I knew, there were 17 chapters exploring work in California, Maryland, Minnesota, New York, Texas, and Virginia, as well as Canada, Australia, the United Kingdom and Pakistan.

I could not be prouder of this book. It shines a light on wide-ranging innovative work and insights. It provides valuable background for anyone seeking to successfully engage diverse students and families. Each chapter has the unique voice and perspective of the author. One of the most rewarding aspects has been that many of the chapter authors, including myself, found the process of writing our chapters brought clarity to our thinking about the work. As we worked to create chapters in direct language that made the insights and lessons learned accessible to anyone who cares about education, we had to reach deep within ourselves to determine *what did I really mean by that.*

Very few of these authors have published before, yet their passion for their work makes their chapters sing. Their words will engage you, challenge you, inform you, and most of all inspire you.

You'll read about the foundations of building respectful schools: *Howie Schaeffer*, a diversity and inclusion consultant, writes an impassioned commentary about the need to close "the culture gap" in our schools, reimagining and reinvesting in public education in a framework of inclusivity for all; College students *Waliha Gani* and *Shriya Adhikary* offer a rare glimpse into the day-to-day life of immigrant students, sharing their experiences balancing the contrasting worlds of American high school with the expectations of their own cultural backgrounds; My own chapter highlights the importance of examining and breaking through assumptions that derive from our own individual culture, a complex web of race, ethnicity, religion, home life and experiences.

You'll read about the special connections that teachers have with their students—*Jioanna Carjuzaa* shares her university work with teacher candidates as they learn to create respectful inclusive classrooms, fulfilling the mandate of Montana's landmark Indian Education for All Act that requires teaching of American Indian history and culture across the curriculum in every class; *Karyn Keenan*, a Chicago elementary teacher, describes the creative ways she brings out students' own stories to help them understand themselves and their peers; *Graciela Rosas*, a middle-school teacher in San Diego, shares the program she developed for long-term English Language Learners that builds literacy in both English and Spanish, building self-esteem along the way; *Sara Kugler* describes the effort in her Brooklyn elementary school that helped her students critically analyze the messages of stereotypes around them, giving them the tools to identify, deconstruct and imagine new messages; *Ashley Harris* takes us on her journey from business professional to a passionate teacher trainer at a highly successful public charter school system in her native Houston.

You'll read the story of courageous educational leaders: *Stacie Stanley* recounts the joys and challenges as a new principal fighting for the needs of an increasing minority population in a school that has long been majority white middle-class; *Nardos King*, the principal of a large diverse high school, describes programs she instituted that forged meaningful teacher-student relationships to enhance learning, particularly for students who sometimes "fall through the cracks;" *Roni Silverstein*, an experienced principal and central office leader, documents the importance of changing both faculty beliefs and actions simultaneously to see equitable improvements in student achievement.

You'll read insights and innovations about the broader community's role in education: *Young-chan Han*, a state department of education official, presents her groundbreaking new model, "The Four Stages of Immigrant Parent Involvement," that helps educators and community members understand the needs and experiences of immigrant families; *Andrea Sobel and Debra Fulcher*, educational consultants, describe the effectiveness of Neighborhood School Readiness Teams, a collaboration among schools, families, preschool educators and the broader community, that helps students enter kindergarten "ready to learn;" *Jesse Bethke Gomez,* leader of a non-profit providing health and human services for Latino families, highlights culturally competent efforts by a school district, a large corporation and his own organization to support immigrant families so they can express and nurture their aspirational hopes for their children.

You'll read perspectives of innovative educators in other parts of the world: *Amineh Ahmed Hoti*, a Pakistani educator, describes the power of a cutting-edge learning resource developed in the U.K., now used around the world, to help students explore and break down stereotypes of "The Other"; *Jeff Scanlan*, a life-long educator in Australia, movingly reflects on the lessons learned from his diverse students over several decades; *Sean Grainger*, a Canadian teacher and administrator, presents a thoughtful discourse on moving from multiculturalism to interculturalism, developing interdependent learners who communicate and learn from people of other cultures.

There are many valuable insights and resources in this chapter that will inform and guide educators and community leaders in increasing their effectiveness in engaging students and families of diverse backgrounds. Every child is our child; every family part of our community. Just ask these innovative educators.

Acknowledgments

What an honor it has been to work with the extraordinary contributors to this book. Their commitment to students, families, and society is powerful. I learned so much from each of them.

As I finished reading each chapter, I would remark to my husband, "This is an amazing chapter," to which he would respond with a smile, "You said that about the last one." And in fact, I had said that, and I would say it again and again.

The chapter authors were unfailingly supportive of this project, even with their incredibly busy lives. They diligently met deadlines and responded to queries with thoughtful interchanges. What a meaningful collaborative effort this was for all of us. I know I learned a great deal.

Another appreciative thank you goes to Jocelyn Meltzer, a talented editor and teacher of English Language Learners, who stepped in to provide invaluable assistance during the last phase of the book. She was a final reader for each chapter, providing insights that greatly improved the book. She helped keep things organized at a point at which keeping details straight for 17 chapters was a quite a feat.

I need to acknowledge another "partner" in this international work. This project was made possible through the wonders of modern communication tools. I was awestruck at times that I could reach Amineh Hoti in Pakistan as easily as Nardos King who works a few miles away. I credit Twitter (I'm @embracediversiT) with helping me find two other extraordinary authors, Sean Grainger (@graingered) and Karyn Keenan (@KarynTeaches).

On a personal level, I thank individuals who recommended potential chapter authors. In particular, I thank Dr. Akbar Ahmed for letting me know about his daughter Dr. Amineh Ahmed Hoti's groundbreaking work in the U.K. and

Pakistan; Jennifer Abernethy and Neen James for putting me in touch with Neen's dad Jeff Scanlan, an Australian educator who truly touched my heart; Natasha Quiroga who connected me with Ashley Harris, a Houston educator with a powerful story to tell; and Alan Weintraut, an extraordinary teacher who has inspired many students himself, for connecting me to Waliha Gani and Shriya Adhikary, students whose brilliant narratives on the daily life of immigrant students will open many eyes. A story by reporter Emily Albert in VoicesofSanDiego.org alerted me to the innovative work of Graciela Rosas. No, not all stories about education in the media are negative!

I want to thank Tom Koerner, vice president and editorial director at Rowman & Littlefield Education, for his constant support of this project, as well as my work over the years. Tom "found" me in 2000 when I was leading a workshop at a national education conference and asked if I would be willing to write a book about my topic, the unique strengths of diverse schools. That conversation opened many doors for me, beginning with publication of *Debunking the Middle-Class Myth: Why Diverse Schools are Good for All Kids,* in fall 2002. Tom is one of the good guys who believes that a well-written book on a significant education issue does indeed serve our educational leaders, our teachers, our students, our families and our communities.

And, as always, I want to thank my family. My husband Larry is an unwavering presence in my life, and has been since we met in high school. A teacher, administrator, and now school-improvement consultant, Larry truly appreciates the opportunities he has had to change lives in his chosen profession. In the South African school where we volunteer together, the community honored him with the Xhosa name "Thando" or love, because "you love all of our children like they were your own." He is there whenever I need him, brainstorming ideas, commenting on a chapter, or just making dinner and making sure I take a break from writing and editing to eat hot food.

I thank my parents, Edith and Milton Gale for their unwavering support of my work and appreciation of its impact. They both passed away as this book was in production, and I believe it is part of the legacy they leave.

It is hard to describe how proud I am of my children, Sara and Alex, who inspire me daily. They see the world through a lens of respect for each individual they meet, and they continue to learn and grow. They challenge me with insights that push my own boundaries. They respect their parents and grandparents and yet are their own unique, wonderful, thinking selves. Love you guys.

Building Respectful Schools

Chapter 1

Closing the Culture Gap in Public Education: A Commentary

Howie Schaffer

E pluribus unum ("Out of many, one") is the Latin motto inscribed on the Seal of the United States. In too many diverse public schools, however, our differences have not been a source of solidarity, as envisioned by our democracy's founders. Rather, our diversity too often has led to exclusion from resources, opportunity, and equitable treatment.

Schools are clamoring to respond to the growing needs of an unprecedented population of new learners. Every day new refugees arrive not only from Mexico and Guatemala, but from Nepal, Pakistan, Bosnia, Rwanda, Timor and Iraq, among other new geographies. With this influx of new students, adding to the different races and cultures in our existing communities, comes increasing demands to respond to a myriad of cultural and ethnic worldviews. Schools must face the challenge of incorporating these learners into a system that values their unique skills and perspectives, to enhance education for every student.

This challenge is daunting. Disturbing differences in the rates of success of students from different backgrounds raise serious concerns not only for schools but for the social cohesion and economic competitiveness of our nation. Language barriers are only the tip of the iceberg leading to these gaps. Economic disadvantage, health disparities, lack of school readiness, parent isolation, hostile classrooms, and under-trained teachers all contribute.

We are all familiar with the handful of gaps that are trotted out to help explain unequal student success. The famous achievement gap underlies the widespread frustration at the difference between the unlimited learning potential of children from all backgrounds and the maddening variation of their test scores. We look to the funding gap. The parenting gap. The digital divide. The nutrition gap. Even the pre-natal care gap. These are all real contributors to educational inequity.

Now more than ever, we also see evidence of a culture gap in schools, which explains a significant barrier that students need to overcome on their journey toward equity of opportunity in schools. This barrier intersects with and impacts many of the others.

Many political and social worldviews compete in the massive marketplace of public education today. Two of the most battle-weary ideological positions are "multiculturalism" and "colorblindness," theories which have become oversimplified and polarized. It is hard for schools and educators to navigate between these poles in their efforts to create high-performance learning environments for all children. In a simplistic view of multiculturalism, schools believe that they must constantly recognize commonalities and differences among groups, leading to intense focus on particular groups who deserve extra attention. In contrast, colorblindness focuses on the belief that people are fundamentally the same. Some exponents of a colorblind view of society believe that racial categories should be ignored or avoided entirely, and that differences in identity should be considered unimportant.

The polarization and oversimplification of these political ideologies has created a false choice between attention to some students to the detriment of others, and political correctness that says we are all the same, devaluing the uniqueness of the individual. On the contrary, it is possible to create culturally competent schools that value the individual without sacrificing academic rigor for any group. In fact, when students of all backgrounds are able to be successful, every student benefits from a more vibrant, enriched learning environment.

Cultural competency is more than a simple set of "tips and techniques" for dealing with different kinds of people. Cultural competency in education requires well-implemented organizational policies, appropriately trained and skilled leaders and teachers, and specialized resources and technologies. Together they systematically anticipate, recognize, and respond to the varying expectations and needs of students and families from diverse backgrounds.

To develop this type of organizational culture is difficult and challenging. But if we are to live up to the dream of transformation offered by a high-quality public education then we must take steps to make this a reality in schools throughout the country. There is also a powerful bottom line. Cultural incompetence destroys the fragile trust between teachers and students that creates the necessary preconditions for learning and intellectual and social development. In our society at large, cultural incompetence costs hundreds of billions of dollars in lost productivity, innovation, and full economic participation by all of our citizens.

We have learned the lesson that a "melting pot" loses some of the unique flavors and tastes that went into it, and we are poorer for it. Today, we are a more vibrant nation because more groups of people are maintaining their cultural patterns in the mosaic of the new "American culture." We need culturally competent people and organizations. Simply put, they need to know and operate in accord with the understanding that human cultures are not right/wrong, better/worse, or virtuous/immoral. Cultural competency goes well beyond cultural awareness. It denotes an individual's ability to effectively interact with and among others whose values, behaviors and environments are different from one's own—through a profound understanding of one's own cultural background.

It is clear that we need to muster the courage to both explore and repudiate our collective willingness to relegate our most vulnerable children to an educational system that too often does not recognize nor value their unique strengths. This repudiation will require us all to question the responsibility we each have for the current situation and the merit we feel we have demonstrated. It will require us to question if those of us well served by our education and society have "earned" our privilege. It will demand that we make ourselves vulnerable to the exploration of how, why, and when we were treated as valuable to society.

The following recommendations for stimulating dialogue in order to make cultural competency a great priority in public education are offered only as ideas that invite participation in conversation, reflection, and action. There are not intended as policy solutions. These ideas are intended to stimulate increased innovation and greater commitment at the individual, group, and systems levels, within and beyond schools and education systems.

1. Do our own internal work about education. It is critical that we understand the story of school that we each carry from childhood and project onto schools today. To do this we must turn inward and grapple with our own experiences in school especially related to merit and equity. All of us tell ourselves a story about our educational privilege. We must reveal hidden systems of power and privilege. An invisible curriculum exists in schools. Whiteness and speaking standard English are just two examples of paths to unspoken educational privilege.

2. Risk caring more about diverse schools. Most of us know very little about education, beyond the headlines. We may feel content to ignore public education or too overwhelmed to investigate. As we shed our protective shells, we expose ourselves to the anxieties that others feel about education and the future of their children. Feeling a touch of this anxiety can be a powerful invitation toward compassion and advocacy for others.

3. Learn to facilitate courageous and difficult conversations. Our most intractable educational problems are hardest to face because they reveal

strong emotions and closely held beliefs. Dealing with change and the complexities of navigating the wide range of human differences can force us to confront and manage anger, polarization, minimization, blame, feelings of loss, and the pain of dreams deferred. Often change requires us to have a breakdown before we can have a breakthrough. Creating safe space for courageous conversations is critical to building engagement, momentum, and constructive dissatisfaction with the status quo.

4. Support schools on their cultural competency journeys. Districts working toward systemic reform quickly discover that any well-intended action brings strong reactions. Schools often reward compliance and non-confrontation. Help schools develop the capacity to see the long-term gain that is the reward for tolerating temporary disruption and discomfort as new skills, systems, and commitments are embraced. Give schools the time to destroy unworkable structures and create new structures that will support cultural competency. Create and support development programs for educators. Examine the current dynamics of authority, learning, and innovation.

5. Imagine and embrace possibility. Only by envisioning alternatives can we create the architecture to support new initiatives. Time, money, interest, and priority will all be cited as reasons that cultural competency cannot be cultivated in schools. Dare to envision schools where all cultures are treated with dignity and respect. Refuse to accept excuses that foster exclusion. Organizations are simply networks of conversations. Change the conversation. Change the system.

6. Focus on developing trust. The primary building block of human systems is trust. Reforms often fail to blossom due to lack of trust, understanding, or cultural relevance to the people and/or communities being addressed by the reform. Trust creates an environment conducive to helping people challenge long-held assumptions.

We need to remind ourselves of what is inscribed on the Statue of Liberty. Emma Lazarus' sonnet "New Colossus" is quoted, "Give me your tired, your poor, your huddled masses yearning to breathe free . . ." But rarely do people go beyond that emotional phrase to what follows: "I lift my lamp beside the golden door."

The challenge before us is to reimagine and reinvest in public education in a framework of inclusivity for all. If we want the students of today to be prepared for the jobs of tomorrow, if we want students to be able to use technology and possess the ability to be lifelong learners of literacies that have not yet been demanded, then we need our schools to be able to engage diverse imaginations, communicate ideas across wide gulfs of human experience, and understand social and emotional cues that are leverage points for unleashing the vast reservoir of untapped human potential. A golden door is within our reach. We must illuminate it.

AUTHOR'S NOTE

I owe a deep intellectual dept to Dr. Linda Powell Pruitt and Howard J. Ross for their input on this commentary. Both agreed to provide me with carte blanche to borrow and build upon their ideas and writings.

ABOUT THE AUTHOR

Howie Schaffer is a vice president at Cook Ross Inc. He is a respected speaker, trainer, and facilitator on cutting-edge topics in diversity, inclusion, and cultural competency. For more than a decade, Howie served as the public outreach director at Public Education Network (PEN) in Washington, DC. He created and edited the award-winning PEN Weekly NewsBlast. Howie has an undergraduate degree in communications from Cornell University and a graduate degree in philosophy of education from Teacher's College at Columbia University. He is a proud husband and the father of two dazzling sons.

Chapter 2

A Foot in Two Worlds

Immigrant Students in U.S. Schools

Waliha Gani and Shriya Adhikary

In 2009, the Annandale High school newspaper, ranked as one of the top ten school papers nationwide, was led by two co-editors in chief who only a few years earlier did not speak English. As these editors, we were both high-achieving students and very involved within our school community. However, although our Northern Virginia high school is known for its vibrant cultural diversity with students from over 90 countries, and we seemed to fit in as well as any other American teenager most of the time, as immigrants, we encountered various internal and external challenges given our background. All immigrant stories share both similarities and differences, as do ours. As you read our individual narratives, we hope that you gain insight into the lives of immigrant high school students. We hope our stories will be valuable to school officials in developing reforms to help students and their families who are encountering similar challenges.

WALIHA GANI

Urgently making the last edits of an article titled "Students Hit Hard by the Economic Downturn," my co-editor, Shriya Adhikary and I felt the excitement of, once more, making history. We were inside our second home, Annandale High School's Publication Lab—the place where we both spent hours after school, intensely editing, writing, and designing pages. We made history every three weeks when the paper came out at the Washington Post plant in Springfield, VA, excitedly reading our names in print as the articles recorded school, community, and global events. By our senior year, this lab had become by far the most comfortable place in the entire school as Shriya

9

and I had become the co-editors in chief of one of the most award-winning school newspapers in the nation, *The A-Blast*.

It was the third issue of the year, and I felt, as I did every time I had to stay late to work, a sudden feeling of worry and anxiety begin to take over me. The time on the clock was 9:30 P.M. My mother had called my newspaper advisor's office at least five times this evening to ensure that I was actually in school, while my father had left several voicemail messages on my own phone, urging me to leave behind my work and simply come home.

So now that I was actually prepared to go home, I mentally prepared myself for I what I knew was bound to come. First, on our car ride home, I would have to hear my father's disappointment in me for causing paramount distress to my mother; admonishing me, for how could I possibly continue to pursue my journalistic ambitions when it created such a tumultuous environment at home?

True to my expectations, the same pattern that has followed for the past two years ensued. My father initiated the same conversation as I quietly listened and said nothing. Upon arriving home, I saw my mother sitting on the sofa, eyes swollen from crying. Without looking up at me, her voice inundated with anger, she questioned, "Where were you?"

My mother knew the answer to her question, yet even after three years, could not get around fathoming the significance of the school newspaper in my life. The idea of coming home late from school and engaging myself in extra-curricular activities was a foreign concept that my mom simply could not understand.

So before I continue, let's rewind. Born in Rawalpindi, Pakistan, my family and I immigrated to the States on October 24, 1999. I vividly remember the unwavering excitement my siblings and I all felt at the thought of living in a land that everyone only dreamed of living in—the good life depicted in Pakistani dramas. Regardless of these dreams, starting life in the world's super power comes with no guidebooks. Coming in, most of us don't receive preparation classes, rules or tips to follow. A common theme of the stories of many immigrants is the idea of overcoming obstacles on our own. The second we landed at The John F. Kennedy Airport in Queens, New York, confusion and excitement set in. We have all been always tremendously thankful for moving to America. Nonetheless, the uncertainty of our new lives was lingering in our minds. Of course, for each of the five members of my family, there were different thoughts dancing in our minds.

A month after arriving in America, I started third grade at William Ramsay Elementary School in Alexandria, Virginia, which had a diverse student population, so I was fortunate to not feel secluded. However, my third grade teacher gave no formal introduction to me as I joined the class I was placed in. The first few weeks of my new life are etched into my memory. Since I hadn't learned any English in Pakistan, with the exception of "Hi! How are you?" I remember feeling completely lost. It was Thanksgiving time, and not being introduced to the Thanksgiving holiday by my teachers, I remember being baffled. I can recall asking myself why we'd ever color turkeys in school. It was this very confusion—complete uncertainty of how everything worked—that drove all my ambitions.

The Pakistani school system relies largely on memorization. So coming in, I had never learned analytical and critical reading. Excelling at everything else, I still remember my teacher's continual disappointment at my poor critical reading performance. What I remember most, however, is my decision in fourth grade to become a news anchor for the school, where I would passionately announce, "Good morning, William Ramsay. This is Waliha Gani with your morning's announcements."

I would report on the school's major events, highlighting the word/person of the day, upcoming events, and of course the lunch menu. There was one dreaded word on that menu that I had to say every single morning: vegetable. In Pakistan, I had learned to pronounce the "v" the same as the "w." Of course, I had never even discerned the difference until students throughout the school began mocking me.

Walking home one day, I heard a student younger than me yelling, "HEY! HEY! Can I have some wegtables?" Once I had given him the satisfaction of my attention, he continued, "I'd really, really just like some of those WEG-ee-tables," he finished. I went home crying that day, but not willing to give up, I took this as another challenge. I was fortunate because my publications teacher sat me down the next day and taught me probably the one thing I am forever indebted to her for. Taking me aside, she sat me down and demonstrated the pronunciation of the word.

"Vegetables," I repeated after her for a good 30 minutes in front of the other news anchors watching.

I went home that day feeling thoroughly embarrassed.

Not giving in, I was adamant to learn to love my "v" words.

The next morning, I walked into the newsroom proudly. I had gotten my VEGetables in my mouth correctly, and knew that I was going to love the lunch menu that morning.

The gap between my parents and me developed during the high school years as all clashing ideologies between the American culture and Pakistani culture came to the front burner. Although my two older sisters had already encountered the cultural gap with our parents, instead of beginning to somewhat grasp an understanding of the American educational system, my mother's perspectives only narrowed. By talking with other Pakistani mothers, my mom only caught on to the negative vines—she heard the stories of girls getting raped, the stories of girls turning "bad," the stories of girls turning against their parents and having a completely different face in school.

As the world was advancing and everything was turning viral, teachers accepted papers and assignments in typed form only, and my mother could not keep up. Typing up any kind of paper for my International Baccalaureate classes erupted in long quarrels between my mother and me. She insisted that I was chatting with a guy and not doing anything academic related. She was just unable to believe that teachers assigned papers that were required to be typed.

Throughout my high school years, my relationship with my mother only deteriorated. We could not see eye to eye on anything, causing the atmosphere in my household to progressively worsen. My father literally begged me to quit my journalistic aspirations altogether to "save everyone at home." However, I was fortunate to have an incredibly understanding newspaper advisor, Alan Weintraut, who attempted to help my mother understand my participation in the paper. He spoke in person to her whenever she came to the publications lab during our long deadline nights, explaining exactly what we did as a staff. Fortunately, this dialogue between Mr. Weintraut and my mother did help my mom understand to some extent. Most importantly, thanks to Mr. Weintraut's patience, my mom received some consolation during my late hours after school by calling his office persistently throughout deadline week.

Although I've never known any of my immigrant friends to go through such disparities in values with their parents, I understand the cause of the rifts in my soured relationship with my parents. My mother barely finished high school, while my father finished college, but didn't pursue his education. My mom never learned English, though my father does speak the language. My mom comes from a culture that is dominantly conservative; a society that holds certain expectations of women. Regardless of their own limited education, both my parents have continually reiterated the importance of education in their children's lives. Unfortunately, the cultural differences have and continued to hinder my mother's ability to understand how things work in America.

The phrase, "But mom. It's not like that here," is commonplace for many immigrant students. My mom just could not get around to understanding that colleges demanded extra-curricular activities or that becoming a well-rounded person was crucial to not only college applications, but most important, to my growth as a human being.

In addition to those struggles, our family was a typical immigrant family at Annandale High School, specifically financially. We barely made ends meet and financial worries persisted all the time. This taught me the value of hard work, and by my junior year, my family was so financially unstable that I began working 16 hours at CVS/Pharmacy every weekend.

I never consulted any of my teachers (with the exception of my newspaper advisor) about the issues with my mom in terms of getting my work done. Many teachers were generally encouraging and supportive. Yet, most of my classes were International Baccalaureate courses and I was surrounded by students who didn't have any such similar issues. The teachers didn't distinguish between the few immigrant students in this cluster of students, and I was expected to get my work done. No questions asked. I honestly did not know how to approach my teachers about this, and perhaps I wrongfully assumed that they would not understand. Nonetheless, I was fortunate that Mr. Weintraut was highly understanding and helpful. I went to him several times throughout the three years I was on the newspaper staff, and he always provided me advice that enabled me to pursue my ambitions. Additionally, all the times that he spoke with my mom about the newspaper work were further valuable.

Although I'm certain my high school years would have been far more enjoyable had things been different, the purpose of this narrative is not to paint a purely ugly picture. We're all born into certain circumstances of our lives, and we are all endowed with the decision to either adapt or let obstacles cripple us. By my senior year, I let these events of my life develop me by ardently seeking refuge in my studies.

Learning from the events of my circumstances, I never complained about what I could not and did not have. I could not afford a cell phone until the end of my senior year, and I was not bestowed with the great gadgets that many of my peers indulged in. Since weekdays were filled with longstanding arguments with my mother, I was not allowed to have a social life over the weekends when I needed to catch up on my schoolwork. Sure, I had friends, but I was not allowed to hang out as everyone else. Prom, the hallmark of many girls' high school life, was something I dared not even ask to attend.

Regardless, I strived to not let the negative experiences get in the way of my education. All my studies made much more sense to me because I could connect nearly everything to my own life. I could interpret the themes of the many plays and novels we read in my IB English class in unique ways. This may sound like a stretch, but learning about the war and international affairs in my IB Topics of the 20th Century class helped me realize how much of the conflict between the United States and the USSR resulted from an inability to communicate with each other.

Leadership on the school's newspaper, *The A-Blast*, fully allowed me to bring my background into play. Not only did it challenge my skills and abilities in various ways, it allowed me to connect to the diverse student population of AHS. Our paper covered everything from sporting events and concerts to the personal journeys of students born in other countries. *A-Blast* was the highlight of my high school years and amid everything else, it was the one thing that never failed to give me solace.

The first official test of my leadership abilities came at the copy meeting when the entire staff gathered to discuss the results of the first published issue of the year. This was my first time speaking in front of the entire staff. My nervousness had gotten the best of me. The broken speech that flew from my mouth went something like, "When interviewing . . . umm," [pause] " . . . do remember to be confident and conversational." [long pause] And that was it. When I made that statement, I felt my stomach churn, face grow crimson red, and my palms were sweating bullets—I knew I sounded like a complete hypocrite. My mind began dancing with thoughts: I was trying to help others understand the significance of being confident? HELLOOO! I could barely form my own thoughts from an intense lack of confidence.

I was suffering from my own worst paranoia as an immigrant: self-doubt. Even after seven years of being in the U.S., I had always put myself down, feeling that my English had an accent, composed of weird "alien" pronunciations of words that would immediately lead others to mock me. As much as I tried to avoid this fear in high school, it always came back to me. It was a fear that I struggled with so many times, and each time I thought I had gotten through it, it would come haunting me once more during presentations.

The staff was largely American-born white, and don't get me wrong, I loved them all, but this fact made me feel more conscious of my English. Back then, I was the one who made my differences stick out, limiting myself from fully being myself. During presentations, I'd find myself feeling incompetent. Most of all, my nervousness would be strikingly visible with my fidgety composure. Nonetheless, not willing to give up so easily, I knew I had to find a solution to my paranoia on my own.

What helped me most was the advice from Mr. Weintraut, the most nonchalant, laid-back teacher I have ever met. His succinct, yet incredibly effective advice was, "Act like the boss you are." And that really had me thinking. ACT like the boss you are. Implicitly stating, he meant that in order for me change, the foremost thing I had to do was discern the significance of my position and play my role as the co-editor in chief.

And it all paid off. Before I knew it, I sounded and acted like the leader I was. I broke out of my shell, and began becoming assertive, clearly dictating what I needed done, and helping others become better journalists.

What has this all taught me? Simply put: There are no limitations to success. As a journalist, I have conducted numerous interviews of immigrants from all over the globe who have experienced challenges similar to mine. At the end of the year, when I had become comfortable with myself, I had one memorable interview with a girl from Thailand. I was asking her opinion of a program in my school called "The Just World Festival" that highlighted different cultures. After I couldn't comprehend her answer the first time, she helplessly said, "You shouldn't ask me. My English is very bad."

At that moment, I couldn't help but laugh inside because I knew the person in front of me had been me not too long ago. The nervous, shameful eyes of that Thai student looking back at me demonstrates the story of many people who struggle with learning English in the U.S., and may feel discouraged by their accents or background. I was one of them for so long before I finally decided to make the effort to prove myself through my skills, and break free from continually feeling victimized by judgments.

SHRIYA ADHIKARY

It was the first day of second grade. Intimidating enough for someone attending a new school, but here I was, dressed in my finest, ready to tackle the first day of school in a new country. It was the first time I had been allowed to wear "outside" clothing to school, and I'd chosen to wear a frilly pink dress that I was sure would make a good first impression.

My parents had just made a life-changing decision, electing to uproot some thirty-odd years of established routine to travel to the land of opportunity. My memories of the journey from Nepal to America are vague, but that first day of second grade remains stark in my memory.

I walked into the brightly decorated classroom as the bell rang, the optimism of a seven year old playing a timid smile on my lips.

"Alright class," the teacher called out, "We have a new friend joining us today all the way from India. Please say 'hi' and show her around the classroom, okay?"

"Hiiiiii," a chorus of voices answered.

I didn't have the heart to tell the teacher that I wasn't from India.

As I took my seat, the pretty blonde girl sitting next to me asked, "How come you look like that?"

"Look like what?" I questioned.

"That," she said again, this time pointing to my skin, which is dark brown, and was at that time further darkened by the unforgiving Nebraskan sun.

"And you sound funny."

Taken aback and a little hurt that she hadn't noticed my beautiful dress at all, I looked around the classroom and observed for the first time that all of the faces there were lighter than mine. I started to cry.

That was my first encounter with any sort of remark about my skin tone or my immigrant background. But the comments did not stop there.

After that first day in second grade, I tried to blend in with my classmates as much as possible. I bought jeans and sneakers, forced my mother to buy cheese and lunchmeat for my packed lunches, and imitated my classmates' way of speaking to the best of my ability. As the year went on, I began to fit in. Yet, ironically, it became increasingly harder for me to forget that I was somewhat different.

During my high school years, we lived in Annandale, Virginia, referred to by many as "Koreatown," and I attended Annandale High School, known for its cultural diversity. By that time, I had established a sense of who I was, what I wanted to be, and where I was headed. My parents, and my peers, on the other hand, had differing expectations.

My parents, born and raised in Kathmandu, Nepal, were caught in a time warp and still lived in the cultural mindset of the land that they'd left behind, even though teenagers in Nepal were going out to clubs, dating, and forgoing traditional styles of clothing for jeans and tank tops. While my parents and I would get into little verbal tussles during my middle school years about whether I could go to the mall with my friends on the weekends, hang out after school, wear ripped jeans, etc., the real battles began once I entered high school.

In high school, my main priorities—reinforced by my parents—were earning the International Baccalaureate (IB) Diploma, becoming co-editor in chief of our award-winning high school newspaper, *The A-Blast*, and keeping a high profile in as many extra-curricular and volunteer activities as I could, all the while attempting to maintain some sort of a social life (not high on the list of priorities as stated by my parents). However, while they fully supported my academic endeavors and thought that I should spend as much time studying as possible, they didn't quite understand why I spent more time at school than I did at home, why I basically lived in the publications lab, or why I had to make more trips to the library than I did to the bathroom. Many times, I would come home after a 12-hour day spent at school, seven hours of classes and another grueling five hours spent editing the newspaper on a computer screen, expecting some sympathy and find my mother upset at how she rarely ever was able to spend time with me.

Needless to say, the way in which she grew up and how I am growing up are vastly different. Although she also attended school, had friends and shared similar aspirations for the future, in her time, it wasn't appropriate or even realistic for girls to consider high-profile, involved careers or participate in activities that would require a lot of time spent away from the watchful eyes of their parents. While my parents trusted me implicitly, as my father repeatedly told me throughout the years, it was the other people he didn't trust. This lack of trust of "others" hindered my many attempts at a social life and I think is prevalent throughout the immigrant spectrum, as many of my friends from other countries have the same issue with their parents.

Ironically, while many in the U.S. distrust immigrants, what they don't real-ize is that the feeling is mutual. It wasn't that my parents didn't trust my friends or their parents simply because they were different from us, but because they didn't know them personally. They also never made an effort to do so because they were either uncomfortable being so forward, or due to the communication barrier. While my parents both received much of their high school and college educations in English, they are still uncomfortable and nervous speaking the language, especially to people they have never met before. However, the trust issue only applied to social situations; when it had to do with school, they had no problems trusting teachers or school officials.

My parents were always supportive of anything that I wanted to do, pro-vided it held some educational, career-related, or other advantage. However, they didn't always see the advantages in the same way that I did. For one thing, they didn't fully understand the way the U.S. education system oper-ates, with an emphasis on practical, hands-on application and training, and the "do it yourself," individualistic attitude, where you are responsible for your learning. And a lot of times, the other issue was money.

Although not true of every immigrant family, many first-generation immi-grant families are financially weak since they have not yet established roots or built up savings. While we never lacked for anything, my family never spent superfluously as many of my peers seemed to do. In my junior year of high school, we were given the opportunity to travel to Spain over Spring Break to "immerse ourselves in Spanish culture and gain a better apprecia-tion for the language and the people." While I desperately wanted to immerse myself in Spanish culture, I never even approached my parents about the pos-sibility because I knew (or assumed) that they wouldn't see the merits of the trip and that the cost was too high.

In my experiences, and for sure the experiences of immigrant kids across the nation, one of the difficulties we face is having to figure out most things on our own. Undoubtedly, parents will always be there to provide emotional and financial support, but generally, they simply lack the real-life experiences or technical knowledge of the workings of the high school system, the college application process, and other practicalities that follow after high school. Many times during high school, I despaired at the fact that while my friends were receiving help and advice from their parents on homework and projects, which colleges to apply to, how to write the best essay, and being taken on college vis-its, I felt like I was on my own. While my parents always listened and advised me based on what I told them after researching and speaking with others better informed than I, they were not a source of information on their own.

However, their continued trust, support and emphasis on the importance of education helped to shape the person I have become and led to my academic achievements. Because of the importance they place on always striving to do and be the best, I usually give a hundred percent to everything I do.

It wasn't always easy to realize the benefits of their parenting, though. Whenever battles were raging in our household, like any other teenager, I would turn to my friends for an escape route. However, the real challenge was when my friends posed the problem. Regardless of how long and how well they knew me, and how much they tried to empathize, the simple fact of the matter was that they didn't come from immigrant backgrounds so they didn't understand the particular struggle of trying to balance one life in two worlds. While many immigrant kids tend to cluster together, I always had a wide palette of friends. But while they were there to comfort me whenever I needed to groan and grouse about how *unfair* my parents were, and how they simply didn't understand, my friends didn't really understand the dynamics of my multicultural life either. For example, I once had a conversation with a friend who desperately was waiting for her 18th birthday—because then she could "do whatever she wanted." In our culture, you listened and respected your parents for as long as you lived—I couldn't (and didn't exactly want to) move away from home and pierce various body parts as an act of rebellion, like some students at our school did.

Also, during Nepali holidays, I would come to school with the red *tika* on my forehead, and be subject to countless questions about our rituals and traditions. Sometimes, it was refreshing to be able to share a bit about my culture—something I clearly knew something more about than anyone else at school—while other times, I wished I could just blend in with everyone else. Then there were the days after large gatherings at home, when the smell of spices and curry would permeate through all of my clothes and I'd frantically spray Febreeze in every nook and cranny where my culture threatened to reveal itself in order to avoid awkward sniffs and stares at school—embarrassing, to say the least. However, I thoroughly enjoyed sharing the highlights of my culture with my friends, such as during our school's annual Heritage Night or the Just World Festival, where I gave a presentation on how dance is used as an expressive means of communication, and then performed various dances for the audience.

Other awkward moments resulted whenever the issue of hanging out with friends arose. For the first two years of high school, my parents, like many other immigrant parents, rarely let me stay out late at night or go to parties, and never allowed me to stay over at friends' houses. Once my friends got cars and I entered my junior year, things got a bit easier, especially since I had long established friendships with people that my parents had also come to know. However, every time I wanted to go out, I faced a barrage of questions about who, what, where, when and why—a string of questioning my friends certainly didn't undergo.

So just like my parents, although my friends supported and comforted me despite our dissimilarities, they didn't quite fully "get it" either. A lot of the times, it basically felt like I was on my own, as far as comprehending the uncomfortable and tricky situation of balancing a foot in two worlds.

Though I was generally comfortable in my own skin, regardless of how brown it was, being in a position of leadership on the high school newspaper brought all my long fought insecurities to the forefront.

I remember what an accomplishment it was to have achieved that role at the end of junior year, and how excited I was to be working with Waliha and our adviser, Alan Weintraut, both people I'd come to respect immensely throughout our years spent working on the newspaper. My family could not have been prouder. As I was the oldest child even in our extended family, any accomplishment of mine was celebrated and displayed as a fruitful result of our combined struggles and sacrifices.

However, not only was there a lot of pressure as co-editor in chief of a top-notch student run newspaper, but in contrast to the rest of the school, our staff of 70 plus students was largely Caucasian—which, looking back, shouldn't have been an issue of consequence and it probably wasn't, to anyone but me. Our staff was very young and we had to personally train most of our page editors and writers as it was only their first or second year on staff. They were frequently rowdy, prone to complaining, and usually past deadline with their material. We soon realized that their behavior reflected our leadership and influence, so we worked harder to enforce deadlines and train them in more effective ways.

As the year wore on, we certainly developed a better relationship with our staff and forged friendships that we still maintain today, yet whenever a staff member was uncooperative or rude, I couldn't shake the feeling that it was somehow related to my status as an immigrant. I didn't speak with an accent—except when I was really nervous in front of a crowd—my written and oral English skills were flawless, and I didn't have any noticeable quirks apart from my obvious skin tone that would delineate my background. So while it was a completely irrational assumption and not one that I'm particularly proud of, it was a thought that sometimes crept into my head nonetheless.

However, coming from a different background was a huge bonus in terms of being able to represent our multicultural student body. Because of every-thing that Waliha and I had experienced, we were able to relate to and under-stand the perspectives of a wider range of students.

Although it sounds trite and full of teenage angst, for a lot of the time in high school, especially in the beginning, I did feel like I was caught in between two worlds and trapped in two identities.

At school, I was loud and bubbly, full of inappropriate humor with my friends, easy to laugh and get along with, but a good student as well. I had social and political opinions that slanted towards the liberal side, I fancied myself in and out of love, ate in the school cafeteria like everyone else (although I never ate any of the so-called "beef") and chatted about the weekend and future plans. At home, I was much more subdued. We generally only spoke in Nepali in the house, ate Nepali style dishes, prayed to our numerous Hindu gods and goddesses, and usually had multiple Nepali relatives and friends over for dinner, when the conversation inevitably shifted to "back in the day."

My parents had instilled in my sister and me their own values, a sort of blend between what they grew up with and what they had gleaned from our lives here, whereas with my friends, I learned a whole new set of values according to the American way of life. For a long time, I didn't know where I belonged.

Although I had mostly grown up in the U.S., my heritage was very important to me and I didn't want to lose any of it. However, I also appreciated and enjoyed many American values, beliefs, and ideas, and wanted to immerse myself in this culture. For a long time, I struggled with the idea of who I was: the person my friends saw at school or the person I was at home with my family. After some time, though, I realized that it was relatively simple to be both persons at once. Of course, I tended to be more subdued at home, as these were my parents! I couldn't be loud and obnoxious with them as I was at school. I had to understand their feelings and way of thinking and respect the values and traditions they had instilled in us, but that didn't mean that I couldn't be my own person as well. My parents had made compromises to their lives by moving here, and I could certainly attempt do the same, crafting a version of the old and new that fit me best.

Two years out of high school, I no longer worry about where I fit in. Perhaps the teenage angst has passed, or perhaps I have matured, but I've grown to be comfortable in my own skin wherever I may be. I've realized that in most cases, my immigrant background is an asset, not a hindrance. It allows me to be more compassionate towards people's differences, take a broader outlook on the issues that concern today's world, and grants me the opportunity to share my unique experiences with others. I've also grown to further appreciate the strength of my values, such as the importance of caring for your family and friends, the emphasis on education and knowledge, and being an independent individual. I love being a part of a culture that is so rich and multifaceted and so very different from what people here experience.

CONCLUSION

While our high school experiences were beset by difficulties, we were fortunate enough to have come into contact with people who helped us along the way. Truly, without the understanding and care of our teachers throughout the years, I doubt we could have been as successful academically or in developing our character and personalities. At times we did not reach out to faculty who might have helped us. But teachers themselves often gave us that extra little push or the occasional "How are you doing?," "Great job" or the interested questions about our culture and families. That made all the difference in terms of being able to talk about our problems or cope with them. Just the simple fact that these teachers were sensitive and sympathetic to what went on behind the façade of a smiling and cheerful countenance, and that they did not make assumptions about immigrant students in general, was sometimes enough.

Both of us also found it extremely helpful to speak with each other about our difficulties, both as students at AHS and in our joint roles as editors-in-chief. While our experiences at home weren't completely the same, we were largely able to relate to one another, and oftentimes, it seemed like it was us against the rest of the staff or school. We are both extremely grateful that we were able to find another wandering soul during our high school years that we could share, laugh, and grow with.

We hope that our narratives will give hope to other immigrant students who are encountering similar situations, and that school systems try to expand their resources and outreach to help those respective students and their parents with their transitions into the American lifestyle. Like we have illustrated, as students of immigrants in American schools, we all have a foot in two worlds.

ABOUT THE AUTHORS

Waliha Gani is a student at James Madison University, majoring in international affairs with a minor in Middle Eastern communities and migrations. Waliha is the current president of James Madison University's Muslim Student Association. Born in Rawalpindi, Pakistan, Waliha came to the United States at the age of eight in 1999, and she and her family have resided in Northern Virginia for the past 10 years. Waliha's ultimate goal in life is "To serve others."

Shriya Adhikary is a student at Wheeling Jesuit University, double majoring in international studies and communications. Shirya immigrated to the United States from Nepal with her family in 1998, and since then has lived in Omaha, Chicago, and in Annandale, Virginia. She is the current news editor of her college newspaper and hopes to pursue a career in the field of international correspondence. Shirya is a firm believer in overcoming "impossibilities" and the idea that laughter is the best medicine.

Chapter 3

Valuing the Individual by Breaking Through Assumptions

Eileen Gale Kugler

The stately grandmother rose from her chair. She began speaking in Xhosa, her mother tongue, to the other families who had gathered that afternoon in a rural South African school. Heads nodded in agreement.

The interpreter did not interrupt the impassioned speech. At the front of the room, I could only stand with respect as she addressed her comments to me, the leader of the meeting.

We had gathered there for a family engagement program I had organized at this elementary school in the rural area of the Eastern Cape of South Africa. For several years, I, along with my husband and daughter—both educators—have spent three weeks each summer volunteering at the school. At the invitation of the principal, we provide professional development for the staff to improve literacy. This year, the principal had agreed to permit me to reach out to families in the community to help them become partners in their children's success.

The program I led, modeled on the *Tellin' Stories* project of Teaching for Change, invites families to the school to make a school quilt, with each family creating a square illustrating their hopes and dreams for their child. While the families come together to sew in a welcoming environment, they also learn about resources both at the school and in the community. Today, at our second of six sessions, the family members were sharing what they learned from discussions with their children about their own dreams.

My mind raced as I listened to Mrs. Nyati speak. Was she challenging my presence as an outsider? Did she think the project was a waste of time and not relevant to their lives? As her words were translated, I wasn't prepared for their power.

"We do have hopes and dreams for our children," Mrs. Nyati said, "but no one ever asked us before. Thank you."

Her words struck me to my core. I was surrounded by impoverished, illiterate families. These are the families who often remain invisible in school, not just in South Africa, but in the United States, and countries the world over.

The teachers in this school are dedicated to educating the students so they can play a role in the "new South Africa," with rights previously denied to the teachers and the students alike because they are black. Yet they assumed the families had little of value to share at school, again not unlike schools in other countries. Even the principal, a great leader who had grown up in this isolated black township created under apartheid, could not see a significant role for township families in the school.

After all, the families are largely uneducated. There are many grandparents raising children, and the parents who are around are too busy working in the nearby orange groves. I was warned that few families would come to the meeting, and those who came would be late. Yet at the scheduled time, the room was filled with 50 family members, who not only came to meeting after meeting, but also brought relatives and friends.

Here was the classic example of assumptions that blocked a real understanding of what people have to offer. In working with families from around the world, many of whom have had limited education and are locked in poverty in their home country or the one they have immigrated to, I've learned they have much to share. I've learned critical lessons about perseverance, determination, hard work, and a commitment to family that entails incredible personal sacrifice. Yet families like these often remain voiceless and powerless in schools around the world.

That is just the beginning of how assumptions, those conscious and unconscious rules we each carry, dictate who has value versus who is The Other. Assumptions keep us from listening to the wisdom of someone with different colored skin, or a person from a different part of the world, or a different part of this country, or a different neighborhood. The Other may be too old or too young, too new to understand how "things are done," and so some think that voice is without merit. Without opportunities to interact on equal footing, misperceptions and stereotypes become further entrenched in our schools, our communities, and our workplaces.

While the gulf between the haves and have-nots in South Africa is so extreme that the impacts are very clear, the messages apply far beyond. So many times we underestimate those around us. Mrs. Pepeta, another grandmother who participated in the quilt project, is a powerful example of what we don't see without looking deeper.

At one of the meetings, Mrs. Pepeta apologized for missing the previous session, but told me she was taking a class. "What are you studying?" I asked. "English," she replied with a twinkle in her eye. Although she had been silent at earlier sessions, I discovered she had excellent English skills and I often asked her to be the interpreter during meetings. I learned from others that she had been a "Gold Scholar" in English in her early schooling, but the opportunity to be a stellar student evaporated under apartheid. So now, in her early 80's, she is continuing the education once denied her, defying the stereotype of a impoverished old woman with few skills.

ASSUMPTIONS WITH JUST ONE GLANCE

The cocoon of the familiar, filled with long-standing assumptions, feels comfortable, and it is as far as some want to venture. But never moving beyond a comfort zone blocks out new learning that is essential to our progress as individuals, schools, communities and as a society. Without this discomfort, there is little opportunity for experiences that can break down assumptions and misperceptions.

The true danger comes when those in power don't move beyond their assumptions. In education, this limits student growth, keeps families at a distance, and blocks new ideas from faculty of all ages. An educational leader can exclude and devalue those who don't fit the assumption of what good parents or high-achieving students look like, or can champion a vision that values every individual, pushing every school employee to move beyond limiting assumptions.

We often make assumptions, faulty assumptions, with just one glance. I was invited to speak about the strengths of diverse schools to the community surrounding a diverse inner-city Indianapolis Catholic school. Cathy, an active school mother who met me at the airport, is a blond and blue-eyed Caucasian. She graciously invited me to her home for lunch, where I met her African-American husband. Their 8-year-old daughter, an African-American who looked like neither parent, was adopted as an infant. Cathy noted that when people see her alone, they make huge assumptions. "They know nothing about me or my life," she stated. "And when people see me with my daughter, many ask if she is my foster daughter. 'NO, she is my daughter,' I tell them, frustrated that they can't see beyond their limited view of what a family looks like."

Assumptions about students are at the core of student success. Research indicates that a teacher's belief in a student's ability is fundamental. Robert Rosenthal and Lenore Jacobsen first identified the "Pygmalion phenomenon" in 1968 and it has been confirmed time and time again over the decades. Basically, when teachers expect students to do well and show intellectual growth, they do, but when teachers do not have such expectations, student performance and growth suffer (1992).

This plays out in our schools every day. Recently, an African-American mother told me about her 9th grade daughter who entered an advanced math class on the first day of school in a diverse neighborhood. Without looking at her name or his class list, the teacher looked her in the eye as she entered the room and said, "I think you are in the wrong class." The student thought she might, indeed, be in the wrong room as a new high school student just finding her way around.

Tanya left the math class and checked her schedule. It was correct. But instead of returning to the class, she went to her guidance counselor. With nothing more than the teacher's comment, the guidance counselor moved Tanya into a lower level math class.

When Tanya told her mother that evening, her mother was incensed. "How dare they make assumptions about my child," asserted the mother, who herself was an educator with several advanced degrees. The issue then became whether she should insist that her child be put back into that class, taught by a teacher who did not believe a black girl was capable of excelling in advanced math. Tanya's mother did go into school and raised the issue with the teacher, the guidance counselor and the principal (much to her teenage daughter's chagrin). In the end, her daughter's schedule was completely rearranged so she could be placed in another section of advanced math.

I wish I could tell you that this is an isolated story. However, I have heard similar versions from numerous parents of color. Their children are simply not expected to excel, and many, without intervention, live up or down to the teacher's expectation.

THAT'S HOW WE DO THINGS HERE

Assumptions abound not just about families and students, but within the faculty itself. One hotbed area relates to generational diversity, a new phenomenon affecting schools, like other worksites. There are now three or even four generations interacting at work, each with different life experiences impacting how they view their jobs.

A middle school teacher in her late 20's told me how excited she was to revitalize the student peer tutoring program that had fallen by the wayside over the past few years. Jennifer is committed to serving her students beyond the classroom and she has enthusiastically volunteered the past few years for an overflowing plate of extra-curricular responsibilities and community activities.

Jennifer emailed the entire school staff about her interest in jump-starting the tutoring program and asked for help from anyone interested. She received no responses. With support of her principal, Jennifer organized the tutoring program single-handedly. The principal announced it at a faculty meeting, asking Jennifer to report on the details.

As the meeting broke up, one of the teachers in Jennifer's department came over and looked her in the eye. "We work collaboratively here. We don't do things that way," she stated icily, walking off before Jennifer could respond.

Jennifer's hands were shaking from the unexpected confrontation. Another young teacher reached out to steady her and reminded Jennifer that she had indeed notified everyone and asked for help. Jennifer felt she was the one who always came up with new ideas and volunteered to carry them out, and now she was being criticized by colleagues who weren't willing to help.

Wanting to smooth things over, Jennifer went to the older colleague's room first thing the next morning. They were both calmer and they talked things out. Carol, a veteran teacher a few years from retirement, felt any new idea should have been personally discussed with all members of the department. Jennifer began to see that everyone didn't consider email as a valid form of communication for important issues.

From the perspective of Carol, a teacher who had witnessed many young teachers come and go, Jennifer still had much to learn. When the principal asked Jennifer to speak at the staff meeting, Carol felt unappreciated and eclipsed by the new "rising star." She assumed the young teacher was making a power play to gain the principal's favor.

In the end, Carol and Jennifer, both dedicated teachers, worked it out. As Jennifer left, Carol said warmly, "You know I think of you like a daughter." Jennifer's defenses rose again. She wanted to be viewed as a peer, an equal, with worthy new ideas. She would be happy for a mentor, but she definitely did not want a mother in the workplace. But this time Jennifer did not say anything.

Few work environments, including schools, provide opportunities to discuss and dissect these generational assumptions. They often remain unspoken, continuing to undermine interaction among colleagues. It remains to be seen how well Jennifer and Carol will be able to collaborate in the future.

SEEING THE VALUE IN EACH INDIVIDUAL

It is important to recognize that our assumptions are based on our own individual culture. That's the prism through which we view the world. Unless we thoughtfully and introspectively look at our own culture and the assumptions that it brings, we never learn to fully appreciate and value the wisdom of others.

Contrary to simplistic assumptions about culture, each of us has a complex culture made up of numerous experiences and influences, including where we grew up, our family structure, our gender roles, and our socioeconomic status, in addition to religion, ethnicity and race. They are interconnected at numerous levels.

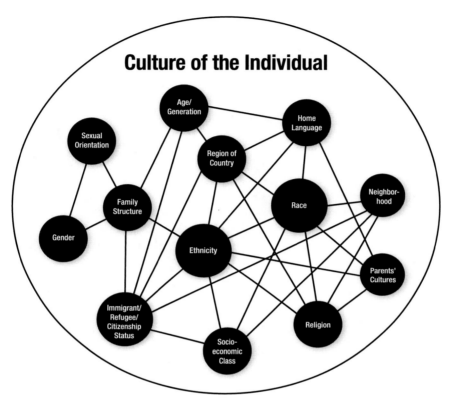

Figure 3.1.   Culture of the Individual

Our own unique culture impacts how we interact with others, influencing how we decide when someone is "right." When I lead workshops on valuing difference, I ask the participants to think for a moment how they expect someone to act if they are showing respect in a conversation. What does a respectful person look like to them?

The first response is always the same—whether I am working with teachers, students, parents, or even diversity trainers. Someone will raise a hand and say that a person shows you respect by *looking you in the eye*.

Then we together take a deep breath and a step back. Once prompted to think more deeply, the participants realize that not everyone looks you in the eye to show respect. Yet, this communication style is so valued in American society that it is always the first answer. On second thought, everyone in the room realizes they have interacted with individuals from different parts of the world or regions of the U.S. who would never look someone in the eye if they wanted to be respectful. One principal said she still has nightmares about her conversation with a young Latino student when Latino families first began moving into her community.

"I started to talk to him about being late for school," the principal said. "He looked down at the ground, and I raised my voice saying, 'You look at me when I'm talking to you!' He started to cry. As I learned more about the families, I came to understand that by looking down, he was indeed showing that he respected me. But I had humiliated him out of my own ignorance."

There are a number of other expectations that people typically raise for what "respect" looks like. One that always comes up is the expectation that the other person will listen quietly and not interrupt. This is actually one of my favorite responses. I grew up in a Jewish home in New Jersey. If you let someone finish a sentence in family discussions, you weren't listening! Deborah Tannen, the noted author on communication, even has a term for it—"overlapping speech." As my workshop participants confirm, Tannen explains this style "can be viewed as an interruption or enthusiastic listenership" (2005, p. 210).

No matter what the background of the group I work with, there are other universal responses. "Someone shouldn't stand too close," a participant will call out. What is "too close?"—a few inches? a few feet? "Someone should not speak in a loud voice." What's loud to each individual? We talk about how some people show their connection to the conversation by raising their voice. Is a parent who is concerned about his child "too loud" if he is animated and intense as he makes his feelings known to the teacher? To some teachers, yes. Others will try to calm the parent but do not take offence at the parent's tone as long as he doesn't appear out of control. The more of these we discuss, the more the participants realize that respect can't be placed in a neat box, with boundaries drawn by your own personal experiences and culture. Yes, there are some basic standards for a respectful conversation, but within those, there is much room for interpretation and indeed respect for others' perceptions.

UNDERSTANDING YOUR OWN CULTURE FIRST

To bring out the strengths of each student, and work effectively with colleagues and parents, educators need to recognize how their own individual culture—their prism for viewing the world—impacts their interactions. Did the teacher grow up as the only girl with four competitive brothers, leading her to believe girls can and should be competitive with boys? Was the teacher raised in a largely white rural area where he knew everyone, with a belief that "people are all basically the same"? Does the principal's life center around the obligatory teachings of her faith which didn't prepare her for the different perspectives of students from eight religions in her school?

Teachers and principals rarely do this type of introspection. There are simply assumptions made about how students, families and colleagues should act. Yet educators need to understand their own individual culture so they know what assumptions they carry with them about themselves and those around them. If not, they view their way of acting or thinking as "normal" and "right," devaluing others. They limit the development of others and shut off their own learning.

One on my favorite exercises to begin to develop self-awareness was created by Linda Christensen (2000), based on a poem by George Ella Lyon called "Where I'm From" (Lyon, 1999). Lyon's poignant poem recalls memories from home—phrases she heard at home, experiences, foods, smells. You learn much just from a few lines of her poem.

In her book *Reading, Writing and Rising Up* (2000), Christensen uses Lyon's poem as a model for an activity that she uses with her students to enable them to share a piece of themselves. "Our sharing is one of the many ways we begin to build community together. It 'prefigures' a world where students can hear the home language from Diovana's Pacific Islander heritage, Lurdes' Mexican family, Oretha's African-American home, and my Norwegian roots, and celebrate without mockery the similarities as well as the differences" (p. 19).

I have found "Where I'm From" to be a dynamic way to help adults understand and share their own culture as well. Lyons herself now has developed learning tools around it and she reports on her website that "People have used it at their family reunions, teachers have used it with kids all over the United States, in Ecuador and China; they have taken it to girls in juvenile detention, to men in prison for life, and to refugees in a camp in the Sudan" (2011).

In working with educators, I ask them to write a poem about home that includes: five phrases they heard, five foods they ate, five items they found. Some finish the poems in the five to ten minutes I allot; some just begin and I urge them to finish them at home. I have them share their poems in small groups and the buzz in the room is enormous as they connect to each other through their words.

Writing these poems empowers educators to think about their own homes, their own schooling, at a time when they rarely have the luxury to ponder this critical time in their own development. There are many damp eyes and tender laughs as they recall memories. Many teachers thank me for the opportunity. Some have said it inspired them to call their parents to thank them.

It doesn't always bring up happy memories, although that is certainly part of the introspection as well. I give the participants the option of writing about "home" as the one they created as an adult rather than the one they grew up in. That way, at least in this public forum, they do not have to dredge up a very painful time. Only a few take me up on this option. Most are willing to do the tough work that introspection about early learning requires.

At the end of the exercise, I ask for volunteers to read their poems to the entire group. We talk about what they learned about themselves and each other. Teachers who worked side by side for years gain new insights about their colleagues. Principals reveal parts of who they are that their staff never knew.

One of my favorite connections took place when I worked with the staff of a large Maryland elementary school. Two teachers listened to each other's poems and heard many similarities in their memories, while also hearing distinct differences. One black and one white, they realized they were both from New Orleans. They saw how growing up in the South, in the city of New Orleans, had impacted them. And they saw how race had influenced their experiences. This was about a year after the Katrina flooding and these two immediately began intently talking at the break, grateful to find someone who truly understood what the flooding meant to those who called this place home.

In another school, a teacher described the words she remembered as a young immigrant, painful words from neighborhood children and adults as well. The other educators remained respectfully quiet and thoughtful. Had they heard words about "those families" around their dinner table growing up? Did they see someone being teased as a child, as The Other, and not stand up for them? Worse yet, did they do the teasing? Or did they themselves feel like The Other because they were poor or new to the community, or just different? After watching their colleague describe the pain she still carried with her, they had new insights about the students and families they worked with.

LEARNING TO VALUE EACH INDIVIDUAL

Activities such as "Where I Am From" help educators to look inside themselves and to better understand others in order to break down long-held assumptions. It is not easy to move beyond the assumptions we have developed as a child or adult. Many are subconscious, learned through generational attitudes, stereotypes in the media, or overheard conversations that repeat in our heads. Breaking through them, like any change, can be disconcerting. But we must begin moving from a cocoon of comfortable assumptions so that we can evolve and thrive, as can those around us.

Be open to learning from everyone

Societal messages tell us that only certain people have wisdom or knowledge. Somewhere along the line, we've developed into a society that says you must be at least middle-class to have anything of value to contribute. This assumption limits us enormously. I hear parents all the time choosing to put their child in a school that is predominantly white middle-class, assuming that has to be the best place for their child. My children were fortunate enough to go to a diverse high school with fellow students from wide-ranging economic levels, cultures, and religions. The lessons they learned in the classroom, and after school, from students of all backgrounds helped to make them the broad-thinking caring individuals they are today. The perspectives of peers who challenged their assumptions, about everything from tasty food to world politics, opened their minds on a daily basis (Kugler, 2002).

I worked on a volunteer project with an extraordinary high school student whose family moved to the U.S. from Sudan when she was 8. Her father had been a lawyer and judge, owning three homes. But he saw the limited opportunities for his three daughters in their homeland. Given the chance to come to the United States through his brother, a U.S. citizen, the father moved the entire family a decade ago. With limited English skills, his job opportunities were few. His brother, who was helping the family acclimate, died of cancer. Today, the father delivers pizza and the family lives in a small apartment. But his daughter is fulfilling his dream as she has earned honor roll status in her college studies. As she spoke of her father, her eyes welled with tears, "He may only be a delivery man, but I know he is so much more. I am so grateful to my dad for bringing our family here."

Do we miss the wisdom of someone with limited English who delivers a pizza or drives a taxi or pours water into our glass at a restaurant? When our children go off to college do we teach them to get to know the custodian and the cafeteria workers as well as their professors and peers from influential families?

Be aware of the sensitivities of those from other cultures, particularly those who are not part of the mainstream culture.

It is unfortunate the pejorative word "political correctness" has been used to describe sensitivity to other cultures. I find it is rarely used by someone who is not part of the mainstream middle-class white culture. If you have ever found your own culture ignored or disrespected, it's hard to boil sensitivity down to being politically correct. It really comes down to the old adage to walk in mile in their shoes. That doesn't mean offering them your shoes, or suggesting they walk your path because it is better. It means seeing what it feels like to walk in their shoes on their chosen path. You might learn something.

Of course it is impossible to always know what is appropriate and respectful to people from different cultures. We've fortunately moved beyond the days where a diversity class just focused on stereotypical ways that Hispanics, Asians, or African-Americans act. Within those broad categories there are multiple sub-cultures; and more importantly, each individual within a culture is just that, an individual. In many regions, such as Northern Virginia where I live, our neighborhoods are rich with immigrants from all over the world, along with people who have lived in the area for decades and those who have arrived from other parts of the U.S. Some struggle with how to interact with people from different backgrounds in this complex mosaic of cultures.

I take my cue in this area from the principal of the high school my children attended, one of my personal heroes. In the school he led, with students from some 90 different nations, it might appear impossible to be sensitive to the needs of every student. Former principal Don Clausen explained to me. "You can't be aware of every cultural difference. But you can develop the sensitivity to ask the question, 'Is this a problem for you?'"

Asking questions is an important way to learn and we too often fear offending someone rather than asking the source. I have found a respectful question is usually very much appreciated. It beats an assumption every time.

A key is not to ask the question from your own perspective, but rather look to learning from theirs. I met with a principal from a magnet high school in a mid-west city, a caring leader who prided himself on developing personal relationships with his students, including a lunch with students each week. He was excited about his lunch the first week of December, explaining to me how he had engaged two Muslim students in discussions about what their families do during the Christmas season. How much more he could have learned, and how much more valued the students would have felt, if he had instead asked how their families mark Ramadan which also fell in December that year.

I asked the principal how the school accommodates these and other Muslim students during Ramadan. He looked at me with a blank stare. Since they fast during the day, I asked, are there arrangements made for them to spend lunchtime in a study hall rather than the cafeteria? Oh yes, he replied, students have a great deal of freedom during lunch hours so they can go wherever they would like. Clearly, the principal had never directly discussed this or other issues relating to their own holiday with the Muslim students in his school.

Don't assume your way is the right way.

From our own experiences and our individual culture, we come to a decision about what we think is the right way. I come from a large extended family that always greets each other with a warm hug, men and women alike. I've been known to reach out and touch an arm of someone while I'm talking if I feel strongly about the conversation. Over the years, I've learned to be a little more circumspect in doing that. I have come to see that some people are warm and caring—but still don't want physical contact from a colleague! My assumptions about how you show warmth and engagement have changed.

Beyond the classroom, teachers need to examine how their own individual culture impacts their interactions with families. Some teachers unwittingly place greater value on students who have parents who "act right"—basically as the teacher hopes or expects. This often derives from how the teacher's parents acted ("My mom came to every one of my soccer games.") or how they themselves view their responsibilities as a parent ("I always sign permission slips the day they are sent home."). There are many ways to be a good parent, like talking about the importance of education around the dinner table, an action that may go unnoticed and therefore unvalued by a teacher.

There are schools around the country that are encouraging teachers to do more personal outreach to families as a critical way to break through assumptions and build partnerships. A high school principal told me how he required each of the teachers to reach out with intention to parents of five low-performing students each quarter. These were often parents who were disconnected from school, and the teachers had made many assumptions why. While not every attempt at connection was fruitful, many teachers reported they did learn much about these families and were able to see them in a new light. One teacher described an immigrant mother who was extremely appreciative for the teacher's personal call, one of numerous calls he made before he finally reached her. That parent felt she had no place in the school because in her home country, parents respected teachers by not "interfering" in school. With a personal invitation from the teacher, the parent was eager to partner with the school on improving the student's success. Another teacher gained new appreciation for a father who had been a poor student himself and felt unqualified, unworthy, to come to school. The teacher met the father at a local fast-food restaurant for coffee and began an informal dialogue. The son's attention at school immediately improved because he knew his father was now getting first-hand reports from his teacher.

I met a Latina mother who is a parent representative on the School Governance Board of her child's high school. She told me about a meeting between her own parents and the school that literally changed her life. "When I was in first grade, the teacher came to visit my family in our home. That visit made all the difference. My English came together that year. Before that, I had been floating through school. That visit told my family we were valued at the school. My parents understood they had a role there." Today she is the president of her own communications firm.

Model respect for other cultures and perspectives.

Educators are formidable role models for their students every day, impacting students for years to come by their words and actions. There is a golden opportunity to model respect starting from the first day by respecting names—our own and our students'. Names are powerful forms of identity. Ask someone whose name was changed by an outsider, like a teacher, and you'll learn that the hurt runs deep.

It is important to pronounce each child's name correctly, pronounced as they and their family want it said. Similarly, each teacher should expect the students to learn her or his name. Think about the message you send about the significance of names when you ask students to call you Mrs. K or Mr. B. Certainly students learn other multi-syllabic words, and names are the most value-laden of our words.

During faculty in-service training, I often use a thought-provoking exercise developed by Lee Mun Wah, called "My Name Was Changed" (Lee, 2004). It looks at the impact on a young Vietnamese man whose name Thuy was changed to Thomas by a teacher. In the exercise, Debbie, a Caucasian, can't understand why it's "such a big deal" because she was called Debbie and her name was Deborah. "It's just a name . . . ," she says. Faculty discussions during this exercise always bring out painful memories of names that were mispronounced or ignored or changed. It's never "just a name."

Teachers should encourage students to openly bring their personal culture into the classroom every day. Classroom discussions filled with insights from students with different backgrounds, different perspectives, different life experiences enrich the class for all.

I visited a kindergarten class to talk with them about a world map on their wall, where they had placed yarn from this town to the places around the world that their families had come from. I chatted with 5 year-old Melissa who told me that Ben wasn't in class that day because he was visiting his grandparents in Korea. I thought for a moment about the power in that statement. First, I don't think I ever uttered the word "Korea" until high school! Melissa could find it on a map at age 5. She knew that not everyone had grandparents who lived nearby, and that some people had to travel days just for a visit. She probably tried some special food that Ben brought from home, experiencing new tastes at an early age. When Ben returned from his trip, he would likely share some things he brought back, providing everyone in the class with an immediate connection to a land on the other side of the globe.

A history teacher in a diverse school told me that he has to be at the top of his game every day because there is always a student who knows more about a topic than he does. "They share their knowledge and perspectives, making everyone in the class think more deeply. My students motivate me to be a better teacher."

This broad range of views and backgrounds inspires students to think deeper in nearly every subject. The insights of students with different life experiences enhance the learning for every student. A board-certified chemistry teacher's eyes lit up when he shared with me a fascinating discourse in his classroom that began as a discussion on the importance of chemistry to society.

The chemistry students started talking about the practice of testing chemicals on animals to see if they are safe for human foods and pharmaceuticals. Some students championed animal rights, asserting that animals should never be used to test for human safety. One student who had recently immigrated from a country on the horn of Africa where starvation was not uncommon looked mystified. "Animal rights? What are 'animal rights?'" he asked with genuine puzzlement. "Animals are food."

There was quiet in the room. The other students, most of whom simply opened the refrigerator door to choose from a wide variety of food, stopped to think. How other people secure nutrients to live was now an issue they had to confront. Several came up to the teacher after class to tell him that the discussion had forced them to think about animals in an entirely new context. "We were so used to thinking about animals one way and not thinking there could be any other way," one student said. Their views on animal rights might not have changed, but their thinking was broader and more nuanced. The teacher recognized that the personalization the student brought to this issue inspired the students to think much more deeply than he could have through texts or lecture.

Use culture as a learning tool to broaden students' knowledge.

Too often teachers are afraid of discussing culture in the classroom except in prescribed ways at certain times. So there are months set aside to learn Black History, Hispanic or Asian cultures. While these commemorations have value in bringing these cultures to the fore, they give the impression that the rest of the year is about "real" history and culture.

International dinners also have their place, but they give us a tourist view of cultures, focused on food and dress, with perhaps some cultural entertainment. It is important that diverse cultures and histories be a part of learning all year long, and not just for their entertainment value.

December is the only time religion, a key element of individual culture, is ever broached in school and then it is typically in the form of some "holiday" music and parties. There are "winter" concerts, largely Christmas music with an obligatory Chanukah song thrown in for balance. Perhaps there is a discussion of Christmas around the world to give an international flavor. But there is rarely a discussion that broadens the context and turns this into a true learning opportunity, such as looking at the many cultures around the world that have winter holidays involving lights to brighten the dark skies.

There are significant religious holidays from major faiths that go unmentioned in schools. In recent years, Muslim Ramadan, Jewish Yom Kippur and Hindu Dawali have fallen within days of each other in the fall. But there is no discussion of these holidays and their significance to millions of people around the world, let alone students sitting in our schools. How much better we would be preparing our students to take part in the global village that awaits them if we opened their eyes to the wide-ranging religious celebrations that take part in months other than December. Instead, we end up with a homogenized secular celebration around an American holiday of the mainstream culture, based on the assumption that it is the only religious holiday worthy of attention.

Take yourself out of your comfort zone.

Everyone needs to know what it feels like to be The Other. For many, that means a conscious effort to get out of those places that are familiar and comfortable. Perhaps it starts with going to dinner in a restaurant where nothing on the menu is familiar. Perhaps it's going to a concert of music created by unfamiliar instruments striking new and different rhythms. Perhaps it is going to an event in a part of town where you've never been. Or traveling outside of the typical spots in which tourists hang out. Whatever it is, the experience challenges you to see how it feels to be the one who doesn't know all the rules, written and unwritten. You will become The Other and know what it feels like to not quite fit in. At the same time, it expands your horizons.

A striking thing happens when you get out of your comfort zone on a regular basis. As your assumptions about what is right and what is good drop by the wayside, you find your comfort zone widens and you realize you have grown in your assumptions and perspectives. When my children were in high school, we went out to dinner at a new spot. "Where is everyone?" my daughter asked. I looked around and saw tables filled with diners. "What do you mean?" I asked. "Where is EVERYONE?" she said. I realized that all the diners looked like us, and to my daughter—used to the thriving atmosphere of her diverse school—this was pretty boring stuff. Difference was her comfort zone.

Expand your thinking.

Reading books that challenge your thinking empowers you to see things from a different perspective. As James Banks, considered the father of multicultural education, states, "Teachers, like students bring understandings, concepts, explanations and interpretations to the classroom that result from their experiences in their homes, families and communities" (Banks, 1996, p. 22). With the vast majority of teachers from white middle-class homes, this viewpoint impacts students with other personal cultures every day.

Reading books from broad perspectives helps enlighten the issue that our history books are filled with references that show our Euro-centric viewpoint. Banks uses westward expansion as one example of how history is presented as fact, although it is actually a highly selective view of social reality (p. 20). Banks asks audiences to simply think about the words "pioneer" or "settler" and then to think what words the Sioux might have used to describe the same people. Were pioneers the "illegal immigrants" of their day?

There are great resources that open our eyes to assumptions we've been taught, such as Howard Zinn's *A People's History of the United States* (2005) and James Loewen's *Lies My Teacher Told Me: Everything Your American History Text Got Wrong* (2007). There is far more than a recognition that Christopher Columbus did not "discover" America. I often think about my own education that never mentioned Japanese-American internment camps in the United States in discussions about World War II. When I first learned about them in my 40s, I was horrified at the omission.

Empower our schools to be beacons of light in our diverse communities.

Schools provide a natural place for students and families of all backgrounds to get to know each other. They can be at the forefront of breaking down assumptions and stereotypes, shining a light throughout the entire community.

Storm Lake, Iowa, like many towns in the United States, watched an influx of immigrants come to take advantage of labor opportunities, changing its population from largely middle class white in the 1980s to nearly 50 percent minorities within a few years. It wasn't an easy transition, but the school leadership led the way in integrating the new residents into the fabric of the community.

The schools in Storm Lake "put the welcome mat out a foot farther," says Juli Kwikkel, principal of Storm Lake Elementary School. She made outreach to parents personal, with home visits to every new family by school personnel, sometimes Kwikkel herself. Recognizing that parents who work at the nearby packing plant often have trouble attending school events, she worked with the plant's human resources director to coordinate important programs with parents' shift schedules.

Since language was a critical barrier for both students and parents, the school marshaled community resources to offer language and parenting skills for parents in one section of the school. Iowa Central Community College and the elementary schools provided the instructors.

The whole town grew from the experience of building a multicultural community, and the school was on the front line. The school created opportunities for members of the community to get to know each other through programs like "Rockin' Readers" which had retirees reading to young immigrant children. The bonds that were formed through that program and others are unbreakable to this day. It was the school that showed how assumptions break down when people have the opportunity to get to know each other personally.

CONCLUSION

Each of us has an individual culture, a complex mix of our ethnicity, race, home life, background and experiences. With our culture comes assumptions about others, and likewise, others see us through their own prism of culture and assumptions.

As educators, we can't afford to limit the learning of students and families, and our learning, by not examining our assumptions, some conscious and some unconscious. We need to be aware of them, dispel myths and misperceptions, and create environments that enhance learning across and among cultures.

When we learn to value the perspectives of students and their families, our classrooms, our schools, and our communities thrive. If we remain mired in our own assumptions, we miss the lessons from a South African grandmother or the Sudanese pizza deliverer or the student sitting in our classrooms, waiting to be valued.

REFERENCES

Banks, James (1996). *Multicultural Education, Transformative Knowledge and Action*. New York: Teachers College.

Bowen, William C., Chingos, Mathew M., and McPherson, Michael S. (2009). *Crossing the Finish Line: Completing College at America's Public Universities*. Princeton, NJ: Princeton University Press.

Christensen, Linda (2000). *Reading, Writing and Rising Up*. Milwaukee: Rethinking Schools.

Kugler, Eileen Gale (2002). *Debunking the Middle-class Myth: Why Diverse Schools Are Good for All Kids*. Lanham, MD: Rowman and Littlefield Education.

Lee, Mun Wah (2004). *The Art of Mindful Facilitation*. Berkeley: StirFry Seminars and Consulting.

Loewen, James (2007). *Lies My Teacher Told Me: Everything Your American History Textbook Got Wrong*. New York: Simon and Schuster.

Lyon, George Ella (2011). *Where I'm From*. www.GeorgeEllaLyon.com.

Lyon, George Ella (1999). *Where I'm From; Where Poems Come From*. Texas: Absey and Company.

Rosenthal, Robert, and Jacobson, Lenore (1992). *Pygmalion in the Classroom: Teacher Expectations and Pupils' Intellectual Development* (Expanded ed.). New York: Irvington.

Sobel, Andrea, and Kugler, Eileen Gale (2007). Building Partnerships with Immigrant Parents. *Educational Leadership, 64(6)* , 62–66.

Teaching for Change. (n.d.) Tellin' Stories Project: www.TeachingforChange.org/parentorg/ overview.

Zinn, Howard (2005). *A People's History of the United States*. New York: HarperCollins.

ABOUT THE AUTHOR

Eileen Gale Kugler is a global speaker and consultant strengthening diverse schools, worksites, and communities. She breaks through dangerous *myth-perceptions* and shares strategies for building on the unique opportunities that diversity brings. Eileen is author of the award-winning *Debunking the Middle Class Myth: Why Diverse Schools are Good for All Kids*, which was called "a community and civic blueprint for the 21st Century." Eileen's articles and commentaries appear in wide-ranging publications, including *USA Today* and the *Washington Post, Educational Leadership, Phi Delta Kappan* and *Education Week*. She has been quoted in hundreds of publications and has been a broadcast guest on national and regional media. Her family's volunteer work in South Africa, including creating a 25,000-book library for a rural school, was featured in *The Washington Post* and on Voice of America television. Eileen lives with her husband Larry in Fairfax County, Virginia, where their two children grew up.

The Personal Power of a Teacher

Chapter 4

Montana's Indian Education for All

Preparing Teacher Candidates to Embrace Culturally Responsive Pedagogy

Jioanna Carjuzaa

While reviewing the multicultural education portfolio of a teacher candidate, I came across a quote she jotted down when she attended our Indian Education for All Professional Development Gallery Walk. Angela incorporated the quote in her final reflective essay summarizing her key take-aways from the course and capturing her fears about integrating Indian content into her future high school English courses. The quote is from *Sisters in Spirit: Haudenosaunee (Iroquois) Influences on Early American Feminists*.

"The key lesson I took away from this event is well-summarized in the following quote by Sally Roesch Wagner (2001): ' . . . the greatest likelihood is that as a white person, I will get it wrong; the highest probability is that I will cause damage . . . I am dangerous. If I wish to create accurate, inclusive history I must first open my ears to hear, my eyes to see, and my mind to absorb the story before me.' This quote was a part of one section of the Gallery Walk workshop. I was humbled and challenged when I read it" (p. 13).

All Montanans, Indians and non-Indians alike, are expected to learn about Montana's first inhabitants, under the state's groundbreaking Indian Education for All (IEFA) Act. Teacher candidates need to be prepared to teach their future K-12 pupils about Montana Indian tribes' unique histories. Integrating Indigenous knowledge across the curriculum at all grade levels is a comprehensive endeavor. In higher education, the responsibility of preparing these future K-12 classroom teachers to implement IEFA in a culturally responsive manner falls on the shoulders of the teacher educators in the education departments across the state. As a multicultural teacher educator, I embrace that responsibility.

This is an account of the struggles and challenges my teacher candidates face, and the successes and triumphs I enjoy in preparing them to integrate IEFA. The student quotes sprinkled throughout come from their reflective essays and their candid comments on surveys and in interviews. Although, in Montana, the focus is on Indigenous education, the principles highlighted here are applicable to the preparation of teacher candidates everywhere. By adopting and adapting this model, teacher educators worldwide can guide their teacher candidates to teach in a culturally responsive manner and create inclusive, respectful classrooms, regardless of their context.

THE LAST BEST PLACE—AND OUR CHALLENGE

Montana is mysterious to most outsiders. Recently at an international conference, organizers wrote the following on my badge: "Dr. Jioanna Carjuzaa, Associate Professor of Multicultural Education, Montana State University, Bozeman, Montana, Canada." I was aware that most people know very little about our state, but I was surprised to learn that many mistakenly think we are a Canadian province. Because of this widespread unfamiliarity with Montana, before I can share our educational reform efforts, I feel compelled to describe "The Last Best Place."

Although the official nickname for Montana is "The Treasure State" because of the rich mineral reserves, many refer to the fourth largest state in the United States affectionately as "Big Sky Country," "Land of Shining Mountains," and most recently as the "Last Best Place." Montana serves as the fodder for many jokes. According to comedian Jeff Foxworthy, you might live in Montana: "if you measure distance in hours; if your town has an equal number of bars and churches; if you know several people who have hit deer more than once; and if you're proud that your state makes the national news primarily because it houses the coldest spot in the nation." Although all of these claims have some truth to them, Montana is so much more.

Larger than Japan, Montana covers over 147,000 square miles; it can take more than a day to cross the state by car. We share a border with three Canadian provinces to the north, Idaho to the west, North and South Dakota to the east and Wyoming to the south. Our only city, Billings has approximately 100,000 inhabitants and only five towns have a population greater than 35,000. In fact, Montana is classified as a Frontier State. Although there are many criteria that define Frontier areas, suffice to say, they "are sparsely populated rural areas that are isolated from population centers and services." In Montana that translates into fewer than six people per square mile on average and more cattle than humans statewide.

In Montana, the total population has not reached the million mark. In fact, the 2010 Resident Population Estimate was 994,416. Yet, the American Indian population in this sparsely populated state is substantially higher than the national average and our 11.6% K-12 American Indian student population is more than 10 times the national average for American Indian students attending elementary and secondary schools. The first inhabitants of Big Sky Country were American Indians, and today 12 American Indian tribes call Montana home: Assiniboine, Blackfeet, Chippewa, Cree, Crow, Gros Ventre, Kootenai, Little Shell, Northern Cheyenne, Pend d'Oreille, Salish, and Sioux. Montana's seven Indian Reservations include: Flathead, Blackfeet, Rocky Boy, Ft. Belknap, Ft. Peck, Northern Cheyenne, and Crow; each is a sovereign nation and each one proudly supports a Tribal College. In addition, the estimated 4,500 Little Shell Band of Chippewa Indians, who are landless, call northern and central Montana home.

Between 85 and 90 percent of all American Indian and Alaska Native students across the United States and in Montana attend regular public schools. In Montana, our American Indian students often attend schools on or near reservations with high concentrations of other American Indian students. What is important to note here is that wherever the American Indian students attend public school, they are unlikely to have an American Indian teacher since only 2% of the teaching corps in Montana is made up of American Indian teachers. Unfortunately, many American Indian students are not successful in their respective learning communities, and a staggering 50% of American Indian students in Montana, as is the case nationally, do not graduate high school.

A lot has been written about the cultural mismatch between the increasingly diverse K-12 student population and what is described as a teaching corps made up primarily of white, middle class females in the U.S. It is our task, then, to prepare our teacher candidates to be culturally competent and to meet the academic and social needs of ALL of their students.

IN A SEA OF WHITE FACES

I am a faculty member in the Department of Education at Montana State University (MSU). I serve as the co-advisor to the American Indian Council and facilitate the IEFA professional development programs for faculty and staff. In the Native American Studies Department I team-teach Powwow Leadership and Powwow Fundraising. I have also taught graduate courses in educational leadership: Indigenous Research Methods and Social Justice in Education and teach multiple sections of Multicultural Education, a required foundations course, in the teacher education program. As is evident by the various appellations, we use the terms Native American, American Indian, Indian and Indigenous interchangeably. In Montana, it is actually more common for Tribal members to use their more specific tribal affiliations, in their respective languages when sharing their cultural identity (i.e., Apsáalooke–Crow).

MSU-Bozeman is a land grant institution of higher learning in the Rocky Mountain region. The school has experienced record enrollment, with nearly 14,000 students in 2010–11. The majority of the student body, 63%, were Montanans. The other 37% included students from the other states across the U.S. and 62 countries. In the Department of Education at MSU, this demographic trend is mirrored for the 1,250 undergraduate education students. MSU offers many majors in elementary and secondary teacher education. Approximately 60% of the students are elementary majors and the other 40% are pursuing secondary education certification. As is the case in the majority of the 1,200 teacher preparation programs across the U.S., the teacher candidates in our program are white, middle class females who are monocultural and monolingual.

MULTICULTURAL EDUCATION

The field-based teacher preparation program at MSU is aligned with the Interstate New Teacher Assessment and Support Consortium (INTASC) standards. These standards describe the knowledge, skills, and dispositions all teacher candidates are expected to know, and display in order to practice responsibly no matter what subject or grade level they teach. These expectations are infused in all coursework; however, certain courses require Signature Assignments focusing on specific standards. The INTASC Standards for New Teachers and the Curriculum Standards outlined by the National Association for Multicultural Education are infused throughout my multicultural education course. In particular, Standard 3: Diverse Learners, is addressed. In multicultural education, for the signature assignment, teacher candidates are required to create an IEFA unit plan that embodies culturally responsive pedagogy.

There are freshmen through post graduates, and majors representative of all eight colleges on campus who enroll in this course. Each semester all four sections are packed and there is always a waiting list. In this three-credit undergraduate foundations course I am charged with preparing teacher candidates to work with culturally and linguistically diverse students. I have designed this course to prepare my students to become culturally competent, reflective practitioners. In this course, we examine the historical, political, and cultural forces that foster systematic disparities based on ascribed characteristics, and critically examine a variety of strategies to address such disparities.

CULTURALLY RESPONSIVE PEDAGOGY

The K-12 student population across the U.S. is reflective of the rich cultural diversity found within American society. On the other hand, the teaching corps is described as a very homogeneous group. To best prepare my teacher candidates to work with students who are different from them, we explore the advantages to embracing culturally responsive pedagogy. Since the late 1980s, there has been a growing interest in how to best design and implement culturally responsive pedagogy in order to meet the needs of our K-12 students. This movement came about in response to the diversity found in our classrooms and the widening achievement gap that all too often leaves many minority students behind, despite numerous educational reforms.

Culturally responsive teaching builds meaningful bridges between the home culture and the school context and uses cultural referents to impart knowledge, skills, and attitudes and create more successful learners. Culturally responsive teaching values students' cultural heritages and validates their life experiences. According to Pewewardy and Hammer (2003), helping teachers to uncover their own biases, become reflective practitioners, and create an inclusive, respectful classroom environment is an ongoing process with positive results for American Indian students. "When schooling provides children with the knowledge, language, and skills to function in the mainstream culture but also honors and provides opportunities for students to learn more about their Native language and culture from elders and others in the community, a true respect for diversity is demonstrated" (Pewewardy and Hammer, 2003, p. 3). Culturally responsive pedagogy is embraced by Montana educators since IEFA and Indian student achievement are closely linked and classroom teachers and tribal members collaborate to support the implementation of IEFA. It is believed that schools that reflect the cultures of the students they serve support student learning.

Unfortunately, American Indian students have not always seen their cultures reflected in their schools in Montana. In class we talk about how ignoring misconceptions and misunderstandings and allowing American Indians to remain "invisible" is damaging to all students and how culturally responsive pedagogy can address these educational inequities. A member of the Little Shell Chippewa tribe captured the discomfort that students feel when their cultural heritage is not validated in the school setting and the hope the promise of Indian Education for All offers: "I think Indian Education for All . . . will help our children understand who they are, take pride in their identity, and see that they have possibilities and opportunities. When I was in school, we didn't talk about being Indian. If we could, we kept it secret. That was a way to get along. But with IEFA, our children won't have to do that. They will see themselves in school. They will know that their classmates are learning important things about them" (Hopkins, 2006, p. 207). As highlighted here, with IEFA, things are changing in Montana's classrooms. We have legal obligations, ethical commitments, and instructional responsibilities to educate all Montanans about the state's first inhabitants.

THE IEFA SIGNATURE ASSIGNMENT

To address the concerns and fears my students have about designing a culturally responsive IEFA unit plan, I have carefully choreographed the phases of the signature assignment for the multicultural education course. I now explicitly cover the evolution of this audacious legislation, highlighting key events leading to the funding of IEFA as well as reviewing the seven Essential Understandings Regarding Montana Indians in depth. I also share a detailed list of Web sites and other materials and resources, review various approaches to the infusion of multicultural content across the curriculum emphasizing James Banks's model for integrating content (1988, 1993), and go over guidelines for preparing a culturally responsive lesson plan for IEFA. After presenting this material, I assign the teacher candidates into groups according to the grade and/or subject they plan on teaching. Developing an IEFA unit plan is an opportunity for teacher candidates to collaborate with classmates and critically evaluate Web sites and resources that have been developed by Indian specialists at the Montana Office of Public Instruction (OPI), Tribal leaders, Tribal Elders, researchers, Class 7 Native American Language and Culture teachers, and other classroom teachers across Montana. Teacher candidates also have the opportunity to develop a unit plan that is tribal specific and meets one or more of the Essential Understandings. The groups share their unit plans with the class. They are also encouraged to add their unit plans to their electronic portfolios.

MUCH THUNDER, LITTLE RAIN

Since the November 2006 issue of *Phi Delta Kappan* featured IEFA, the spotlight has been shining on Montana and its leadership role in integrating

Indigenous knowledge in all disciplines at all grade levels, but our success did not come overnight. Before my teacher candidates can embark on preparing an IEFA unit plan in their respective disciplines and/or at a specific grade level, I need to familiarize them with the evolution of these legislative mandates.

Indian Education for All is an unprecedented reform effort some 40 years in the making. A Montana Supreme Court lawsuit and special legislative session resulted in funding for IEFA as part of the state's definition of a quality education. Funding allocated to school districts in 2005 and accompanying reporting requirements caused IEFA activities to begin in earnest (Carjuzaa, Jetty, Munson and Veltkamp, 2010). Mike Jetty, an Indian specialist at the Office of Public Instruction affectionately known locally as the "face of Indian Education for All," explained he first heard the expression "Much Thunder, Little Rain" from his friend, Dr. Lionel Bourdeaux, president of Sinte Gleska University in South Dakota. Dr. Bourdeaux was referring to what folks say regarding reform efforts in Indian education. We have used this saying in Montana to describe our journey.

In 1972, the Constitutional Convention met in Helena to revise the state's constitution. Although there were no American Indian representatives present, the other delegates were inspired by the moving testimony from high school students Mavis Scott and Diana Luppe from the Ft. Peck Reservation. It is amazing to think about the courage it took for these students to ask if they could learn about "themselves"—the Assiniboine and Sioux—in addition to covering the Roman empire, ancient Greece, the Mayan temples, and so on in their social studies curriculum.

It was delegate Richard Champoux who challenged his fellow legislators to preserve and protect American Indian cultural integrity. The delegates' response was formalized when they added language specific to preserving the cultural integrity of Montana's 12 tribal nations to the state's constitution. Article X, Section 1 (2) pledged, "The state recognizes the distinct and unique cultural heritage of American Indians and is committed in its educational goals to the preservation of their cultural integrity" (Mont. Const. art. X, §1.). By adding this language to Montana's constitution, delegates ensured that the state would have to honor the mandate (Carjuzaa, Jetty, Munson and Veltkamp, 2010). In recognizing the importance of including the distinct histories and heritages of cultures in its educational system, Montana took a step no other state has matched.

The following year an Indian Education Master Plan laid out how the state was expected to implement Article X. All Montana teachers teaching Indian students were required to complete Indian studies coursework. Unfortunately, the Office of Public Instruction (OPI) and the teacher education programs in

Montana were not prepared to provide said coursework for the 3,400 teachers affected by the Indian studies law. Regrettably, the requirement was repealed and the circumstances led many to think of this legislation as an exercise in futility. More than 15 years passed before the Montana State Accreditation Standards, which included recommendations that the schools include the contributions of Montana's Native Americans and address the unique needs and abilities of Native American Students, were developed in 1989. Unfortunately, as legislative researchers confirmed in 1995, little was being done to realize these recommendations.

In an effort to reinvigorate the provisions of Article X, in 1997, the Montana State Legislature designated the fourth Friday of September as "American Indian Heritage Day." Two years later, in 1999, the state constitution was codified when the Legislature passed House Bill 528 into law—MCA 20-1-501 which has become known as Indian Education for All (IEFA). It states, "Every Montanan . . . whether Indian or non-Indian, [should] be encouraged to learn about the distinct and unique heritage of American Indians in a culturally responsive manner. . . . all school personnel should have an understanding and awareness of Indian tribes to help them relate effectively with Indian students and parents. . . . Every educational agency and all educational personnel will work cooperatively with Montana tribes . . . when providing instruction and implementing an educational goal" (Mont. Code. Ann. ttl. 20, ch.1, pt. 5, § 1 Indian Education for All, 1999).

Once it was decided that all educators would be held responsible to integrate IEFA, decisions had to be made about what should be taught. In 1999, OPI brought together representatives from all 12 tribes in Montana and created the Seven Essential Understandings, guidelines which form the basis for all the IEFA curriculum efforts.

In 2005 the Montana Quality Education Coalition sued the State of Montana asserting that its educational funding scheme was unconstitutional. Then the special session met and provided the funding to implement their definition of quality, which includes IEFA. Consequently, we are required to integrate IEFA in all areas, in all classrooms, in all content, in all assessments, in all professional development programs, and in all teacher education programs across Montana. Then the legislature appropriated funds which were used to create model curriculums, assemble classroom materials, provide professional development, and fund grants for schools to develop best practices. In fact, under Governor Brian Schweitzer's administration, $13 million in funding was allocated to the OPI to enable K-12 school districts to implement IEFA in all Montana's classrooms and an additional $2 million was appropriated to the Tribal Colleges to write their tribal histories for use in K-12 classrooms.

IEFA IS FOR ELEMENTARY EDUCATION OR
SOCIAL STUDIES, NOT FOR ME

Even though Montana educators have a constitutional obligation to integrate IEFA across all disciplines at all grade levels, implementation does not always come easily. Some teacher candidates feel a natural fit to their discipline, as expressed by Camy, an art student who had this to say about her discipline: "This is a FANTASTIC subject to integrate Indian education in because there is so much space for understanding the various Indian cultures through their art. It will be awesome to have a subject that can so easily reach across any language or cultural barriers and get students to recognize similarities between cultures." Many are supportive and eager to integrate IEFA as demonstrated by Amanda's statement, "I am very excited to teach IEFA. I will try to incorporate it in most of my lessons. It is good for students to learn and have respect for all cultures," likewise Frank says, "I think integrating IEFA into the curriculum is an excellent idea and will work to try to integrate unique Indian cultures into every lesson so it feels natural." Some teacher candidates, however, feel that IEFA does not pertain to their discipline and/or grade level, that the integration seems forced or superficial and that they will have a difficult time seeing the purpose and/or connection. Often secondary majors in science and math have the hardest time understanding how they can integrate IEFA in their disciplines. An elementary teacher candidate shared what many voiced: "At first I thought IEFA would be more difficult to incorporate in the curriculum than it really was. I think it will be easier to incorporate IEFA into elementary school, English/literature, and history classes than it will be to incorporate it into math and science classes."

Ashley, a secondary math major, had this to share: "I think IEFA is a very important thing in our school. However, I don't believe a math classroom is the best place to learn about Native Americans. Story problems could encompass facts about Native Americans, but it would be difficult to create an entire lesson using IEFA. Also, history isn't our area of expertise. So, if a math teacher is going to integrate IEFA, they're going to have to be creative." Still, most teacher candidates majoring in math and science are willing to try. Hillary, a biological sciences major, said, "I think initially it will take time and effort to figure out how to integrate IEFA into my high school science classroom, but it will be worth it to see students as well as myself gain a better understanding of and appreciation for other cultures." Casey, another math major, shared this after his experience creating an IEFA unit plan with his group on patterns using Crow bead work: "For math class it may be challenging to incorporate IEFA into a lesson plan. However, I do feel that if I can find ways to incorporate IEFA into my lesson plans it would be a great change of routine for my high school students. It was great to see how much the class enjoyed our beading lesson. Making math fun and relevant is important. The main resource we used for our group teaching offered several examples of how IEFA could be incorporated into a lesson plan. I'm excited to try out the geometry teepee unit with my future students."

WHY DO WE HAVE TO LEARN AND
TEACH ABOUT INDIANS, ANYWAY?

The resistance I have observed among in-service and pre-service teachers, administrators, and community members alike usually results from a misunderstanding of the goals of IEFA. At MSU, many teacher candidates voice their concern about what they perceive as an unfair bias when the focus is put on American Indians. Mark, a teacher candidate with a double major, had this to say, "I'm going to teach both music and math. I don't see much use or help to integrate IEFA in math curriculum. This is a social issue and has nothing to do with math. I could definitely see its application in music. Overall, though, I question why we specifically focus on Indian education. If we really strive for diversity, then doesn't focusing on one or even two Indian cultures kind or detract from teaching about general diversity? Why just the Indian and general history as curriculum? Diversity should include everybody."

According to Bobbi Ann Starnes (2006), a former reservation classroom teacher, "Whether or not there are large numbers of Native Americans or reservations in every region of the country, Indian Education For All under-scores a national challenge to our education system to improve our teaching about Native America history and culture more evident than during the month of November" (p. 186). The state of Montana has made this mandate clear, as IEFA is a constitutional requirement, a state law, and a Montana Supreme Court mandate. In fact, educators in other states have voiced their frustration in not having the backing of similar legislation.

While the legal obligation is clear, it is the ethical commitments and instructional responsibilities which were mentioned earlier that get at why we really do this work. In a model social studies lesson plan designed by the OPI, students are asked to brainstorm why they should learn about American Indi-ans. Then they are instructed to read through a collection of primary source documents, from the 1972 Montana State Constitutional Convention, Montana state law and an excerpt from a Supreme Court case. This quote in particular, by delegate Richard Champoux, discussing the Indian Education amendment (Quotes, Const. Trans. 1972), explains the ethical reasons for IEFA: "Every other ethnic group in this country has a country of origin to relate to in their pride of heritage, and we have learned in our schools about their countries.

All of us have taken Greek history, Roman history, English history, French history, and so forth. Why not Indian history? . . . Why not a Chief Charlo day, Chief Joseph, Chief Hungry Horse, and so forth? What is the country of origin for American Indians? It is America. What have the average Americans learned in our schools about our American Indian people? Very little, if not nothing." Delegate Dorothy Eck had this to add during the Constitutional Convention after hearing the pleas from the Ft. Peck high school students (Quotes, Const. Trans. 1970): "They came asking what . . . the Convention could do, to assure them that they would have the opportunity . . . to study their own culture, perhaps their own language, and to develop a real feeling of pride in themselves for their own heritage and culture, and also a hope that other students all over Montana would recognize the importance and the real dignity of American Indians in the life of Montana."

When we think of our instructional responsibilities to carry out the intent of IEFA, it is also important to emphasize our commitment as multicultural educators. It is our duty to combat stereotypes, address misconceptions and inaccuracies, and confront educational inequities. If we expect our teacher candidates to act as change agents and their future K-12 pupils to challenge the status quo, then we need to empower them to demand social justice by treating all people with fairness, respect, and dignity.

Montana's mandate to teach Indian cultures and histories in a culturally responsive manner has impact beyond the classrooms of our state. If we truly are to embrace the diversity we have, and provide equal educational opportunities for all of our students and promote social justice, then the ethical and instructional aspects play very important roles. In our classrooms we have to value our students' cultural heritages, and validate their life experiences. Adrienne Rich (1986) eloquently stated, "When those who have the power to name and socially construct reality choose not to see you or hear you, whether you are dark-skinned, old, disabled, female, or speak with a different accent or dialect than theirs, when someone with the authority of a teacher, say, describes the world and you are not in it, there is a moment of psychic disequilibrium, as if you looked in the mirror and saw nothing" (p. 199). For far too long, our education system has rendered too many students invisible.

This concern was echoed by multicultural education theorist James Banks at the IEFA Best Practices Conference in Bozeman, in 2007. He said, "In order to endorse the national culture, people must see themselves reflected and valued within that culture. We must make all children feel included in our national identity" (Carjuzaa et al., 2010, p. 193). To create a space for an inclusive "we," we have to understand the importance cultural identity plays in the teaching-learning process, be humble enough to admit that we do not have all the answers, and be willing to collaborate with others who are different from us. We need to heighten our awareness, avoid assumptions, ask questions, and model cultural sensitivity.

Indian Education for All exemplifies tenets shared in the numerous definitions of multicultural education. Neither a prescribed curriculum nor an add-on program, IEFA is a comprehensive approach to be infused in every aspect of education. The primary goal of IEFA, like all other multicultural education approaches, is to promote the education and achievement of ALL students, especially those who are traditionally ignored by and underserved in our education system. According to Banks, the father of multicultural education, challenging and confronting misconceptions, untruths, and stereotypes about American Indians and other minority groups allows educators to effect social change by making curriculum more inclusive of all groups (1993).

AN INDIAN IS AN INDIAN IS AN INDIAN, RIGHT?

As mentioned earlier, once a decision was made to teach about the cultures and heritages of American Indians, Tribal members representative of all Tribal nations in Montana gathered to create the Seven Essential Understandings. These guidelines serve to help teachers decide what should be covered in their classes. As John, a social studies broadfield major points out, "As a future history teacher, Montana's IEFA requirements provide a great framework for incorporating a multicultural curriculum in the classroom. As with any such requirement, however, these guidelines should serve as a benchmark for the lowest effort exerted, rather than as the target for teaching a good, culturally sensitive lesson. A good instructor will go above and beyond the guidelines and truly incorporate Indian history/culture into the curriculum whenever it is possible."

Essential Understanding 1 and Essential Understanding 2 address the problems that result when American Indians are all lumped together and discussed in a Pan-Indian manner. The Essential Understandings encourage educators to learn the differences among the tribes' histories, cultures, languages, traditions and to explore individual cultural identity. These two Essential Understandings are a great starting place for teacher candidates and K-12 pupils to learn about the similarities and differences among Montana's Indians. Essential Understanding 1 states, "There is great diversity among the 12 tribal Nations of Montana in their languages, cultures, histories and governments. Each Nation has a distinct and unique cultural heritage that contributes to modern Montana." Essential Understanding 2 states, "There is great diversity among individual American Indians as identity is developed, defined and redefined by entities, organizations and people. A continuum of Indian identity, unique to each individual, ranges from assimilated to traditional. There is no generic American Indian."

One elementary education major shared this regarding the importance of learning tribal-specific information: "I feel like IEFA is very important to a 5th grade curriculum. In 5th grade was the first time I learned anything about Native Americans. I learned about "generic" Native American history; I did not learn about different cultural groups or modern issues so I had many misconceptions. I thought all Indians were the same and I actually thought that all Indians ceased to exist after we put them on reservations. I want to make sure that my future students aren't misled in the same way."

BLAME, SHAME, GUILT

My teacher candidates are often unaware of the federal policies, except for maybe the colonization period, that have had and continue to have an impact on American Indians with devastating effects. Therefore, I familiarize them with Essential Understanding 5 which states, "Federal policies, put into place throughout American history, have affected Indian people and still shape who they are today. Much of Indian history can be related through several major federal policy periods: Colonization Period 1492–; Treaty Period 1789–1887; Allotment Period 1887–1934; Boarding School Period 1879–; Tribal Reorganization Period 1934–1958; Termination Period 1953–1988; Self-determination 1975–current." Since my students plan on being classroom teachers, I think it is important to review the history and foundation of American Indian education policy with them; I do this by focusing in on the boarding school era.

In a class activity, I introduce my students to the K-W-L-H technique developed by Donna Ogle (1986) to help students organize their knowledge about Indian boarding schools. I place students in groups and start the activity by asking them to brainstorm and record their responses to the first two categories, K and W. K—stands for what they KNOW about Indian boarding schools, W—stands for what they WANT to learn about Indian boarding schools, L—stands for what they LEARN from our "intervention," and H—stands for HOW they can learn more.

After the students have recorded what they already know about Indian boarding schools, which usually is very minimal, they come up with questions they would like to know the answers to that they think will help them to better understand their American Indian students, their families, and their communities. Then I share three video clips with them so they can begin to answer some of their questions. We start with the PBS special *In the White*

Man's Image, which chronicles how Indian children were forcibly removed from their homes, transported across the U.S. and "imprisoned" in boarding schools. The film focuses on Captain Richard Pratt and the founding of the Carlisle Indian Industrial School in 1879. It depicts the experiment in forced assimilation led by Pratt to "kill the Indian and save the man" by stripping the Indian students of their identity and forcing them to learn English and become "civilized."

Second, we watch excerpts from *Our Spirits Don't Speak English* by Rich-Heape Films, Inc. This film shares an American Indian perspective on life within the boarding school institutions between 1879 and the 1970s. The moving interview excerpts from Andrew Windyboy and others detailing the abuse they endured are heart wrenching. Third, we watch the trailer from *Something's Moving/The Thick Dark Fog* by Randy Vasquez. In this film Vasquez explores the legacy of American Indian boarding schools through the voices and stories of survivors. The survivors retell the horrors they experienced while attending boarding school. They share accounts of the brutality and loneliness they suffered and recount the painful reality of being separated from their families, their culture, their spirituality and their identity. The devastating impact their boarding school experiences have had on their lives is evident as is their courageous efforts at healing and confronting generational trauma.

When my teacher candidates learn about the abuse that took place in these boarding schools they are horrified and outraged. One student remarked, "It disgusts me that this aspect of history was hidden from us for so long. It's hard to understand how terribly the children were treated in the Indian boarding schools." Another student had this to share after our K-W-L-H activity: "IEFA is an incredibly important curriculum because of its historical relevance and current impact on history and events today. No wonder so many Indian kids are reluctant to trust teachers. No wonder there is such pathology in Indian country. I had no idea they had suffered such trauma. Students deserve to be safe in school. I want my students to learn about these different cultures, different lifestyles and tragic events so they can diversify their understanding of the world."

Some students have a hard time learning about the Indian boarding schools as well as most historical accounts of massacres, forced migration, genocide, etc. They internalize the events and feel like we are pointing the finger at them. It is important to stress that we need to learn about all of this because it is our shared history and we can not change what we do not acknowledge. I emphasize that playing the "blame game" benefits no one. Here a student shares why he believes it is important to critically evaluate what is taught and question what is left out of the history curriculum, "I think it is important to teach students about Native Americans' history, especially in the western states. Even if it's ugly, it's something we should have a common knowledge of since it is part of our everyday world. But, honestly, it makes me so uncomfortable. I feel like I am being blamed for all of the atrocities that took place. Still, I know we all need to learn this."

HOW COME I NEVER HEARD OF THAT?

Students are often disturbed and shocked to discover that in their K-12 educations and college courses several "inconvenient truths" have never been broached. "The closest I ever came to studying Indians was looking at Lewis and Clark's journey. Of course it was from their perspective," one student remarked. Many teacher candidates share their frustration in what they describe as an incomplete education. We talk about Essential Understanding 6, "History is a story most often related through the subjective experience of the teller. With the inclusion of more and varied voices, histories are being rediscovered and revised. History told from an Indian perspective frequently conflicts with the stories mainstream historians tell."

We explore revisionist histories by reading excerpts from Vine Deloria, Jr. and Daniel Wildcat's *Power and Place: Indian Education in America*, James Loewen's *Lies My Teacher Told Me: Everything Your High School History Textbook Got Wrong*, Howard Zinn's *A People's History of the United States: 1492—Present* and Ronald Takaki's *From Different Shores: Perspectives on Race and Ethnicity in America*, among others. We discuss the meaning of "the truth" and settle for an explanation of "a truth." We conclude that there is no one reality, only multiple perceptions. We talk about being inclusive and how important it is to include Indigenous voices in our study of American history. As one history major commented, "There really is a need for Native American history to be taught in our schools, because most of us know very little. Not a separate Indian history course, but an American history that tells both sides of the story." He added, "Native American oral histories should be counted as legitimate histories and should be taught as such." Another student shared, "In a science class or any other subject, really, I think it's important to implement IEFA into the curriculum because we need more exposure to cultures and perspectives other than the European-American mainstream culture and the beliefs in the status quo. But also because it is a chance to get another perspective as well as gain insight and relate better to those who are different from ourselves." Another student commented, "I am definitely going to integrate IEFA into my social studies curriculum. It is very important to give students differing perspectives and provide information that was NOT available to me as an aspiring student. I could use many different subject topics to demolish stereotypes my students may have already come across."

I CAN'T TEACH WHAT I DON'T KNOW

Among teacher candidates, there is a shared all-too-common journey which I first depicted in an article highlighting the professional development of teacher educators (Carjuzaa, 2009). For too many generations, Indian and non-Indian students alike have graduated from their respective secondary schools across Montana having learned virtually nothing about American Indians. They were unlikely to have been presented curriculum from an Indigenous perspective, exposed to lessons that were framed from an Indigenous worldview, or required to read about Indigenous contributions in core curricular areas.

If these high school graduates decide to pursue teaching careers, their educational gap concerning Montana Tribal histories and cultures is compounded. Even with the recent IEFA implementation efforts, this predicament still exists. It is especially problematic for teacher candidates currently enrolled in our teacher preparation programs because most of these teacher candidates had already graduated from high school before their respective schools started implementing IEFA. Since these teacher candidates were not exposed to information on the unique cultures and histories of Montana's American Indians, they need to gain this background knowledge in their teacher preparation programs.

In fact, when I surveyed my teacher candidates about their concerns in integrating IEFA, many of them expressed uneasiness and shared that they were not confident they could do it. They felt they were inadequately prepared. When asked about whether she felt ready to teach K-12 pupils about the unique histories and cultures of Montana's tribes, one teacher candidate commented on how she had never been exposed to Indian content before enrolling in her Native American Studies course. She shared her disbelief regarding this grievous omission by saying, "I took Intro. To Native American Studies last semester and prior to that class I have never learned ANY Native American history, laws, or even heard stories. SAD!!! How can I teach it???"

In *An Imagined Educational Journey*, Juneau (2000) related the typical limited exposure to Indian culture and history teacher candidates are likely to have had in their K-12 educational journey and the need for increased Indian education in our schools. The superficial, spotty exposure to Indian education that is typical is described here. In first grade, sometime in the fall between the Halloween and Thanksgiving holidays, students are likely to make and wear paper feathered hats and role play Indians and Pilgrims enjoying the first

Thanksgiving. In fourth grade, students usually play Oregon Trail, a game which emulates the crossing of the Western United States in the year 1848 from the American settlers' point of view. In eighth grade, students often take Montana history which might make mention of General Custer and the famous local Battle of the Little Big Horn from the mainstream perspective. In high school, students usually cover world history, which is framed in an old world/new world dichotomy; even though they may touch on American Indians, their curriculum is likely to ignore civilizations before Columbus' discovery. In college, students wanting to be K-12 classroom teachers enroll in courses in their respective teacher preparation programs and are introduced to the requirements of IEFA in a limited manner. These teacher candidates graduate and start their new teaching positions with little background knowledge and minimal exposure to culturally responsive instructional strategies (Carjuzaa, 2009).

Because of this one-sided view of history and lack of basic exposure to Indigenous perspectives, my teacher candidates are concerned that they do not have the necessary background information to integrate IEFA. One general science major expressed his feelings of inadequacy: "IEFA was a provision put in the Montana Constitution that requires schools to teach all students about Indians, especially Plains Indians' cultures and histories. Teachers need to have enough knowledge about Plains Indians or, if you teach, math or science, understand the Indian perspective on those subjects."

PLEASE DON'T LET ME COMMIT A FAUX PAS

Of all the concerns that teacher candidates voice in regards to integrating IEFA, the fear of getting it wrong or offending American Indian classmates, peers, students, their families and communities is the most paralyzing. One of my elementary teacher candidates gave this advice, "Make sure you know the facts, not just common misconceptions, to present. You have to know what you are talking about so you don't offend anyone." Another teacher candidate had this to share after receiving constructive criticism from a Crow classmate, "Coyote stories, gosh, I didn't know they could only be told certain times of the year, by certain individuals. I am so embarrassed. I feel so terrible." Another teacher candidate made this confession during her IEFA group presentation: "We wanted to do our IEFA presentation on American Indian powwows. We thought it would be great to tape the Grand Entry, some of the dance competitions, the vendors, etc. at the 36th Annual MSU American Indian Council Powwow to share with you guys. I attended the powwow and did all of the filming. When we were reading Dr. Murton McCluskey's

"Your Guide to Understanding and Enjoying Powwows" I realized I broke etiquette. I had taped Assiniboine Cree, the Host Drum without getting their permission. I was horrified. What if I had shared that tape with you guys, my classmates, or worse yet, my future students? I felt so bad."

Students are afraid of stumbling over unfamiliar words/terms and mispronouncing words from an Indian language that seems impossible for them to learn and remember. They are also afraid that their actions will be seen as inappropriate. A female music major borrowed a hand drum from the museum collection and spent hours memorizing the vocables to a Blackfeet honor song in order to bravely stand up before all of her classmates and perform her solo, only to be told by an Indian classmate after her performance that only men, Indian men, are allowed to sing honor songs for individuals who have accomplished great deeds. He went on to explain that the Blackfeet also use songs for courting, traveling, lullabies, and praise. He explained, "like some Elders and Traditional Indians, I think anyone who is non-Native should not play Indian hand drums" (a perspective not shared by all American Indians—see Essential Understanding 2). He claimed that since the hand drums are sacred, they should only be played by Indians. The female music major was really crushed, embarrassed, and dismayed. Another music major had this observation: "I think integration is tricky. You are trying to protect something in a authentic, accurate way that you may not totally understand. I think if there were more examples and collaboration between music teachers and Native Americans it might be easier to come up with plans that are accurate both to IEFA and the content area." In fact, collaboration between classroom teachers and tribal members is modeled for the teacher candidates. Instead of having this end as a "disaster" we used this incident as a teachable moment emphasizing what we learned from the experience and how to ask tribal members for assistance.

IN CONCLUSION

All eyes are on Montana as the IEFA initiative sets a valiant national precedent for K-12 education across the nation and around the world. The attention is evidenced by the educators and scholars from as far away as China and Australia who have visited Montana to observe and study our practical application of culturally responsive pedagogy so that they may adapt the model for their context. Only recently, since the 2005 redefinition of "quality education," and allocation of funds to support curriculum development and professional development, has IEFA truly taken off.

Still, integrating IEFA across the curriculum in a culturally responsive manner is a challenging task for teacher candidates. The OPI Indian

Education Specialist Mike Jetty captures just how daunting it can be, saying, "It's a work in progress—like building an airplane as it moves down the runaway!" Asking elementary and secondary education majors enrolled in multicultural education courses to complete a survey, participate in interviews, and write reflective essays has provided me with helpful information to scaffold their learning. From their responses, it became evident that teacher candidates need specific instruction in the benefits and goals of culturally responsive pedagogy as well as an overview of the chronology of this landmark legislation, and the Seven Essential Understandings that serve as guidelines for what Indigenous knowledge is to be integrated across the curriculum. They also need some handholding while exploring how to create lessons that are meaningful and appropriate. I discovered that teacher candidates are likely to have had minimal exposure to culturally responsive pedagogy as an approach and lack a clear understanding of the requirements of IEFA. They also have very limited background knowledge regarding the unique histories, cultures and contemporary issues facing Montana's Indian tribes.

Helping teacher candidates design lesson and unit plans that teach core curricular concepts from an Indigenous perspective and that also satisfy the expectations of the third and fourth levels of curriculum integration of Banks model (1988, 1993)—the most difficult levels but those with the greatest potential to meet the goals of multicultural education—can be quite challenging. But if we expect transformation, we must provide students with the opportunity to participate in equitable education.

Yes, IEFA does result in many positive outcomes, including promoting human relations, increasing self-esteem, and helping to preserve students' native languages and cultures. However, these are not the primary goals of multicultural education in general or IEFA specifically. Indian Education for All reaches beyond Montana's borders, inspiring educators around the world to become more culturally inclusive in their classrooms and communities, embracing the ideals of social justice and educational equity.

REFERENCES

Banks, J. A. *Multiethnic Education: Theory and Practice*. 2nd ed. Boston: Allyn and Bacon. 1988.

Banks, J. A. "Integrating the Curriculum with Ethnic Content: Approaches and Guidelines." In *Multicultural education: Issues and perspectives*, edited by J. A. Banks & C. A. McGee Banks (pp. 189–207). Boston: Allyn and Bacon. 1993.

Carjuzaa, J. "Professional Development for Teacher Educators to Help Them Prepare Their Teacher Candidates to Integrate Montana's Indian Education for All Act

Across the K-12 Curriculum," *International Online Journal of Educational Sciences*, 1 (1), 2009, 29–47.

Carjuzaa, J., Jetty, M., Munson, M. and Veltkamp, T. "Montana's Indian Education for All: Applying Multicultural Education Theory, *Multicultural Perspectives,* 12 (4), 2010, 192–198.

Essential Understandings Regarding Montana Indians—Retrieved August 10, 2010 from www.opi.mt.gov/pdf/indianed/resources/essentialunderstandings.pdf.

Hopkins, W. "Indian Education for All through our own eyes: The promise of IEFA," *Phi Delta Kappan,* 88(3), 2006, 207.

Juneau, D. (2000). *An Imagined Educational Journey.* The University of Montana Press.

Mont. Code. Ann. ttl. 20, ch.1, pt. 5, § 1. Indian Education for All, 1999.

Mont. Const. art. X, §1.

Pewewardy, C., and Hammer, P. C. "Culturally Responsive Teaching for American Indian Students." *ERIC Digest*, Retrieved from ED482325 2003-12-00 ERIC Digests, 2003.

Quotes from the 1972 Montana Constitutional Convention courts.mt.gov/library/mt_cons_convention/index.pdf.

Roesch Wagner, S. *Sisters in Spirit: Haudenosaunee (Iroquois) Influences on Early American Feminists.* Summertown, TN: Native Voices Book Publishing Company, 2001.

Starnes, B. A. "Montana's Indian Education for All: Toward an Education Worthy of American Ideals," *Phi Delta Kappan*, 88(3), 2006, 184–192.

ABOUT THE AUTHOR

Dr. Jioanna Carjuzaa is an associate professor of education at Montana State University-Bozeman. She holds a Ph.D. in multicultural, social and bilingual foundations of education from the University of Colorado-Boulder. She has over twenty years teaching experience as a multicultural teacher educator, diversity trainer, and English for academic purposes instructor. At MSU she teaches multiple sections of multicultural education in addition to offering graduate courses in social justice in education, indigenous research methodologies, American Indian studies for teachers, and Teaching EFL/ESL. Of Greek heritage, Jioanna is well aware of the challenges culturally and linguistically diverse students face when competing with native English speakers in demanding content courses. Jioanna is grateful to serve as the co-advisor to American Indian Council and has had the very enjoyable opportunity to team teach Powwow Leadership and Powwow Fundraising with Jim Burns numerous times. In addition, Jioanna serves as the facilitator for Indian Education for All professional development opportunities for MSU faculty, staff, and students. She resides in Montana with her husband Gilles and their two keeshonds, Lance and Arthur.

Chapter 5

The Importance of Student Stories

Karyn Keenan

The January wind rushed in with the students as I stood in front of my classroom door. As Thomas poked my side for the second time I pulled myself away from the thoughts of my unchecked mailbox, the teacher who wants to borrow a flip cam and the ringing phone. "Did your mom have the baby?" I asked. "Not yet, but she says she is going to soon." Thomas sighed as he moved into the room to unpack. My focus has to be on Thomas, especially as he will become a big brother any day and that has him a little scared! I have to remember to look him in the eyes and listen to his stories, especially in those early rushed moments. Each student has important stories to share and as a teacher I must give them the opportunities to share them.

It is important to build times throughout the school day and school year when students are able to tell their stories. Giving value to the words, actions and thoughts of students helps them understand that what they say and do is important. By listening to each others' stories in a respectful environment, students learn to give more consideration to their own actions and thoughts, as well as those of their classmates. Carving out time for students to listen to each other's stories, while not an easy task in a busy classroom, is vital to establishing this respectful environment.

Teaching at an urban school that focuses on immigrant, refugee and neighborhood students means that my class is incredibly diverse. I have taught students whose families are from more than 15 different countries and who speak at least as many languages. When all of these students come together in a classroom there is a need to help students understand one another. Building a common set of class community values is important to this understanding.

One of the best ways we can do that is to listen to each other and tell others what is important to us.

In my classroom, our storytelling begins during our Morning Meeting, which I base on Roxann Kriete's *The Morning Meeting Book*. Each student is assigned a day of the week when he or she may bring in an item or simply speak to the class. It is during these moments when students can announce that they are taking a family trip, show us a photo of a loved one or even let us know that today is a brother's birthday. Carving out the 15 minutes for the Morning Meeting can be a challenge with all the demands facing teachers and their schedules. However, this time to share is crucial for students. On the mornings when we do not have time for the full Morning Meeting, I still make sure that we have time for sharing.

In addition to Morning Meeting, students share important things about their lives through projects such as creating personal timelines. Students work on their timelines with their parents and have to include at least eight events, including their birth year and when they entered second grade. Photographs or carefully drawn pictures accompany the explanation of the events in the child's life. For me, this is a wonderful way to learn about what my students and their families believe are defining moments in their lives. After we hang these timelines on the wall and students can see each other's timelines they make connections to each other's lives.

One year after I hung the timelines on the wall, Deondre noticed that Janeya had also been to the Wisconsin Dells the previous summer. Deondre had never really talked to Janeya, but now they had a starting point for a never-ending conversation on the merits of different water slides.

One of my favorite parts of the timeline project is creating my own timeline. Students learn about my graduations from high school and college. They can ask questions about the 1999 Women's World Cup soccer matches that I attended. They see when I started teaching at Passages. By seeing a visual representation of my story students are able to make connections to me, as well as understanding that their stories will extend long beyond where they currently end.

STORYTELLING THROUGHOUT THE CURRICULUM

When my students have the opportunity to share relevant personal stories they are more connected to their learning. Each October the second grade studies immigration, as part of the Core Knowledge Curriculum. My colleague, Brianne Pitts, and I have developed a series of activities that help students investigate and present their own immigration stories. Each student interviews a family member about how their family came to Chicago, and that interview becomes the basis for a family history map and ancestor doll. Many of my students know that their parents came to the United States from somewhere else, but few know how their parents came here. Last year one of my students learned that his grandfather was the leader of a town in Nigeria. I love learning alongside my students about the paths their families have taken.

On the history maps, students draw outlines of their countries of origin, as well as an outline of the United States. They then illustrate the way their families came to the United States. My colleague Brianne's beautifully drawn example showed her family's path, by boat, to the United States from Poland.

Our children bring rich examples of how their families came to the United States. There were cars traveling from Mexico to Chicago. Many other students took planes from Bosnia, Iraq or Nigeria. And still other students illustrated boats traveling from Africa, the exact location of where their ancestors originated unknown. After creating these maps my students were full of questions for each other about why their ancestors came to America.

Because each student had created their own map and interviewed their own family member, they knew their immigration story more intimately. One student knew that her parents had left Bosnia during the war. Another remembered her mother describing the hot, sticky weather as they drove north from Mexico. And yet others informed our class that their families came to the United States not out of choice, but because they were forced onto boats and brought to America to be slaves.

Each student is supplied with a cardboard cutout of a human body and, with the help of his or her parents, transforms the cutout into an "ancestor doll." Students bring in intricately created dolls wearing traditional clothing, enabling them to share cultural norms and traditions of dress. Sharing the dolls is a fun experience as we all practice learning words such as *barong tagalog*, the name of dress for Filipino boys, and *gele*, the name of a Yoruban head tie.

This project not only gives students the opportunity to tell their own stories, it provides a way for students to understand both their own backgrounds and those of others. Education about other people and their cultures turns into better understanding of each other. Making each child feel welcome in a classroom, which is crucial to their learning, is only possible if students understand each other.

During the ancestor doll presentation, Abeja's face kept lighting up. As a student who was new to our school, Abeja was delighted to learn that so many of her classmates also had families who came from Nigeria. During the question session after Amra's presentation, a classmate asked if everyone had left Bosnia because of the war and Amra informed us that not everyone had left and she still had family in Bosnia.

MAKING TIME FOR DAILY WRITING

Giving students the opportunity to tell their stories does not need to involve elaborate lesson plans or home projects. Each day my class has a Writing Workshop in which, after a read-aloud and a mini-lesson, students have time to write. English language learners "need to know from the very beginning of their exposure to English that writing is an act of communication and everyone is capable of engaging in this form of communication, albeit with varying degrees of sophistication" (Samway and McKeon 2007, 58).

Daily writing time in class is a fantastic way to allow students to work on communicating their stories through writing. We use the Lucy Calkins writing curriculum; as she notes, "human beings come to know each other through the sharing of stories, and beginning the year with a narrative unit provides opportunities to build community" (Calkins 2009, 2). The early narrative unit allows me to introduce myself to my students in a unique way. By modeling that day's mini-lesson in my own writing, students can learn about some of my personal experiences (like the time my sister and I rang the bell in our church, moments before her wedding).

One of the most important parts of our Writing Workshop occurs at the end when students share what they have worked on that day. Each day I pick a few Popsicle® sticks with students' names written on them out of a jar and those students share a few sentences of what they have written. At the end of a writing project I have the students form groups and share their writing with the other students in their groups. Afterwards they put their writing on their desks and everyone walks around to look at everyone else's work.

Students find a partner and read their writing (or have it read to them). Each student is encouraged to give a compliment to the writer whose piece they just read. After a few minutes students find a new partner and read a new piece. During a fairy tale unit students complimented each other on the ways they adapted the original tales in unique ways. Students also love looking at each other's illustrations and the different touches they put in their work.

As teachers we hold students responsible for what they are working on by setting standards, such as having them write at least five sentences and assigning grades to the work they have done. Giving students an opportunity to share what they are working on provides a measure of accountability that goes far beyond grades. My students love hearing what others read and love sharing what they have written. It is my job to carve the time out of the day to give them that important time to share their stories.

HELPING STUDENTS START THEIR STORIES

All teachers have faced the student who reports he or she has nothing to write about. We normally try to follow it up by suggesting things that we know the child is interested in or asking questions about their weekend. By providing "story starters" that the students choose we can help them break through their writer's block. Providing activities that appeal to multiple intelligences, or learning through a variety of ways, as these activities do, gives students the opportunity to story-tell in ways that best suit them.

Literacy centers in the elementary classroom lend themselves well to giving students opportunities to write stories. Incorporating different writing prompts and strategies allows students opportunities to write creatively. It is important for students to have opportunities to tell their fiction stories, as they reveal a great deal about their thoughts and dreams.

Two of the favorite "story starter" activities in my classroom are cutting pictures out of magazines and using stamps to create scenes. My students love picking interesting designs out of a magazine to describe or picking a picture and making up a story to go along with it. Stamping is fun for students and they enjoy carefully picking stamps, creating a picture and then writing about it. One of my students, Tyshawn, recently chose space-themed stamps and carefully recreated the scene of an astronaut blasting off towards the moon. He made his story personal, writing, "I went to go to the mune as an astrawnut."

In Brianne's classroom, students use a digital camera to take pictures of each other and the happenings of their classroom. The pictures are quickly printed thanks to a photo printer. Her students then write about the pictures and the experiences they were having at that time. This makes the pictures and their accompanying stories very personal. Oluwa took a picture of five classmates reading on the couch. Underneath his writing he wrote the students' names and positive things about each one.

Another literacy center that lends itself to storytelling is a Drama Center. Puppets and a puppet stage invite students to take on different personas and explore different stories. Dramatic play gives students an opportunity to tell stories of the different ideas they have in their heads. For many children, having puppets act out their own life experience makes it easier to share. When Rubia's parents decided they were getting divorced, Rubia performed a puppet show in which the tiger and gorilla puppets decided to get divorced. Her story did not end with everyone miraculously getting along, but rather this was Rubia's format for telling us what was happening in her life.

A great way for students to summarize their learning about a topic is to create a script based on their learning. In addition to providing students with story ideas, dramatic play can help students remember or think of experiences to write about.

USING TECHNOLOGY TO CONNECT STUDENTS AND THEIR STORIES

Bringing technology into my classroom has enabled me to provide students with many more opportunities to tell their stories. I have secured five computers for my classroom through Donors Choose, an online education charity that allows teachers to post funding requests for classroom projects. Without these five computers the only computer in the room would be the school-provided teacher computer. All of my current and past Donors Choose projects are available at www.donorschoose.org/Ms.Keenan.

We begin our digital storytelling by creating a Wikispaces page. Wikispaces is a secure, easily editable website that runs much like Wikipedia; individual users can go on to the page and add content. Wikispaces offers advertisement-free sites for educators, in addition to having tools that make it easy to create, edit and manage the site.

I create a page on Wikispaces for each student where they respond to prompts about their favorite things (favorite thing to do in the summer, favorite season, etc.). Students can view the entire site and read what their classmates enjoy doing. At the beginning of the year this lets my students learn about each other without the pressure of striking up a conversation with someone they do not know.

Wikispaces has a feature that allows the creator of the site to check what information has been changed. I knew that this format of communication was helping my students make connections with each other when I viewed the edits and saw that Tala had edited her page at home to write "I love the beach, just like Priyam." What a delightful thing for a seven-year-old to realize that the classmate who has been sitting next to her also loves going to the beach!

Reading each other's digital writing helps push students to think through the expectations they have for one another; I have found that some very shy students will write a large quantity of material for their classmates to read, and it is sometimes my least talkative students who write the most digitally.

One student with autism wrote about topics he wouldn't normally discuss with his classmates, like his favorite things. About his favorite subject in school Trip wrote, "My favorite thing to do is recess to excersise." After reading Trip's posting, I overheard a classmate tell him that her favorite thing to do at recess was to play tag. Without the Wikispaces page these two students would probably not have talked about recess. The digital format allows for a different type of interaction among students.

Another way we tell our stories digitally is through the website Storybird .com. Storybird provides beautiful, professional artwork that can be arranged in any order and the children then add their own words. My students type with ease when presented with pictures. It is a low-pressure way to tell a story with their ideas sparked by the pictures they choose. Giving students pictures for ideas (whether online or printed) encourages students to share the stories that they really do have inside of them.

On Storybird, Amra picked quirky, colorful pictures of monsters. Her story started with an explanation that each night the monsters came to a little girl's bedroom. Under each picture Amra wrote a compliment that the little girl gave to each monster. Beneath the last picture Amra wrote, "'Okay,' the monsters said, 'we will be your friends and stop scaring you.'" Without Storybird, this student would not have had the inspiration to tell about how she handles her fears of monsters under her bed.

My class also enjoys using Voice Thread, a digital storytelling method. We can upload pictures (or, as my students often have, images they have created in paint) and then narrate with their voice. Oral language often develops before written language and a Voice Thread is a fantastic way to support a child in their oral storytelling. On field trips, I love to have students take a picture of something that caught their eye and then use Voice Thread to record their thoughts on that picture, as we did in our Voice Thread after visiting the majestic Garfield Park Conservatory (voicethread.com/share/1173009/).

Flip cameras are a fantastic way to record student experiences. The cameras are relatively inexpensive and, more importantly, are incredibly easy to use. I secured my four flip cams through Digital Wish (www.digitalwish.org). One of the best parts of the flip cam software is that still images can be taken from moving images. For my second graders, capturing a still image can be a hard task. The flip cam makes it possible to go in, review the entire movie and create a good still image from the movie.

One of the best uses I've found for the flip cam is to allow students to record elements of our classroom day. They can then share these movies with their parents who are unable to join us in the classroom because of their work schedules. In the days leading up to our Winter Concert, as my students practiced Jack Johnson's "With My Own Two Hands," Ana told me that her mom could not come to the concert because of work. After I recorded the video and uploaded it to my website, Ana's mom viewed the video on their computer at home. Ana was so happy to be able to share her fantastic performance with her mom. The most common response I get from parents is that now they understand an activity, such as morning work, that their child tells them about.

CREATING A SPACE FOR STUDENTS
TO SHARE THEIR STORIES

Creating an environment where students feel comfortable sharing their stories orally takes time, particularly with those who are still learning English. For the first few days, I carefully select the Popsicle® stick identifying the next student to share. Letting some students hear many examples before they are asked to share helps to ease their anxiety. Depending on the student, the teacher might need to put an arm around them as they share, or even echo their words for the rest of the class.

Some students are reluctant to share their stories, whether they are hesitant to write or hesitant to speak to the class. The silent period, a time when those learning a new language say "nothing (or very little) in the new language being learned for periods ranging from several days to several months" (Samway and McKeon 2007, 27), can be a roadblock to having a student share their story. Other students are not in a silent period, but do not feel comfortable sharing their story. As teachers we have to find a way to help these students tell their stories.

A student whom I have struggled with to get her to tell her story is a refugee from Iraq. When she first came to my class she had little formal schooling and often spent the whole day crying. I can only imagine that if I had to move from the only place I had ever known to a freezing cold city like Chicago that I would spend my days crying too. This particular girl had been through nightmares that would terrorize any child. Her lack of participation in class and unwillingness to write could be attributed to her lack of schooling and the fact that she had just started learning English.

However, this Iraqi student made great strides in her academics. With a picture dictionary, she could add words to her beautiful illustrations. But, I was still left frustrated with what appeared to be her refusal to share her stories in class. After parent-teacher conferences (with a translator), her mom revealed that she liked school and was talkative at home. Being talkative at home in one's first language does not mean you will necessarily be talkative at school in a new language. However, this student was very talkative to other staff, including her English language teacher and the after school staff.

Still, academic English in the classroom is significantly different from social English that is used in the cafeteria or after school.

I would like to write that this student now is the first to jump up to participate and share what she has written. I would also love to share that this child writes sentence after sentence, but this isn't the case. This student still struggles to get much written on paper or on the computer, and doesn't contribute much when we use Voice Thread. She is hesitant to participate and tell her story. Due to her previous lack of formal schooling this student stayed with me for a second year. She continues to grow academically, but still resists telling and sharing her story. The days when she speaks a full sentence to me or writes without cajoling are huge successes. I relay my experience with this particular student because even with academic support and a myriad of opportunities not all students will be willing to share their stories and we must understand that as teachers. Some students just need more time to feel free enough to share.

INSPIRING WRITING THROUGH NEW EXPERIENCES

Experience should be the middle name for the second grade at Passages. Last year we took our students on ten field trips. I am lucky to have a supportive administration that sees the value in these experiences. And I am also lucky to teach in Chicago where many of the major museums invite Chicago Public School children to visit free of charge for field trips. To go on so many field trips, my colleague Brianne and I applied for bus grants and field trip grants, pursued opportunities within walking distance and completed Donors Choose projects.

By working to find the resources to give our students these experiences, Brianne and I are helping to make their lives full of stories. Many museums have bus scholarships for those who qualify, which make it possible for us to visit the Museum of Science and Industry each year. Our Park District operates a program that allows our students free bus service to visit the shore of Lake Michigan. This year I received a Target Field Trip Grant (targetfieldtripgrants.target.com), which will allow us to go to the Chicago Children's Museum.

One of my favorite experiences from last year was traveling to the LEGOLAND® Discovery Centre in suburban Chicago. The day was made infinitely more exciting because our bus driver accidentally took the wrong highway and we ended up going through O'Hare Airport. The students were amazed to see the airplanes taking off up close. One student, Linda, told me about the last time she was on a plane. With her father, two brothers and a sister, Linda boarded a plane in her hometown in Nigeria. She doesn't remember all the details of the two other stops, but she does remember the meal she got, complete with a toy, while she was flying over the ocean.

When we finally got to LEGOLAND® we were led up to a large open room that had table upon table of Legos® for the kids to play with. During the day we got to see how Legos® are made, built towers that withstood an earthquake table, and even enjoyed a pizza lunch in the party room. Many of our students left exclaiming that this was the best day of their lives!

The day was made possible through Donors Choose and the hospitality of LEGOLAND®. The day provided my students with a thousand things to see and do. In turn, this means that they had a thousand things to talk about, draw about and write about. It is important to give our students experiences that encourage them to tell stories about what happened.

These experiences can also happen in the classroom. With funds raised through Donors Choose, we were able to raise butterflies. We watched them grow from creepy crawlers in the plastic jars to hardened pupas and then on those miraculous spring days when we would enter the classroom to see a new butterfly flying around the mesh cage. I had never raised butterflies during elementary school and so I was experiencing this for the first time with my own students.

The most powerful day had to be the day we let our beautiful Painted Lady butterflies go. We had our flip cameras ready to record the whole experience. We marched out with our mesh cage down the front steps right outside our school. I heard later that a first grader saw us heading out, announced it to her class and the entire class lined up at the door to convince their teacher that they too could come outside to watch. Luckily their teacher was able to convince them that they would do it next year!

Outside we unzipped the top of the mesh cage and at first, nothing happened. There we stood, ready and anxious for the flight. The butterflies, on the other hand, did not want to leave the cage. Finally, one butterfly emerged from the cage (with a little coaxing) and, to make things more exciting, landed on several students before it took off into the world. In one of those moments it feels like the students conspired before it happened, they all stopped, stared and waved, "Bye butterfly!" as it sailed off.

One by one our butterflies slowly made their ways out of their mesh cage and off into the busy city of Chicago. For the rest of the semester, whenever we saw a butterfly (Painted Lady or not), students would rush over as if it surely had to be one of our butterflies.

When we reviewed the footage taken by the students, I was glad I hadn't eaten lunch yet because the jerkiness of an eight-year-old filmmaker is quite jarring! For me, the most moving part of the entire experience was hearing my student who is so hesitant to speak in class speak enthusiastically in the film. When she had the camera, she narrated the entire experience, speaking vividly about what was happening and even asking her classmates how they felt!

For Gabriella, who checked on the status of the butterflies everyday from caterpillar to release, the departure of the butterflies was particular devastating. In the days that followed Gabriella drew several pictures of the butterflies flying away and described where she thought they were now. Her invented continuation of the butterflies' lives helped her adjust to the loss of the butterflies in our classroom.

As a teacher, it is hard to predict which moments will have such a great impact on a student or class. By supplying the students with a large number of experiences, we increase the odds that each experience will have an impact on at least one child. After our shared experience we created a Voice Thread (voicethread.com/share/1116324/). This Voice Thread was made incredibly richer by connecting with students in Philadelphia who left comments for us.

REFLECTING ON STUDENT STORIES
THROUGH PORTFOLIOS

A comprehensive way that we support storytelling in the second grade is by creating student portfolios. At the very basic level the portfolio is a keepsake for students. A portfolio is memory of the work and experiences a student had in second grade. Ideally, students select the materials for their portfolios and include a written reflection with that item in their portfolio. Students can choose items they feel are their best work, items that upon reflection show room for improvement or reminders of an experience. Within the portfolio it is important for students to answer the question of why they have chosen to put each item in their portfolio. The reflection element of understanding their choices helps to tell their story.

A portfolio has great potential to show the growth of a child over the year and can be used as an assessment. With a class of 28, as my colleagues and I each have this year, it can be hard to set up a management system in which students select pieces for their own portfolio. Instead, I keep all published writing pieces that students complete during the year. At the beginning of the year the published pieces are simple works, but as the year continues we are able to see the students' growth in all elements of their writing. For students the most striking changes over the year are seen in their handwriting, story length and drawing ability.

GIVING VOICE TO EVERY CHILD

Every student has a story to be told. Incorporating the opportunity to tell stories throughout the school day and school year are crucial to building a community within the classroom. For students who are just learning English, it is important to have storytelling strategies that do not force them to write their stories. In my classroom, the act of the storytelling and the sharing of our stories have allowed us to create a classroom community in which members understand each other. Most importantly, giving time for students to tell their stories lets them know that they are valued members of the classroom community.

REFERENCES

Calkins, Lucy. *A Quick Guide to Teaching Second-Grade Writers with Units of Study*. Portsmouth: Heinemann, 2009.

Kriete, Roxann. *The Morning Meeting Book*. Northeast Foundation for Children, Inc., 2002.

Samway, Katharine Davies and Denise McKeon. *Myths and Realities: Best Practices for English Language Learners*. Portsmouth: Heinemann, 2007.

ABOUT THE AUTHOR

Karyn Keenan is a second grade teacher at Passages Charter School in Chicago, Illinois. She has taught students from more than fifteen countries. Her passion is helping each of her students tell their unique stories. Karyn earned her B.A. in Elementary Education from DePauw University, as well as her certificate to teach English Language Learners through National Louis University. As a SMART Exemplary Educator, Karyn works to improve instruction through the use of an interactive whiteboard. Raised in Wilmington, Delaware, Karyn now lives in Chicago where sunny summer days at the beach outweigh the long winters.

Chapter 6

Serving Long-Term English Learners by Building Literacy in Two Languages

Graciela Rosas

The question that I have been asked time and time again is, how can English language learners learn English by learning Spanish? Believe it or not, it's possible, but it's not just teaching them their native language. There is a lot more that goes into teaching English language learners and, in this case, long-term English learners. It is important to understand and know who your students are in the beginning. This applies to any class, but is essential in the creation of the biliteracy class.

There isn't a lot of research and my class is the first biliteracy class at the secondary level in San Diego Unified School District. I write this chapter during my prep time, after school, and on the weekends to be able to share my story about my misunderstood class. I am a teacher at Pacific Beach Middle, which is also an International Baccalaureate School. This biliteracy class is unique, difficult to prepare for, and sometimes overwhelming, but I love it. The benefits these students will gain now and in the future make it all worth it for me.

Alexis R. is an eighth-grade student in my class; he is considered a long-term English language learner, based on California English Language Development Test (CELDT) scores and performance in the last seven years. When we think about English learners in San Diego, we assume they are from Mexico and have had language struggles along the way. Alexis was born here and started school in kindergarten. However, after conducting a few in-class surveys, I learned his family only speaks Spanish and he was never really taught how to read or write in Spanish. As a child he didn't get the language support he needed in either language.

In my class Alexis is always on task, and makes every effort to do his best work. He believes his weakness is not English, but Spanish. However, after reviewing his writing samples and test scores the lack of language skills in English are evident.

In this class there are students from 7th and 8th grade, but every student's story is different and unique. They all complained at first about learning Spanish and asked, "Why are we learning Spanish when we already know it?"

Alexis R. sat in class writing his warm up. He looked up, raised his hand somewhat hesitantly, and asked me, "Why do we have to write the warm-up in Spanish?"

I replied, "We are starting to practice Spanish."

He said, "I can't write it. I don't know where to start."

I smiled back and said, "Do your best. We are all learners and are all at different levels. Some know a lot [of Spanish] and some only know a few words; just do your best."

He grimaced and said, "OK, but you won't understand it."

I laughed and said, "Its OK. I'm sure I can figure it out."

My goal was to have students write any way they knew how; this was already my way of assessing their writing. Having the students write whatever they could was essential in the early stages of the biliteracy class. I needed to know what each student was capable of in Spanish, so I could build the curriculum around what they knew and didn't know.

MEETING THE NEEDS OF LONG-TERM ENGLISH LANGUAGE LEARNERS

The English language learner concept is not a new one; however, California has become more active in identifying long-term English language learners. In the study *Reparable Harm*, the coalition Californians Together conducted a survey that identified 175,734 English learners in California in 2009-10 in grades 6–12. This is approximately one-third of the state's secondary school English learners (2010). At my school, we identified 25 students in 7th and 8th grade, a small percentage of the 700 students at our school. However, when you think about the problem in terms of an entire district, an entire city and then all of California, these small numbers add up. These students can no longer be ignored, and they deserve a future.

Creation of the class was inspired by studies like *Reparable Harm* and the work of Kate Menken of the ong-Term English Language Learner Project at The Research Institute for Study of Language in an Urban Society. We needed to do something to meet the needs of long-term English language learners (LTELLs) who were falling behind year after year. The urgency to do something to help these students is necessary; if nothing is done, these students may drop out in high school. When my principal Dr. Julie Martel began her research on the problem, she asked me to investigate and research LTELLs, schools with biliteracy programs in California and within our district K-5, and language acquisition strategies that could be implemented at our site to aid our LTELLs in their language development.

BUILDING STUDENT CONFIDENCE

An essential element of this class that grew organically was building student confidence and personal strengths. Unfortunately, most of these students have had little success in school. They feel like failures. A comment a student made to me in the beginning of class was, "Why should I try? I'll probably get an F anyway." This made me reflect on these students. They have fallen into the self-fulfilling prophecy of thinking there is no longer a point in trying, that they are failures. I am Mexican-American and thought, maybe if I share a little of my life with them, I can show them that success is possible. When I shared my story I could see interest in my years in college and my career. I also reiterated to them that any further education they choose to do is a good one; there is no bad choice. But they need to graduate and get there first. The class visits the local high school and university to trigger motivation in their future. For many, if they attended college they could be the first in their family to graduate from college, which I also tell them is very important.

I can relate to the students, because I've been there. I had the same trials and tribulations while I was in elementary and middle school. I was born and grew up in San Diego to my Spanish-speaking parents. My parents divorced when I was six years old, which led to my mom working all the time, and I was left at home watching television. My mom only spoke and understood Spanish, so if I needed help on my homework, I was on my own. I remember that as I got older I started to need help in math and science and just felt frustrated, because no matter how hard I tried, I just never got it. I honestly felt dumb and insecure about my future in school.

For a long time my grades struggled. Finally, when I reached high school I had an English teacher, Mr. Adair, who took that extra time to help me not only in English class, but in anything I needed help with. He motivated me to not give up, and was also my motivation to do something like he did for me when I grew up. So I did just that: I went to college and pursued my dreams. I became a teacher just like him, and now I want to help students out of that failure feeling. I want to give these kids hope and an opportunity for a future, hence my teaching this class.

TEACHING SPANISH TO STRENGTHEN ENGLISH

The idea is simple: teach reading and writing in the students' native language to strengthen their academic language and literacy. By teaching students Spanish we are strengthening them as a whole, getting them ready to take on another language, English, and the benefits will trickle down to other classes as well (Krashen and Biber, 1988).

Some students do not have a strong foundation in either language, thus reaching a point where they just can't attain a higher level in English. Think of these students as strong trees with no roots; they can only grow so big without falling down, because they have no foundation. Trees need roots and without roots in any language, there is no way these students can grow. The idea is if we can strengthen their roots they will be able to continue to grow in both languages. Foundation is a necessary component of learning.

The goal for these students is to reach reclassification. This is the process through which English language learners (ELLs) become reclassified as Fluent English proficient (RFEP). This occurs when they have demonstrated academic English proficiency based on district-established criteria. The eligible students are identified through test scores on an annual test and academic achievements. Unfortunately, these students haven't been reclassified after all the years in the district because they don't have the strong foundation in either language.

The challenge now was to develop a curriculum and develop strategies to implement these theories. I had some familiarity being the ESL (English as a Second Language) teacher at the site, but preparing myself to teach a biliteracy class, a first for our district, was overwhelming. I relied heavily on studies by Dr. Jill Kerper Mora, a professor at San Diego State University. She has done extensive work with English learners and the benefits of biliteracy in schools. I also read several publications by Teresa Walter, a local educator and curriculum writer for San Diego Unified for English Learners, who is also a major advocate on biliteracy teaching. Her belief is that learning their native language will help students attain a higher level of English.

Pacific Beach Middle School is also part of the International Baccalaureate (IB) Program. I needed to align our class with the International Baccalaureate

Middle Years Program (MYP) which aims to develop internationally minded, independent learners. The curriculum must be written in a way that students can reflect, problem-solve and analyze lessons. Within each unit is a central focus which develops connections across the curriculums, so that students will learn to see that everything they learn is interrelated.

Jennifer Sims, the IB coordinator at our site, was kind enough to take me up to the Semillas School in Los Angeles, which shared a similar philosophy in creating a strong foundational language. We met with the administrator and several teachers to brainstorm which direction we should take with this class. Jennifer helped me evaluate my class and create units that not only meet students' standards in both English and Spanish, but also the requirements of the IB program. After trying to meet all the elements, and evaluating the work and research, we formulated a thorough summary and report to present to the school administrators.

The final step was discussing our proposed pilot program using the biliteracy approach beyond the elementary level with the Office of Language Acquisition (OLA). This would be a new class for our district at the middle-school level. The OLA office helped in initiating the focus and planning of the class. The language director of the Office of Language Acquisition, Mary Waldron, suggested I attend Quality Teaching for English Learners (QTEL) trainings, English Language Development (ELD) trainings, and several Write Institutes, to become familiar with English learner methodologies and teaching strategies. San Diego Unified School District stands behind biliteracy in its K-5 programs and approved our middle school class as a pilot program for the district.

The class that was constructed is now called Academic Enrichment. We didn't want to label this class as a remedial or support class. This is a unique class with unique goals; we want students to gain skills, but build their confidence as well. The overall goal is to help strengthen the students' academic language by giving them a foundation in their native language, Spanish, which will strengthen their language acquisition in their second language, English. We wanted to find out if the Academic Enrichment class could help these students improve and keep them from falling further and further behind.

When I began creating the class, the challenges arose immediately. As I noted, there is no other class like this in our district at the middle school level. There are no textbooks for this class, which required me to do extensive planning and create a curriculum with very little resources. Curriculum writing and planning was done over the course of three months, during summer break. Dr. Mora's website, *A Road Map for Effective Biliteracy Instruction: A Knowledge Base and Teaching Strategies* (2004), was useful in the early stages of production of the biliteracy curriculum.

I also had to include the English support component within the curriculum, to meet English standards. Trying to meet English standards while integrating academic language in Spanish, an essential component of the class structure, was very difficult. Finally, after getting feedback from administrators and colleagues on possible curriculum, we decided to create a curriculum that would reflect the English curriculum units and teach similar concepts in Spanish. The students would then be getting the same structure and curriculum in both languages and gain substantial instruction in Spanish literacy development, while tying it into our International Baccalaureate school expectations.

IDENTIFYING STUDENTS FOR THE CLASS

A team consisting of the principal, English learner support teacher (ELST), and myself began the process of selecting students for the class. First we had to identify the characteristics of students who need this class. Some of the criteria we identified were:

- Students were 7th or 8th graders
- Six or more years in district
- Strong oral language in both English and Spanish (non-academic)
- Struggling academically
- Inability to be reclassified (based on CELDT scores)
- Lacking academic language in both English and Spanish
- Lack of interest in school, unmotivated
- Students with individualized education program (IEPs) and special education (SPED) students were excluded based on needing additional support classes

Students were also given a unique assessment tool created by our ELST Wade Plunkett to identify students' oral language, reading comprehension and writing in Spanish.

The testing process took approximately a month. The results showed us that the students we were considering could articulate well using both English and Spanish. However, after giving a vocabulary-like test, we realized that their language was not at an academic level. Their spoken language would be considered conversational or low level. Their reading comprehension and writing was also very low and in some cases, students had made little effort to complete or answer questions. We also looked at a variety of state testing data. Other contributing factors included years in the district and the last year the student's English grades were approximately a C or below.

All of the students who were chosen to participate in the Academic Enrichment class have a strong conversational, oral language in their native tongue and second language, but lack literacy skills in both English and Spanish. Students in the class have been in the district for longer than six years, some up to eight and a half years.

LEARNING ABOUT MY STUDENTS
BEYOND THE CLASSROOM

Evaluation of my students started even before I met them. I had to review their previous grades and try to identify their individual needs in both languages. Then as early as the first day of school it was a *getting to know you* moment for the students and myself. I asked them to describe themselves, physically, mentally, education wise: how did they feel, and what were their goals in this class and other classes? I wanted to get some background on each student, and get to know who they were and what their family life was like. After reading their stories in their daily writing journals, I discovered that typically both parents work until late in the day. Some students don't live with parents; they live with family members while their parents are away working or still in Mexico. They don't really get any help on school assignments at home. The vast majority of students said that they get home and don't do the work because they just "don't get it."

Many teachers often forget to learn more about their students; however, it is a major element in teaching. You need to know who your students are. How can you address an issue without having the full picture? By learning about my students I became very aware that many students had little to no support in their homework at home. Parents typically were working late and even if they were at home, the homework is at a higher level of understanding than most parents' education or language. Their educational level may be at the elementary level or below and their children are learning more complex information; so unfortunately, even if parents want to help their children, their best intentions are thwarted. The pitfall for these students is that instead of getting help from peers, family or teachers, they just don't do the assignments.

The students in my class sound like all the kids at the middle school; as they walk through the halls they speak English with friends. They walk in and say, "Hi, Ms. Rosas." Most people wouldn't even think they are having struggles in English. There are a few teachers who see this group as lazy and not doing work. These students have strong oral language skills in both languages; however they do not have strong literacy skills in either language. Many at the middle school level have already given up. Their English ability varies as well, and some just cannot see that. It is important that all educators get to know student needs and provide additional help if needed.

PROVIDING A STRONG FOUNDATION

Most of these students do not have a strong grammatical foundation; without this foundation a student cannot grow in either language. For example, many students could not tell me what a noun is in English or a *sustantivo* in Spanish. For some of the students the concepts were new and others just didn't recall learning these concepts. Therefore I had to start teaching them in mini grammar lessons to trigger their background knowledge and in some cases give them the opportunity to learn something they just didn't know. Most students did well and often commented, "Ms. Rosas, this is so easy."

After the students would do something relatively simple in English, I would teach the same concept in Spanish. This type of lesson is interchangeable depending on their ability in both languages and I would have to modify to meet student needs. This lesson may not work with another student population.

For the first two months, I primarily focused on re-teaching grammatical structures and basic language in both languages. My students were confused in the beginning. Students like Jenny G., an 8th grader who is at best at a fourth grade level, showed very limited writing skills, low vocabulary and incorrect use of grammatical structures. She was born in the United States and has been in the school system since pre-school. One would not expect a student who was born in the U.S. to have these struggles. After asking her a little about her family, she said they always speak Spanish at home. When I asked about homework help or studying at home, she said her parents never help her because they don't understand her homework. She had a limited understanding of how nouns and verbs had anything to do with her everyday life and really didn't see any importance in the lessons.

In class she said, "Miss, don't get mad, but I don't get anything about the sentences. This is dumb."

As a class we were learning simple and complex sentences and how we identify them in English and Spanish.

I said, "What do you mean, what are you not understanding?"

She said, "I know what verbs and nouns are, but does it matter how I write them in my sentence?"

I asked the rest of the class to be honest and raise their hands if they didn't get the lesson either. Most of them raised their hands. I was shocked, needless to say.

I had to build a foundation, by teaching them essential components of these sentences like subjects (nouns) and verbs. Breaking up my lesson was the only way that this group could learn effectively.

The process was simple. First I would do a simple definition and grammar lesson on basic structures in English. Then, after I taught it in English I would then teach the same concept in Spanish. Students in the beginning complained, "Ms. Rosas, I already know this, but I can't do it in Spanish." I laughed and said, "Yes you can, and you just don't know it yet." We started by reading small articles together sentence by sentence. They realized that they could read, but just needed to learn more vocabulary and cognates. After I taught them what sentence structure was, it was easier for the students to read sentences and understand what they read. It was a process, but by making baby steps I saw improvement in their reading and writing in both languages, within the first half of the semester.

COORDINATING BILITERACY AND ENGLISH CLASSES

By mid-year, the students were learning how to write a persuasive essay in both languages. This is one type of writing structure they need to have when they graduate from middle school and is also part of the district benchmark requirements in English. Many of my students struggle with the writing process. In the biliteracy class, it is important to frontload essential vocabulary, and students can use what they have learned as a reference when they are beginning to write in English. The structure for writing is essentially the same in English or Spanish.

Students began writing introductions and reviewing thesis statements and how to use them within the paragraph. The expectations at this grade level are that students can successfully state a claim and be able to support their claim with facts and examples. Unfortunately, some students have no idea how to begin writing. In the class I show them writing structure, before we start the actual writing process. I had several students tell me how it was easier for them to write in Spanish than in English, "It just flows, Ms. Rosas. I can say what I want easier, you know," said Brenda O.

Exposing students to similar lessons in Spanish and in English proved to be effective. Students in the biliteracy class learn the basics which they can then apply to a more academically rigorous class that doesn't include basic structure as part of the lesson. The lessons are taught a week or two before the lessons are taught in English class. Students can take what they learned in my class in both languages and apply it. English teachers update me on the topics they are working on and then I structure the class so that similar lessons and academic language students need are integrated into the class.

Students were asked individually what they felt their improvements were in Academic Enrichment as well as in their English class. This class is working for most students like Perla B. a student who has been in a California school since kindergarten:

> "I'm learning both [English and Spanish] in this class, because we are doing similar things," Perla B. said.

> I asked, "So do you think learning how to write in Spanish is helping you in English?"

> She responded, "I think so. I get it better now."

ENGAGING STUDENTS WHO HAVE BEEN DISENGAGED

Keeping students involved and engaged is a major component of this class. I didn't want this class to be a repetition of what they are doing in their English class. However, I still want students to gain writing and reading skills in both languages. I use the class Promethean Board, an innovative tool that allows me to use handouts or flip charts to create interactive lessons. I have created several fun flip charts that have simple, funny, unique sentences with pictures that they can relate to.

I use pictures of someone in their age range or that they admire because they are more inclined to pay attention and stay engaged. For example, I use pictures of a celebrity such as Justin Bieber, and create a sentence. I will write, "Yo fui al concierto de Justin Bieber." I will then ask students to come up and first read the sentence and circle the subject, then underline the verb and finally tell me in English what the meaning of the sentence is.

These activities have been very effective, because they are interactive and fun. Most of the class is consistently raising their hand to participate. Students like to come up to the board and participate. They like using the different colors available to circle and underline. This is an excellent lesson for visual learners. These lessons also work great for kinesthetic learners, because they are able to take part in sentence construction and identification using the drag feature on the board. Some of the flip chart activities require students to construct a complete sentence by moving words around on the board. While students are at their seats observing or waiting for their turn, they are being productive by taking notes.

These lessons take a great deal of preparation and planning to create, but do keep the students engaged and motivated. Similar lessons can also be created using PowerPoint slides, if a Promethean Board is not available.

IMPROVING BEHAVIOR

In the beginning, behavior was a major issue. Students expected yet another class they would do poorly in, and students came into class with an imaginary chip on their shoulder. I was a little worried by some of the feedback I had received from other teachers, because this particular class has many students labeled as having behavior problems by other teachers.

The students quickly realized this class would be different. I started by introducing myself and asking them questions about themselves. The students quickly raised their hands to ask me why I even cared about their opinion and lives. I told them, "How can I teach you something if I don't know who you are?" That surprised students, and one student said, "Ms. Rosas, you are the first teacher who has ever asked me what I think about a class." Several students chimed in, saying that they were never asked for their opinions. I was shocked that students felt this way. I wanted to make these students feel like they could contribute and participate in their own learning.

Our first project in this class was a "Me Bag" that they were all required to present. After this lesson students seemed to feel at ease in the class, and participated more fully. I reiterated to them that this is their class.

The students are typically well-behaved, but there are behavior problems. They aren't as bad as I expected and they could have potentially been worse. Many teachers complained about certain students and how their behavior was impossible, disruptive and defiant. I didn't see this, but I did encounter some issues. For example, I was having a discussion with a student, Rogelio B., who came to United States when he was three years old. He is such a bright student, but his disruptive past seems to loom over him and hinder his progress in other classes. When I addressed an issue he had in my class, I asked him why he acts up in my class and in his other classes.

He laughed and said, "I don't like my other classes. They're boring and I don't like to listen to boring classes."

I said, "OK, so you're telling me my class is boring?"

Rogelio looks at me with a big look of disbelief on his face and says, "Ms. Rosas, you don't get it."

I was bewildered, and asked him again, "So my class is boring to you?

He just smiled and said, "I am behaving good in your class; I don't listen to the other teachers."

I smiled and said, "Oh, so this is you being good?"

"Yes, Ms. Rosas. I behave good, better than the other class and I promise to try not to get kicked out of your class, because it's fun."

After our talk I had to laugh and I thought OK, so how bad is he in his other classes? I talked to his other teachers and quickly realized Rogelio was being honest. Compared to other classes, he was well behaved in my class; he never talks back, is rude or defiant. He sits for most of the period, raises his hand and attempts to answer questions, occasionally speaking out and getting a little squirmy, but overall listening and paying attention. Unfortunately, in other classes, he speaks out of turn and talks back to teachers, maybe due to a lack of interest or understanding of the class content.

As an educator I believe that if I can help at least one student do better in school and reach their goals, I have done my job. So are these students little angels? The truth is, no, but I can tell you that I care about them very much and they know that. That is why I believe they behave and make an effort in my class. The students who typically have behavior issues in other classes are usually engaged and participate in my class. When Dr. Martel walked into my class she was in awe that students who don't participate in other classes were raising their hands and taking part in class.

TECHNOLOGY GAP AT HOME

Another issue that I discovered while teaching this class was brought to light by Desi B. He told me that he really didn't like his English class or his other classes. He said that he had to type things out and had to take tests online in history and science, but didn't have Internet at home.

Desi said, "I don't really like it too much. Sometimes it's hard, and I don't have a computer at home to do my assignments."

I asked him, "Have you improved and turned in the assignments, when you work on them in my class?" and reminded him he can always use the computer in my class if needed.

He responded, "I like this class, because I get help in my English class homework and still learn Spanish."

Desi highlights a major issue students are facing in school. With technology today, students at Pacific Beach Middle are required to type essays or use *moodle*, an online site used by our district, to complete assignments or take quizzes. Unfortunately, most of these students do not have a computer at home, while some have a computer and don't have access to the Internet.

Teachers do often give students the opportunity to use computers at lunch, after school or in the district's free after-school program for working parents. I provide additional support for students in their English class by setting some time for them to work independently using the classroom computers to get some work done for English. I also stay in at lunch and after school so students can use computers for work for my class or any other class. Students become motivated after seeing positive changes in their grades when they use the computers. It is important for teachers to not only make the technology available to their students, but to personally encourage the students to take advantage of it. That is another reason teachers need to develop personal relationships with students.

PROGRESS BEGINS

As we move through the year, the students begin to feel successful. They come into class showing me their grade reports for other classes, showing me how they are now A or B students when they used to get C's and D's and yes even F's. Motivation and confidence are traits that they have attained with this class. They never feel discouraged and even when they don't understand the information, they are not afraid to ask for help anymore. They know that I will try to review the material with them, and reteach it if needed.

Keeping the kids motivated and excited to learn makes all the hard work pay off. I want to see my students be successful and graduate, hopefully making it to college. This class has been difficult and it does require an extensive amount of planning, but it is definitely worth it. I realized that not one student was the same as the other. The population may appear the same, but assessments reveal that students have all sorts of differing educational backgrounds and needs. I do my best to meet these needs.

I have seen a positive change; when I see students understanding the concepts and improving in English and Spanish, it is a major accomplishment. The class has been successful in many ways; we monitor students' grades and test scores to document their improvements. In the last documentation there has been a general trend of progress for the majority of students. There are some outliers, but overall the results have been positive.

I would be lying if I said all of my students were passing all their classes, and receiving A's in English or in my class. However, what I can say is that we are making small steps towards their reclassification and building their confidence. I strive to have them believe in themselves and their capabilities as learners. It is definitely a long tough road ahead, but I am willing to put in the time and effort for these students. If this program takes off in the next few years, I am sure that the gap for long-term English learners will be drastically reduced. This class is giving students the opportunity to apply themselves and truly see that they have potential and hope for the future.

REFERENCES

"Educational Leadership: Supporting English Language Learners: The Difficult Road for Long-Term English Learners," *Membership, Policy, and Professional Development for Educators" ASCD.* Jan. 31, 2011. www.ascd.org/publications/educational_leadership/apr09/vol66/num07/The_Difficult_Road_for_Long-Term_English_Learners.aspx.

"IB Middle Years Programme Curriculum," *The International Baccalaureate Worldwide Community of Schools.* Jan. 11, 2011. www.ibo.org/myp/curriculum/.

Krashen, Stephen D., and Douglas Biber. *On Course: Bilingual Education's Success in California.* Sacramento, CA: California Association for Bilingual Education, 1988.

Menken, Kate and Kleyn, T. (2010). "Long-Term English Language Learner Project." *The Research Institute for Study of Language in an Urban Society.* Jan 8, 2011. web.gc.cuny.edu/dept/lingu/rislus/projects/LTELL/index.html.

Olsen, Laurie. "Changing Course for Long Term English Learners," *Californians Together.* Web. Jan. 10, 2011.

Olsen, Laurie. "Reparable Harm: Fulfilling the Unkept Promise of Educational Opportunity for California's Long Term English Learners." *Californians Together.* Jan. 14, 2011. www.californianstogether.org/.

Walter, Teresa. *Teaching English Language Learners: the How-to Handbook.* White Plains, NY: Pearson ESL Longman, 2004.

Zehr, Mary Ann. "Study Finds ELL Students Languishing in California Schools," *Education Week* 2 (3), June 9, 2010).

ABOUT THE AUTHOR

Graciela Rosas is an ESL, biliteracy, and Spanish teacher at Pacific Beach Middle School, part of San Diego Unified School District. Ms. Rosas has earned an M.A. in education and a B.A. in political science, and is enrolled in the Administrative Credential program at San Diego State University. She has both a Multiple Subject and Single Subject Credential and has taught Kindergarten through eleventh grade. She has been an educator since 2006. Most importantly, she is a Mexican-American who was also a language learner, and she has found her calling and passion for helping struggling long-term English language learner students. She lives in San Diego with her son, Erizen, and her two dogs.

Chapter 7

Addressing Silences

Creating a Space for Classroom Conversations That Matter to Students

Sara Kugler

The group of fifth graders ran up to me one September afternoon after recess, grabbed at my shirt and furiously announced, "Boys from another class were calling Mona a terrorist!" I looked at Mona, who wore a *hijab*, a headscarf which covered her hair. Despite being one of many Muslim girls, she was one of only a few students in the school who wore a hijab every day.

Many thoughts ran through my mind as I struggled to decide how I would react. Should I shake off their comments and declare the immediate start of reading time? Should I reveal the anger and frustration I felt toward those boys, marching into their classroom and demanding an apology for Mona? Should I scold the girls for "tattling" on other students, as I had seen a couple of my colleagues do? Should I sugarcoat this topic and explain to Mona that "everybody looks different and that's what makes us all special"? That day, I chose not to do anything immediately, but to acknowledge their frustration and promise to think about the next steps we should take.

Similarly, my third graders returned from lunch one day in October, having called one another "gay" with little understanding of its meaning, but just knowing that it was a word forbidden in school because it was a dangerous insult. Each time this happened, I wondered what my reaction should be and what message I was sending my students by choosing this reaction.

Choosing to ignore and move onto another area of the curriculum would send the message that my classroom was not an appropriate space to discuss such issues, but it would not stop the teasing from happening again. Demanding an apology from the students may slow or stop the teasing but would not empower the girls to take action themselves next time this happen, nor would it help any of the students understand why or how their words were damaging. Scolding the girls for tattling would encourage their passivity and victimization next time something like this happened. And sugar-coating the topic just didn't feel authentic and honest; it just felt like a simplistic answer that would make my job easier, but not make Mona or her friends feel any more empowered.

As a teacher, I realize the impact of my words as I stand in front of a classroom full of students who are eagerly awaiting my reaction after a moment like this. They watch and listen for messages about how to deal with these struggles, the conflicts and conflicted messages that arise daily in classrooms, hallways, cafeterias, playgrounds, and, frankly, neighborhoods all over the country.

So what is the message that we are giving to kids when we say, "Sit down. Enough. Don't say that. You can't use that word." What are we *really* saying to them? We're really saying, "We can't talk about that. We don't know how to deal with it. Just don't talk about it in *here*." Many teachers admit that when issues of race, class, gender, or physical ability arise in their rooms, that is exactly how they feel: ill equipped to lead any sort of discussion. Despite our implicit ban on these topics in the classroom, they continue on the playground, out of earshot. And without adult guidance, stereotypes are perpetuated, misinformation is spread, and bullying continues to escalate.

Our hope as teachers, parents, and adults is that by not drawing attention to these topics, by not discussing them, the children will not notice the problems we are aware of as adults. Many parents wish that their children will grow up "colorblind," or unaware of the cultural, racial, and religious differences and the value placed on different groups by society.

Unfortunately, research on diversity consistently points to the fact that *despite* these efforts to raise children in a colorblind world, a world where differences go unnoticed, we are surrounded by covert and overt messages about difference that even our youngest children are picking up on and living by. As Carlos E. Cortes points out in *The Children Are Watching: How the Media Teach About Diversity* (2000), it is a fact that "media *contribute* to the construction of beliefs and attitudes about" groups in our society. We are not our children's only teachers; the media, from films, to commercials, to books found in their classroom, are constantly teaching our children about cultural norms and these messages are internalized. However, as Cortes says, "much of media teaching remains hidden in one sense. Its subtle messages generally go unnoticed, even when learned and acted upon." Without even knowing it, we are all influenced by messages from media; messages which often promote stereotypes.

In those moments when students raise issues, point out these messages, beg us for some guidance, we often choose to silence them with easy, and often dishonest answers. These topics, that students are faced with multiple times a day, become the silenced curriculum in our classrooms and schools because we, the adults, are unsure of how to navigate these tricky waters.

HELPING STUDENTS ADDRESS
THE SILENCED CURRICULUM

When I worked in a public school in Brooklyn, New York, I began to notice the insults being thrown around by the students during recess, lunch, while transitioning from one activity to another, and during instruction. I began talking to my colleagues about this. "Has anyone else noticed this?" I asked. "What have you done about it? Has it worked?"

Teachers all around the school were struggling with similar problems. Students arrived in their classrooms first thing in the morning, already angry about an insult, already offended by a verbal attack against a friend. At staff meetings after school we began discussing the problem further. We looked into hiring outside consultants who could come help us address issues of bullying and classroom management. But for the teachers at my school, something seemed to be missing from these programs. They all promised to address the *behavior* of bullying, to make sure there were consequences for their *actions*. But nobody was talking about the *motivations* behind the bullying. None of these programs helped children get to the root of the insults and the attack, to help clarify misconceptions and stereotypes, to assist children in identifying issues of power that played out in every corner of the school and their homes.

It was then that the teachers realized that we needed to become the experts on helping students address this silenced curriculum. It was up to us to create spaces in our own classrooms where students felt comfortable talking to each other in ways that felt risky at first; to help them become skilled at holding difficult conversations. Teaching the silenced curriculum is also about helping kids develop a critical lens for messages, whether from media or from other people in their life, about identity. We want students to be able to read their world in such as way that they can identify, dismantle, talk about, and reconstruct these messages. This is work that will serve them well in school, but also in life, as adults must contend with these messages as well.

I was lucky enough to be surrounded by other teachers who were curious and passionate about helping their students navigate these topics. With the support of our administration, we formed a voluntary study group that met after school once a week to develop a school-wide approach. The study group consisted of a classroom teacher from each grade, kindergarten through fourth, as well as the P.E. teacher and the English as a Second Language (ESL) teacher.

The school is located in a neighborhood that has a demographic mix in terms of race and socio-economics. About 30% of the students live below the poverty level and about 3% of the students receive ESL services. The school is approximately 50% Caucasian (which included an Arabic population), 15% Black, 25% Hispanic, and 10% Asian or Pacific Islander.

THE FRAMEWORK OF ADDRESSING SILENCES

We began our inquiry by watching a video entitled "It's Elementary" (1996) by Debra Chasnoff and Helen S. Cohen. This video specifically addressed ways to help students talk about "gay issues in school." However, from the start, our study group did not set out to merely address homophobia and stereotypes about the gay community. We studied the video in order to identify methods and pedagogy the teachers used while supporting students in their discourse about a socially taboo issue.

Our study group hypothesized that in order for teachers, parents, and administrators to be comfortable enough to navigate such tricky terrain, there needed to be some predictable structure that teachers might follow in their classrooms. We drew on the methods used in the video, our beliefs about how children construct knowledge, and the format of many other respected curriculum programs. What we developed was a framework for addressing silences inside of a classroom.

---

1. Choosing Topics for Your Own Classroom
2. Eliciting Students' Background Knowledge
3. Reflecting on Our Background Knowledge
4. Studying Myriad Resources
5. Reflecting and Taking Social Action

CHOOSING TOPICS FOR YOUR OWN CLASSROOM

As every teacher and parent knows, free play or free time is often the time when comments about race, class, gender, and physical appearance come up. Every parent has a story of their child returning from school, tears welling up their eyes, recounting how a classmate commented cruelly on their clothes or haircut or choice of backpack.

Likewise, each day, as my students run to line up as the whistle marks the end of recess, they often race over to me to recount the list of today's insults hurled around by other children on the playground.

Reading aloud is another time I pay particular attention to students' reactions and comments. The book *William's Doll*, by Charlotte Zolotow, brings out a variety of responses from our students, no matter their age. In this book, a young boy yearns for a doll for which he can care. His brothers call him a sissy and his father dismisses this want, instead encouraging him to play basketball. At the first mention of William's desire for a doll, many students often snicker and look uncomfortably at each other.

This, too, is a confusing situation for me, as a teacher. I can glare at the giggling student and decisively declare, "That's not funny. Stop laughing." Or I could stop reading and provocatively challenge the student by asking, "What's so funny about *that*?" Both of these send the message that students should not be laughing and that their opinions or feelings of discomfort are not allowed in my classroom.

On the other hand, I could lead my students in a discussion in which I highlight the belief that anybody can play with whatever kind of toy they want, that the father is the "bad guy" in the story and that the grandmother, who eventually buys him a doll, is the hero. I can count on a couple of my students jumping on board quite easily with this argument and with little effort, I could build consensus around the idea that "there are no such things as girl toys or boy toys." In this case, the message I send is there is one way to think about this and any other idea is wrong.

I have to admit; I have reacted in both of these ways before. Mainly, my simplistic reactions came from a place of feeling pressured as a teacher. I felt pressure to make it OK or safe for my students. I felt pressured for time. I felt pressured to get through the book, the unit, the subject area. I felt pressured to get to the "real" curriculum.

But this year I decided that instead of moving past these issues to the next subject area, I decided that this *was* the curriculum I should be studying with my students. So, instead of any of these responses, I took furious notes, then met with my study group to ask for help in making a plan for our classroom community curriculum. I told my students that I noticed they were angry, uncomfortable, sad, and nervous about these topics. And then, I promised to make some time in the future when we could think about these issues more. These issues, the ones that come up naturally in students' interactions with each other and with texts, can become the topics that we help our students study and discuss.

It is not always easy deciding how you will frame the issue for your students. For example, although my third graders were teasing each other about being gay, I was not comfortable leading them in a discussion about sexuality. Nor did I really believe that this was the issue at hand. Instead, I decided that our focus would be on gender identity, such as stereotypical roles, which all students had experience with. In a kindergarten class on the floor below mine, the teacher Carol taught three children whose families were going through divorces. She decided that, rather than studying divorce, she would broaden the topic to "loss" so that all students could bring some knowledge to the class discussions. While some children knew about loss through a parent moving out, others might know about the death of a grandparent, while other might bring their experiences with the loss of a beloved toy or pet. And in the gym, our P.E. teacher Kathy decided that she had heard enough teasing to warrant spending some time on studying students' perceptions about physical ability. And the ESL teacher, Amelia, decided that she would study how immigrants are perceived and constructed with her group of English language learners.

When choosing a topic to study, it is important to listen to what students are already talking about in and outside of the classroom. In this way, we will not be planting ideas and thoughts in students' heads, but instead creating a safe space for what is already being talked about. It is also essential that all students have some sort of access or way of contributing to the discussion. By so doing, we are making our students experts and helping them feel invested in the construction of new knowledge.

ELICITING STUDENTS' BACKGROUND KNOWLEDGE

As in any area of the curriculum, such as math or science, it is essential that we start with what students already know, or more specifically in this case, what they *think* they know about this topic. However, it is also important that we make it clear that this is only the first step in a process of our study of the topic; it is not merely a listing of information or facts. We often begin by asking questions such as:

> - What do you know about _____?
> - What have you heard about _____?
> - What do other people say about _____?
> - What do you associate with _____?
> - What do you think about _____?

We felt that it was important not just to ask students what they think or know about a topic, but to also ask what they've heard *others* saying about the topic. In this way, we hoped to create a safer space for students to share what would normally be considered controversial opinions and ideas.

There were a couple of different formats for leading this discussion. The first option is to lead a whole class discussion. In my classroom, students gathered in the meeting area in the corner of the room, the same space we often held class meetings and where I read books aloud to them. The students sat in a circle while they talked about their background knowledge; I took notes on chart paper.

Another option is for students to sit in small groups and record their own ideas on pieces of chart paper. In a first grade classroom, a group of students made a chart using pictures and labels of what they considered "Boy Things," "Girls Things," or "Both." In this way, students were sharing their ideas about gender roles.

Amelia, the ESL teacher, decided to start by inviting students to share what they had heard kids and adults saying about their getting pulled out of class each day for the ESL services. While the students listed the comments, Amelia took notes. Her students admitted that other kids had said, "He doesn't speak English" and teachers had declared to substitutes or other children, "She can't understand you." The students also talked about finally building up the courage to speak, only to be mocked by another student for their accent. She also asked them, "What do people think of immigrants? What do people think about kids who speak other languages?" Her students, especially the 4th and 5th graders, had no hesitation in articulating their ideas about this. Jamilah declared, "They think we can't understand or talk. They think we don't get it."

Kristen, another first grade teacher studying gender roles with her class, took a different approach in order to elicit students' ideas about gender. She took a picture book that had a drawing of a classroom of students. She then covered the words of the text and the faces of the characters and asked her students, "Which of these is a girl and which of these is a boy? How do you know?" Her students' responses were varied and confirmed her hunch that they had many strongly held beliefs about gender. One student responded, "It must be a girl because she's not raising her hand. That means she's shy." Another, with a different perspective said, "That one must be a boy because he's wearing jeans and that's what boys wear." A third student offered, "I think that's a girl because I see pink in her shirt and girls wear pink." For Kristen, the important information did not lie in whether each character was identified as a girl or a boy, but in the students' explanations of their thinking. It revealed so much about the messages they had received and internalized in their lives.

Often, when one idea was shared with the class, another student would pipe up and declare, "That's not true!" For example, after a third student shared that nail polish was a girl's thing, another student angrily pointed out that he had seen high school boys and a couple of rock stars wearing nail polish. I decided that at this point in our journey, it was essential that students *not* be allowed to comment on each other's ideas and I told them this. I often started the discussion by saying, "We are sharing our ideas about this topic. Each of us may have heard different things or have different beliefs and so it's important that today, we don't shoot down each other's ideas." If every comment was met with an argument, I thought students would be less apt to share, for fear that their idea would immediately be shot down.

Likewise, I decided that this was not the time for me to chime in with leading questions. As a teacher, I desperately wanted to ask students, "Is that true? Who says that's true? Who agrees? Who disagrees? Is that ever *not* true?" I stopped myself though, knowing that at this stage, I was trying to reveal what information and ideas the students held, not silence them. More significantly, I was also working to send the message that my classroom was a space in which you were allowed to say things that might not be true or "right" and you would still be safe.

REFLECTING ON BACKGROUND KNOWLEDGE

This next step in our process marks a turning point in our classroom. We are no longer passive recipients of knowledge, accepting what books, television, ads, adults tell us to think. Instead, we begin the important work of questioning the information and even the sources of this information. We have called this next step "Reflecting on Background Knowledge" because we hoped to help children see that beliefs are not facts. They are opinions and therefore reflect views of the people who express them. Also by doing this work, we hoped that children would see that there are myriad ways to view a single issue, and therefore would be empowered to make choices about their own views, rather than being passive recipients of messages.

As in every step of this process, I began by thinking about the questions that would help students do this difficult metacognitive work. Here are some questions that I began with:

> - Where did you find this out?
> - What did that source teach you about _____?
> - Who decided that this is true?
> - What are the "rules" that this source has created?

I used two different formats to help my students explore these challenging questions. First, we began with a whole class conversation. We looked back at our charts and thought about where these ideas about "boy things" and "girl things" came from and how these messages were put into our heads so that we had this collective idea about gender. It's also important to start using more sophisticated vocabulary so that students start to see that concepts such as "gender," "race," and "class" are socially constructed and so they can eventually understand that they can also be reconstructed to reflect a different set of values.

It was during a whole class conversation that my third grade class started exploring a couple of very mature ideas about gender. At first, when I asked them who makes these "rules," they had definitive answers. Kayla suggested that older kids make them, but Chloe, a self-proclaimed "tomboy" who often deliberately broke gender rules, disagreed, stating that they were created "when our grandmothers were alive." Savannah wondered aloud if "maybe teachers made it up." These were all important suggestions, though, because the students were starting to think about the stereotypes, not just as facts, but as messages that had been communicated to them, usually from older people with more authority.

The conversation quickly took a turn when Kayla pointed out that often these stereotypes and messages can be used against you. She pointed out that "older kids are always taking out their feelings about it on the little kids." Many students agreed that there is a lot of teasing going on at the playground and in their neighborhood about these ideas. Many kids said they had been called names like "wimp," "gay," or boys being called "girls." This was another important part of our conversation because so many students were sharing how stereotypes were not harmless images but were actually the source of bullying for many of them.

Then, Chloe took the class talk in another interesting direction. She pointed out that "it's not always used to hurt people's feelings." This confused many of the students and so Kayla asked if she meant that it doesn't really hurt if "you're just being honest." But Chloe was suggesting that when someone is teased, they can actually reclaim the language of the bully and use it for self-empowerment. Cesar, a boy in the class who often avoided the large groups of boys playing sports at recess, chimed in and gave the example, "When someone gets called a wimp, they say thank you and start playing around with the word." This was a critical point in the conversation because what Cesar was suggesting has actually been done many times throughout history as a way for disempowered groups to reclaim the language which has been used against them. For example, the gay community reclaimed the word "queer," which, in the past, had been used as an epithet. In the 1990s, however, they incorporated that word into the abbreviated description of their community: QLGBT (Queer Lesbian Gay Bisexual Transgender).

At this point in the conversation, I felt that we had veered from our original inquiry about who was responsible for the messages that were prevalent. So I asked once again. This time, Mona, a very shy student who rarely spoke during our whole-class discussions, piped up with a revolutionary idea. "In the commercials," she said quietly, then waiting to see if someone else would finish her sentence. When nobody did, she continued, "They only show girls playing with the toy, so you are supposed to think it's for girls." The class erupted in many side conversations after this comment; Mona had clearly hit on something big that the students had not previously articulated but felt strongly about. Chloe ended our conversation that day by adding on, "Companies advertise it as 'girl stuff' and 'boy stuff.' So they want the girls to buy it." Although we did not explore this point further that day, we had come up with a comprehensive list of groups of people who forwarded messages and helped form our socially constructed ideas.

In other classrooms around the school, teachers were leading similar conversations about physical ability, immigrants, and homelessness. Although the topics were different, students discovered that the messages often came from similar groups: previous generations, adults, older children, and media or advertising. We were all beginning to see how cultures agreed upon certain social norms and then perpetuated them through a variety of communication.

Here is the transcript from a discussion that took place on November 28, 2006.

S. Kugler:	Who makes these rules? Who says that they are "girl things" or "boy things?"
Steven:	People in my house.
Kayla:	It came from older kids.
Chloe:	I disagree. It came when our grandmothers were alive.
Summer:	I agree with Kayla. Maybe teachers made it up.
Kayla:	I think you misunderstood me. Older kids are always taking out their feelings about it on the little kids.
Jane:	Yeah. Like you have it in your head already.
Chloe:	Well, it's not always used to hurt people's feelings.
Kayla:	Like if you're just being honest?
Cesar:	I get it from other people, but I don't know much about it.
Alex:	Like sometimes it *is* to be mean to other people.
Charlotte:	I wonder why you don't hear "boy-boy" the way you hear "girly-girl?"
Chloe:	There's such thing as a tomgirl. It doesn't always hurt people's feelings.

Cesar:	When someone gets called a wimp, they say thank you and start playing around with the word.
Charlotte:	Like with "gay." The bad meaning is used and the good meaning isn't really used anymore.
Ruby:	It's not really bad. It's just different.
Steven:	Somebody called me gay.
Henry:	That happened to me, too.
S. Kugler:	So who makes these rules?
Clara:	There's no such thing as the rules.
S. Kugler:	So who decided?
Ruby:	A long time ago, boys said, "I like these things so these are boy things."
Chloe:	Companies advertise it as girl stuff and boy stuff. So they want the girls to buy it.
Mona:	In the commercials, they only show girls playing with the toy, so you think it's for girls.

It is also interesting to note that we had not yet begun the discussion of whether or not we agreed with these messages. As a class, the students were merely noting that such clear messages did, indeed, exist in the world, that these messages had come from a variety of sources, and that often, in the case of physical ability or gender, for example, these messages were used against people who didn't exactly fit into expectations. This is important because in order to have such an honest discussion, students need to feel that their ideas and the opinions of those who they love and respect will not be attacked. In order to foster feelings of safety in the classroom, I did everything I could to ask the question "Who makes the rules?" without any judgment. In fact, I struggled with whether or not to use the word *stereotype* instead of rules but decided again it at this point because of the negative connotations in the word *stereotype*. However, the word *"rules"* is not solely good or bad but is up for constant interpretation.

Not only did I need to be aware of my questions, I also needed to be diligent about my reactions to the students' answers. If Kayla had commented that "our grandmothers made the rules" and I had immediately asked why we assume the *women* are the ones making the rules and not the *men*, this may have sent a clear message that only some answers were permissible. As teachers, we also have the tendency to ask presumably innocent questions that lead students clearly down one path of thinking. For example, I could have also asked, "Is that true? *Did* our *grandmothers* make the rules?" However, often merely the intonation of a question like that leads the entire class to join in unison, "Noooooooo!" I was constantly monitoring my own questions and reactions as well as those of the students in order to create an environment that fostered, rather than stifled, honest dialogue.

I also recognize that not all students will ever feel comfortable participating in a discussion with 25 of their peers, no matter how "safe" the space. Many adults can sympathize with the feeling of having something to say at a meeting, but being uncomfortable with the format of public speaking. In order to allow all of my students an opportunity to share their views, I also sent home a survey for each of them to complete for homework. I asked similar questions to those I asked during the whole class conversation, but because it was written, it allowed my more introverted students to reflect and respond.

In one of these take-home surveys, Jason reflected on the use of the word "tomboy" and how it was being used during lunchtime and recess. While others in our class suggested that words like "tomboy" were not necessarily insults, but could be reinterpreted depended on the person, Jason felt strongly that this was a punishable crime. In his survey, he wrote that if he overheard someone say that he would "get a teacher" in order to get the student in trouble. He also writes that he would remind that person about "guideline #1," which was the first rule of our classroom: Take care of the people in your community. It's also interesting to note that the use of the word "sissy" was actually more egregious in Jason's eyes than the use of the word "tomboy," prompting him to get not one, but "two teachers." This difference, between comparing a girl to a boy or a boy to a girl, is one that my students would return to, to ponder and discuss, weeks later.

SURROUNDING STUDENTS WITH
A VARIETY OF RESOURCES

Up until this point, students are relying purely on their prior knowledge of these topics to participate in class conversations and activities. This next stage in the process is a time for students to expand their knowledge by studying a variety of resources and thinking critically about what each particular text has to say about the topic. As is always the case, we begin with questions:

- What does this text have to say about the rules?
- Do the characters in this text break the rules or follow the rules?
- What happens when people and characters break the rules?
- What happens when they follow the rules?
- How is this group depicted in this text? Who has the power here?

Based on my study of critical literacy, I encouraged students to think about a text not just in the traditional sense of the word, meaning only books and words. Rather, text was used in its broadest meaning to include people, images, advertisements, books, newspapers, and signs. After all, all of these "texts" send us messages, obvious and covert, that help form our ideas.

It was now my responsibility as a teacher to expose students to as many different texts as possible, while still representing a variety of ideas on the subject. I realized early on in our gender study that if I truly wanted students to become aware of how these rules or stereotypes played a constant role in our world, it would not be as easy as reading a single, didactic picture book. I can imagine an earlier time in my career when there was bullying among my students and so I chose to read them a single moralistic tale of a bully who later was punished or befriended, or some other equally neatly-packaged ending. These books told similar tales of victimhood and redemption and sent the clear message that bullying is wrong, that the victim should speak up, and there will be a clear and easy resolution.

And while these texts serve an important purpose in our classroom dialogues, I was usually left feeling that the whole story had not been told. There was little discussion in these books about why students were bullying each other. There was no acknowledgment of the personal risks it took to stand up to the teasing, and the stories always ended in ways that didn't match my own experiences with standing up to those who very often have more status and power. I wanted to provide my students with not just one image of prejudice and stereotyping in action, but multiple, conflicting images. In this way, I wanted my students to recognize how stereotypes and prejudice are created and perpetuated not just with overt teasing on the playground, but also with images, by comments from our closest friends, and through texts that we read.

My class began our exploration of resources by studying the books in our classroom library. I began by reading aloud books that specifically addressed the issue of gender stereotyping and prejudice, such as *William's Doll*, *The Sissy Duckling*, *Pinky and Rex and the Bully*, and *Oliver Button is a Sissy*. As I read each of these texts, we discussed the questions listed above. What were the messages about gender in this text? How did different characters react when the main character followed or broke the rules? What were the consequences of following or breaking the rules?

Earlier on in my teaching career, I felt that it was my job as the teacher to forward the messages of the text and make them as explicit to students as possible. In the cases of the texts listed above, the message was usually, "You can be anyone you want to be" or "Just be yourself" or "Stand up to the people who tell you to be somebody you are not." What the texts never seem to be acknowledging or addressing, however, was that it is never that easy. Breaking rules or acting out of expectations can be risky and takes tremendous amounts of courage. The risk and need for courage does not end the minute you declare yourself a "rule-breaker" or the day you stand up to the bully on the playground. In fact, that is when the risk and need for courage *begin*. And yet, many of these texts began with the main character as a victim and ended when the main character stood up against the prejudice, broke the rule, and transformed into a hero. This led me to ask my students other vital questions:

- Do you agree with the way the main character handled this?
- Do you agree with how the author wrote this story?
- Do you think that would happen that way?
- Does this match your experience?
- How else might this have gone?

Later, we read through texts that didn't explicitly claim to address issues of gender but forwarded these messages in more covert ways. In *Fantastic Mr. Fox*, by Roald Dahl, one of the class's favorite read-alouds, we examined a scene in which the father fox and four small sons have boundless energy to dig their way out of trouble, while the mother lies helpless and exhausted. We asked the question, "What is the author saying here about the gender rules?"

In other texts, such as *Sarah, Plain and Tall* by Patricia MacLauchlan, Sarah defied the stereotype by putting on a pair of overalls and climbing on to the top of the barn to fix the roof with the father of the household. Just as I read that scene, Marco, a usually quiet child, gasped and blurted out, "She's breaking the stereotype!!!" At this point, students were starting to see that messages about race, class, language, and gender could be found in every text if we had our eyes and ears open to it. More significantly, we could identify what message this particular author was forwarding and then ask ourselves if we agreed or disagreed.

I also thought it would be important to bring in some people who had first-hand experience dealing with these issues so students could hear how difficult it can be to deal with others assumptions. I invited a few fifth graders who considered themselves "rule breakers" to visit. They were interviewed by my students and answered questions such as:

- Why were you teased?
- What did the teaser do?

- What did you do?
- How do you break/follow the rules?
- Why do you break/follow the rules?

These fifth grade students became another resource for us to study, helped put a real face to the theoretical issues at hand, and also gave my students a vision for what it looked like to be teased because of who you are, different ways to deal with this teasing, and the real life consequences for defying people's expectations.

Lastly, we studied advertisements by combing through the local paper, looking at ads in magazines, and the circulars for toy stores to see how this medium could also forward messages in obvious and not-so-obvious ways.

On the first floor of our building, in the ESL room, Amelia had no difficulty finding resources that depicted immigrants in a variety of ways. They read books such as *My Name is Yoon, One Green Apple, I Hate English, The Name Jar, and My Name is Maria Charlotte.* As you can tell from the titles, many of these books use the name of the child as a metaphor for how they felt they needed to leave a part of their identity behind when they entered an English-speaking school.

REFLECTING AND TAKING ACTION

Beverley Daniel Tatum, in her book *Why Are All the Black Kids Sitting Together in the Cafeteria* (1997), compared racism (and any "–ism," for that matter) to a people-mover at an airport. She suggested it is not enough to stand still because the direction the culture automatically heads is toward that of stereotyping and prejudice. She suggests that in order to combat racism, you must actually turn around and walk quickly in the other direction. In my classroom, this meant that it wasn't enough to merely raise awareness of sexism, racism, and any other form of prejudice. If we were aware and inactive, we were still passive bystanders and therefore compliant in the prejudice. Instead, we now have to *act* on this newly discovered knowledge. But first, we had to reflect on our new learning and understanding.

We began with these essential questions:

- What do you think about the rules/stereotypes now?
- Has your thinking changed? How? Why?
- Are there times when the rules are broken? How?

In my first grade class, when I asked these questions, the students began a series of confessions about times when they had each acted out of the gender stereotype. Willow, a Native American boy who had hair down to his waist, admitted, "I have long hair and *sometimes* I don't care." Dillon boldly claimed that going to the art center during choice time was not something that most boys in our classroom did. And Jack, a tough boy who often led the rest of the boys in our class in block construction, admitted for the first time that year that he took ballet after school. The class sat in shocked silence for a moment after this particular confession. Even in this first grade class, students recognized that stereotypes and expectations affect the minute decisions we make, even at 6 years old. These children were admitting that when they choose a crayon or a when they pick their clothes out of their closet each morning, they are aware of the effect that decision will have on them.

In the gym, just a few rooms down the hall, the students had spent the last few weeks discussing the topic of physical ability. One class decided that it would be a good idea to create a bulletin board of images outside of the gym that portrayed "surprising athletes." The students began cutting out and posting pictures of paraplegic athletes, Special Olympics athletes, and women weight lifters. Their point was to broaden other students' idea of the word "athlete."

What Can I Say?

If I'm getting teased...

- I'm allowed.
- Who said I can't?
- Go away.
- What's the problem with that?
- How would you like it if you got teased?
- You're just saying that so *you* don't get teased.
- That's not true.

If someone else is getting teased...

- Come on, let's go.
- How do you think she/he feels?
- He can play with whatever he wants.
- He's actually *brave* to break that stereotype.

In my third grade classroom, the students were much more concerned with the bullying that continued at lunch and recess. Their action plan included a list of "comebacks" they would try to use when faced with bully about gender. They titled the chart: What Can We Say?

One of my main goals at this point in the study was to help students see that there is no such thing as duality when it comes to culture and identity. Despite the messages our culture sends us, it is not true that you are either a "girly girl" or a "tomboy." If you are biracial, you do not have to choose between your black and white self. You do not have to be identified solely as an immigrant or completely shed your cultural and family heritage. Within each of us are multiple identities and truths. This was a complex concept for my elementary school students, who continued to struggle with this idea. They either wanted the rules to be true or for there to be no rules as all.

This cognitive struggle came out one day when Savannah, the self-proclaimed girly girl, and Chloe, the girl who passed as a boy, got into a discussion. Savannah confidently proclaimed, "There are no rules. Actually, there's no such thing as 'rules' in the first place!" Chloe placed her hands on her hips and asked, "Then why do I get teased?" For me, this conversation represents the heart of this work. While social norms are constructed and might not be true, they still exist and are forwarded to us in a variety of ways. So while you *can* break stereotypes and social rules, this behavior often comes with some level of risk.

Through this process, students became aware that they had already internalized many messages about gender, race, culture and physical ability. Then, they learned to question and ponder the sources of this information. Next, they explored multiple resources, which sometimes confirmed and often contradicted the simplistic ideas they had previously thought to be true. And finally, they were allowed to reconstruct and re-imagine more complex ideas about identity and cultural norms. Mostly importantly, they left feeling empowered to act on this knowledge, to use it to change their own behavior or address other's prejudices.

CONCLUSION

It was never my goal to indoctrinate students into one kind of thinking. From the beginning of our journey together, I avoided and even discouraged students from using clichés about stereotyping and prejudice. We all want books to teach us neat, simple morals like "We are all the same" or "You can be whoever you want to be." But the hard truth is that in many ways we are different and being different is often a challenging experience. Of course, most of those "differences" are socially constructed through media, language, and social interaction. However, it does little good to tell children that the constant covert messages they are receiving about these social constructions do not even exist and that they should operate as if everybody is the exact same.

When I first moved to New York City, I was teaching in a school that was predominantly Catholic Hispanic. For decades, the teachers had been putting on a huge assembly at Christmastime, with the guidance counselor dressing up as Santa Claus and handing out candy canes to each student. In more recent years, there had been an influx of immigrants from Yemen and the school was now 20% Muslim. On this particular year, the Muslim holiday Ramadan was being observed throughout the month of December. This meant that hundreds of Muslim children were going to be ushered into the school auditorium, led onto the stage to tell Santa Claus their Christmas wish, and then handed a candy cane, which they were not allowed to eat because they were fasting for the holiday.

About a week before this event, I approached the administration in a private meeting. I explained how I truly understood the conflict many of these children faced because it had often been difficult for me, as one of the few Jewish children at my school, to participate in Christmas events. I further explained that there was an added challenge for the children who were fasting to be surrounded by candy that all the other children would be allowed to eat. I then offered to host an alternative celebration in my classroom, playing my guitar, singing, and organizing games unrelated to a particular holiday.

There was silence around the table, and then the assistant principal said calmly, "My daughter has a teacher like you: a teacher who's trying to ruin Christmas for the rest of us. Why can't you just enjoy the holiday?" Even as an adult, who had clear ideas about and confidence in my own identity, I was unsure how to respond. It was clear from the assistant principal's reaction that I was supposed to silence the part of my identity that didn't fit into the culture of this school as were all the students who did not have the same perspective on this religious holiday. Instead, I decided to offer the alternative celebration in my classroom for the students who did not feel comfortable celebrating Christmas.

The day after the Christmas assembly and my alternative sing-along, one of the mothers of a Muslim student approached me on the sidewalk during dismissal. "I know you had a sing-along yesterday," she told me. "And I told Mahdi to go to the assembly with Santa Claus instead." I stared at her in disbelief. Mahdi had been one of the students on my mind when I met with the administration in the first place. She went on to explain that she didn't want

Mahdi separated from the majority of the students because she didn't want him ostracized any more than he already was. It was easier, she said, to just let him participate in a Christmas celebration.

The uncomfortable, and sometimes dangerous, thing about sending the message of "we are all the same" is that it requires certain people to deny the parts of themselves that are actually different. By acknowledging the differences, we are acknowledging and validating our students, their lives, their experiences.

This is not just a curriculum that aims to help students read and write their way through elementary school, although that is where it begins. The curriculum of addressing silences intends to teach young students to become the kind of adults who see unfairness in the world and have the knowledge and the language to stand up against it. As I helped students recognize stereotypes and identify where those ideas came from, my goal was to send students down a life-long path of reflecting on their beliefs and behavior. Is this *really* what I believe or is that just what I've heard from others? Is this really true or is that just what the book says? Can I imagine another way this could be? Can I think of this in another way? In asking these questions, we hope to raise students to be the kind of adults who feel empowered to talk back to bias and take action against it.

REFERENCES

Ada, Alma Flor and K. Dyble Thompson. (1996). *My Name is Maria Charlotte*. New York: Alladin Paperbacks.

Bunting, Eve. (2006). *One Green Apple*. New York: Houghton Mifflin Company.

Chasnoff, Debra and Helen Cohen. (1996). "It's Elementary: Talking About Gay Issues in School."

Cortes, Carlos E. (2000). *The Children Are Watching: How the Media Teach About Diversity*. New York: Teachers College Press.

Dahl, Roald. (1970). *Fantastic Mr. Fox*. New York: Puffin Books.

Fierstein, Harvey. (2002). *The Sissy Duckling*. New York: Simon and Schuster Books for Young Readers.

Howe, James. (1996). *Pinky and Rex and the Bully*. New York: Simon and Schuster, Inc.

dePaola, Tomie. (1979). *Oliver Button is a Sissy*. Orlando: Harcourt Brace & Company.

Levine, Ellen. (1995). *I Hate English!* New York: Scholastic, Inc.

MacLachlan, Patricia. (1985). *Sarah, Plain and Tall*. New York: Harper Collins Publishers.

Recorvitz, Helen. (2003). *My Name is Yoon*. New York: Frances Foster Books.

Tatum, Beverly Daniel. (1997). New York: Basic Books.

Yangsook, Choi. (2003). *The Name Jar*. New York: Dell Dragonfly Books.
Zolotow, Chalotte. (1972). *William's Doll*. New York: Harper Collins Publishers.

ABOUT THE AUTHOR

Sara Kugler is a reading teacher with Bailey's Elementary School for the Arts and Sciences in Fairfax County, Virginia. Prior to that, she was a literacy staff developer at the Reading and Writing Project at Teachers College, Columbia University, leading workshops on balanced literacy and critical literacy throughout New York City public schools as well as in Florida, Illinois, California, Minnesota, and Gothenburg, Sweden. She has taught in multiple elementary schools in Fairfax Country, Virginia, and in Brooklyn, New York, co-leading one school's Diversity Committee. Sara has also volunteered as a literacy staff developer in rural South Africa. She earned her master's degree in Reading and Writing Education from Teachers College, Columbia University. Sara lives with her husband and daughter in Fairfax County, Virginia.

Chapter 8

A Calling to Teach

Providing Every Child with an Opportunity for Success

Ashley Harris

Tan. As a small child, this is how I described my caramel colored skin. Proud of my biracial heritage, I never hesitated to let people know my background. When I was four years old, my family joined the Interracial Family Alliance of Houston. My mom often recounts my reaction as we walked into the first function. Wide-eyed and anxious to discover what was in store, I exclaimed, "Look at all these tan kids!" I remember the sense of belonging I felt being surrounded by kids who looked like me. Their hair was like my hair—crazy curls and waves everywhere that obstinately stuck out, claiming independence rather than laying flat on their heads. Their parents were like my parents with skin tones at opposite ends of the color spectrum. This social network became a crucial part of my development as I began to realize the possibilities for defining who I was. Without brothers and sisters, ultimately, this group helped me to establish my identity.

Despite the stereotype that mixed kids are confused, I was just the opposite. When people asked, "What are you?" and sometimes even before they could ask, I professed that I was both black AND white. There was no reason to be ashamed of the hue of my skin or the texture of my hair. I was proud to be me.

Another thing I was proud of was my parents. They both came from humble beginnings and were the first in their families to attend high school and graduate from college. Though I've asked him about it several times, I still can't fathom what it must have been like for my father to attend a one-room school house until eighth grade. In the world of education, differentiation is not only a buzz word but a best practice that is used by the most effective teachers to tailor the content to meet the needs of diverse learners.

With multiple grade levels in one classroom, his teachers had no choice but to differentiate, to provide instruction and/or resources at a variety of skill levels.

My mother, on the other hand, literally grew up on the wrong side of the tracks, in the South. She was encouraged by her grandmother who raised her to focus on her studies. She knew that college was her only way out of the small town and more importantly out of an environment that stifled her growth as an intellectual person of color, striving to know more and do better for herself.

Regardless of race or upbringing, both of my parents realized that education was the only way to expand their horizons. They didn't stop at bachelor's degrees. My mom went on to receive a master's degree and my dad earned a Ph.D. Ultimately, they became educators. Given their backgrounds and chosen profession, of course that meant that my education was of the utmost importance.

In my last few years in high school, I wasn't really sure what I wanted to do with my life. My option was not whether or not I would go to college but rather which college I would attend. Though I was uncertain about the direction in which I should focus my energies, my parents, my mom in particular, had a clear plan for what I should major in to ensure my career prospects would be vast and prosperous.

Business. Without a clear sense of purpose for my life, my parents urged me to pursue this field of study. I would be able to earn a good salary while working a reasonable amount of hours. I took their advice as usual and did well in college though I wasn't terribly interested in accounting, finance, management, and the like. Upon graduation from college, I moved from Houston to the Washington, D.C., area to pursue my career as an assistant buyer for a major retailer.

I loved living among and learning about people who were different than me. This was the first time I had been exposed to 1st and 2nd generation immigrants from Africa. The Ethiopian and Somalian community especially intrigued me. In fact, the secretary that worked in my department was Somalian. She often informed me of cultural practices from her home country and let me sample foods that she brought for lunch. I began to know and understand her as a person.

Unfortunately, others in our department did not value her contributions. At times it felt like they were forcing her to assimilate to the American way of life. They were often impatient when explaining processes to her and were noticeably upset when she took an extended vacation to Canada twice a year to visit her family. I also began to notice that almost all of the secretarial staff were people of color, and in this large corporation, only two buyers were black. No one seemed to care. The hierarchal structure of the organization, the lack of focus on bridging the communication gap from one level to the next, and the lack of meaningful relationships created a toxic work environment. Despite the individual relationships I was nurturing, I hated my job.

Toward the end of my second year as an assistant buyer, I remember my manager calling me into her office for my annual review. I can still see the look in her face, a look of contempt and frustration. I knew I wasn't really doing my best work, but I didn't realize that other people were noticing as well. Halfway through the meeting, she paused and then asked, "Do you even HAVE drive?" Dumbfounded, I had no idea how to respond. How could she even ask me that? I had graduated at the top of my class in both high school and college, co-founded and led numerous student organizations, and always strived to be the best at everything I did.

That was my light bulb moment. I knew that I could no longer work for this organization. I just didn't get it. We were selling dresses, not saving lives, yet the people around me hustled and bustled about like the world would end if a bestseller wasn't reordered on time.

I realized I had always pushed myself to be *my personal* best, not better than everyone else. Perhaps because I was an only child and didn't have siblings to compare myself to, my sense of competition was more of an internal struggle rather than an external battle. Whatever the case, I knew I was unable to muster up enough personal conviction to connect to the goals of the organization. I asked myself, "Why am I here? What's the point in making money for a huge corporation?"

I knew that I needed to find a career where I was working for a greater cause, and after some serious soul-searching, I thought this might be the time to explore the realm of education. I knew I eventually wanted to be a teacher, to follow in the footsteps of both my parents. I had seen the impact education had on them and the impact they were having on their own students.

I had a friend from college who was living in the D.C. area and was in her 2nd year as a Teach For America corps member. I visited her classroom and talked to her about her experience as a teacher in a low-income community. After watching her teach, I remember commenting, "Your students just adore you. They would do anything to please you." Seeing her in action confirmed my desire to become a teacher. Thankfully, my epiphany happened at just the right time, because the final deadline for TFA was the following week. Needless to say, I applied.

One day, all children in this nation will have the opportunity to obtain an excellent education. That's what I dreamt about, prayed about, and truly believed when I applied to join TFA. At that point in my life, I didn't realize what an impact this mission statement would have on how I would spend my time and who I would become. Teach For America was my way back to Houston and my way into the realm of education, a realm where I would find a home and *eventually* thrive.

MY FIRST CLASSROOM ASSIGNMENT

My first experience in the classroom was a bit unnerving to say the least. I was placed at a middle school that was about 85% African American and 10% Hispanic. Over 90% of the students qualified for free or reduced-price lunch. As a person of color, I assumed that I would be able to naturally connect with my students. Boy, was I wrong. I found that I had little in common with them as we lived very different lives. They did not see me as one of them.

TFA encouraged me to build relationships with my students. Meanwhile, veteran teachers cautioned me not to drive around the neighborhood. It was too dangerous. On a weekly basis, tires were slashed in the teachers' parking lot. The second week of school, a student brought a gun to school. In my own classroom, one particular student tried to start a fight with her classmates at least three to four days out of the week. There were fights in the courtyard almost every morning before school. There were fights in the cafeteria during lunch. Violence was pervasive. Overwhelmed and just trying to get by, relationships were not at the forefront of my mind. I was just trying to survive.

How was I supposed to provide an excellent education for our nation's children when I couldn't even provide them with a safe environment to learn? I reached out to my assigned mentor in numerous ways, but he brushed me off. I even asked my principal to assign me to a new mentor. I recognized that I was struggling and wasn't afraid to admit it to my colleagues, but I couldn't figure out where to get help or how to improve my circumstances.

This is not what I had signed up to do. I knew the obstacles would be numerous, but I felt like I was alone in facing them. I felt like I wasn't making a difference at all. Period. Every morning I was physcially ill due to the anxiety of facing another day. I remember having a conversation with two of my brightest students. I told them, "You two should transfer to another school. You're doing well here, but you deserve a better education." They were living up to their potential and making the most of the limited opportunities offered to them. At the time, I don't think I fully realized that they may not have had other options. Futhermore, what about the other students in my class? Did they not deserve more as well? Did they not deserve an environment of encouragement, high standards, and accountability that would lead to achievement?

I often thought about my initial interview when I applied for TFA. The interviewer asked, "What would make you quit Teach For America?" Without hesitation, I declared, "I'm not going to quit. The only way I would even *consider* leaving TFA would be if my life is in danger." I was on the frontlines now and while I was reminded of my answer, I had such passion, such drive, that quitting never really crossed my mind. I had taken a significant paycut to join this movement, and I was doing something that I truly believed in.

That first year in the classroom was rough. At the beginning of the school year, my principal informed the staff that enrollment was down and two teachers would need to be let go. I prayed that it would be me. I even asked my program director at TFA if I could volunteer. She said no, so I waited. One day at the end of October my principal called me into his office, and let me know that since I was a new teacher, I was being let go, but he had arranged an interview for me at a nearby school that very afternoon. In a matter of a week, I went from teaching 6th grade math to 4th grade self-contained. I was now responsible for 22 students and five lesson plans each day. I was the 3rd teacher my students had that year—and it was only October.

At first glance, my second school seemed to be more conducive to teaching and learning, but I soon found out that shiny outward appearances can conceal systematic issues below the surface. Though the school had been rated as Recognized the year before (the second highest rating from the state education agency), students' test scores were not authentic. A couple of teachers explained techniques I could use to "help" the students do well on the exam. One of the teachers made it pretty clear that the principal knew this was going on and encouraged it.

What made the situation worse to me was that my principal and several of the teachers professed to be Christians. My faith in God was stronger at this point in my life than it had ever been before, so I was thoroughly perplexed by this situation. I just didn't understand how they could knowingly compromise themselves and our students and still claim to be people of faith. What faith did they have in our students when they assumed that they couldn't achieve without cheating? What faith did they have when they yelled at students because "that's what they're used to" instead of honoring them for who they were as individuals?

Although I wasn't afraid for my safety in this school, I was infuriated by the behavior of the other adults around me. My students were not physically in harm's way, but the emotional damage they were enduring was just as severe. One electives teacher in particular was especially intimidating and demeaning. After picking up my students from her classrom one day, many of them were visibly upset. I asked what happened, and they informed me that she told them, "You're the stupidest fourth grade class I've ever taught!" I was almost in tears *with* my students hearing such a cruel comment. I never approached the teacher. I hadn't yet developed my voice as an advocate for children. This teacher was best friends with the principal, and I felt that if I had stood up to her, it would only make my situation worse. Again, my students were being shortchanged of a quality education. How could anyone expect them to thrive in an environment of disrespect?

When my class received our score reports for the Stanford exam, at least 4 of my students appeared to have unlearned material because they were a full grade level below the score they had received the year before. Teach For America wanted corps members to track significant gains, defined by 1.5 years of growth in math and reading. How could I track gains when the last year's data was completely skewed? Again, I couldn't understand how anyone could think that cheating was a viable option to ensure students did well on a standardized test. I was furious, and yet I didn't speak up. I didn't know who was involved in this scheme and was fearful of being fired and released from Teach For America, fearful of completely disrupting my future in education in my first year in the classroom. I just knew that that was not a place I wanted to be. My students, all students, deserved more. I wondered if other seemingly high performing low-income schools operated with the same crooked values. The acheivement gap was being exacerbated rather than diminished due to unethical behaviors of adults. How did our students have a chance at life when they were taught that cheating is the only way to get ahead, to get by?

BECOMING A TRUE TEACHER

At the completion of my two-year commitment with TFA, I was eager to move to a school where my integrity would not be challenged, a school where students were safe and respected. I knew I still wanted to work with a racially diverse low-income population, but I knew I needed a school community and ultimately a principal that would allow me to teach to the best of my abilities without expecting me to compromise myself. My third school was just what I had hoped for. My principal was more supportive of her teachers and had students' best interests in mind. She trusted my abilities as a professional and let the success of my students speak for my instructional strategies.

The students at the school were treated with respect more so than at the other two campuses where I had worked. Yelling as a form of discipline was used signifiantly less at this campus, and ultimately, students were held to high expectations for behavior and academics. I worked on a grade level team that appreciated my work, a team that was willing to collaborate rather than use insults and political ties to coerce colleagues. I spent many a late night on campus surrounded by my co-workers who were working equally as hard for our students. I was especially appreciative of my team leader who had a special knack for working with parents. I learned a lot from her about the importance of involving parents in the educational process. It wasn't just my grade level team but the school as a whole that was efficiently run. I would probably still be there today if I hadn't decided to leave the classroom.

By my third year in the classroom, I realized that this was something I could do; I could become, and indeed was becoming, a successful teacher. I reaffirmed my commitment to education and decided to pursue my masters degree. Not having majored in education, I wanted to further my knoweldge of best practices in the field. I was also interested in exploring opportunites outside the classroom. All in all, I was tired of grading papers. As a middle school English teacher with upwards of 160 students, I was up to my neck in essays. I wanted to explore avenues that would allow me to to have a larger impact on the educational reform movement, beyond my individual classroom. I happened upon a blurb about an instructional coach position at YES Prep Public Schools in a TFA alumni email blast and decided to apply. I wasn't sure if I was qualified, but I thought it was worth a shot. With each step of the interview process, I realized how much I wanted the job.

In researching YES Prep, I began to realize the values of the organization were in sync with my own values. YES Prep Public Schools exists to increase the number of low-income Houstonians who graduate from a four-year college prepared to compete in the global marketplace and committed to improving disadvantaged communities. In fact, acceptance to a four year college is part of YES Prep's charter. One hundred percent of YES Prep's graduating seniors have been accepted into four-year colleges, 90 percent of whom are first-generation college-bound. How could someone not want to be part of such an awe-inspiring organization?

BECOMING PART OF THE MAGIC

I was elated when I was offered the position. I felt as though I had finally arrived. In my previous experience, the exterior of the school buildings masked broken systems. I had a positive experience in my third school, but the options outside of the classroom were limited. I soon discovered that YES's five campuses made up of old portable buildings, a warehouse, and a wing in a large public school were home to a whole, functioning, progressive organization authentically bridging the achievement gap. I remember thinking there must be magic happening in these buildings, in these classrooms. Sure, they weren't fancy; they were actually pretty barebones, but there must be something, some way of teaching, extra motivated students, parental support, *something* that allowed this organization to achieve such amazing results.

The night before I set foot in my first YES Prep classroom, I anticipated seeing this magic in action. I truly thought I would see a completely different world. I soon found out, it wasn't magic; it was skilled dedicated people willing to do whatever it takes to ensure all students achieve. Everyone was on board with the mission and a true sense of collaboration thrived, which made the mission come to life. I had seen some of this at the third school, but it seemed to be intensified here. Everyone believed in the students and believed that as the adults teaching and guiding them, they had the power to change the trajectories of the young people in their care.

The students YES serves are quite similar to the students I had worked with before. Eighty-four percent of the students at YES are Hispanic, and 13% are African American. As I mentioned before, I had a difficult time connecting to my students at the beginning of my career as a teacher. Since then, I had gained more confidence and had so many culturally rich experiences. I grew up in a multi-cultural environment, and as an adult I've had more exposure to African American culture. Thus, at first, it was easier for me to connect with the African American students at YES. Now, I feel like I'm able to connect to students of all backgrounds. When I see them in the hallways or when I'm teaching them during model lessons, I'm much more comfortable asserting my authority while bringing a piece of myself into the school or the classroom. This being said, many of the faculty members at YES are white. So the myth that in order to be successful, minority students need to be taught by people who look like them is just that—a myth. I repeatedly see white teachers able to build strong relationships with their students despite the lack of cultural sameness.

I am impressed with the responsibility YES Prep places on the students themselves. The organization has a set of tenets called the "Thinks and Acts Statements" which were created by students a few years ago. Statements such as "We always leave a place better than we found it" and "The strong take care of the weak" guide the values instilled in students by teachers. Students are constantly reminded to make good decisions and ultimately do so on their own. For example, a group of YES Prep students attended a program at another school and noticed that trash was left around the auditorium. Without being prompted to do so, five or six students collected the trash and disposed of it properly. I am by no means claiming that every YES student has angelic qualities and only does what's morally right. I am, however, saying that YES works to create civic-minded students who look outside of themselves.

Since its inception in 1995 as Project YES, the organization has been creating opportunities that would otherwise not exist for a growing numbers of students. Chris Barbic, founder and CEO, and a group of concerned teachers, parents, and community members started Project YES with 58 students. As a fifth grade teacher, Chris was distressed by the dim prospects of his students once they left his classroom and moved on to middle school.

Project YES became YES College Preparatory School in 1998 and in 2006 was renamed YES Prep Public Schools. YES now serves 4,200 students across eight campuses, with two additional campuses slated to open in July of 2011.

YES utilizes an online lottery to randomly select incoming students. There are no admission requirements and zip codes are a major determining factor regarding which campus a student is "zoned" to. The organization strategically places its campuses in low-income areas so that the students in surrounding zip codes are the target population. YES has an extensive bus system, so that transportation is not a concern for families, and every year roughly 85% of YES's students are eligible for free or reduced-price lunch. While the lottery is probably the fairest way for students to gain admittance to YES, it's heartbreaking to think about the number of students that are rejected. Multiple school directors have shared stories with me about conversations with parents who are in tears, begging for their sons and daughters to have a chance to attend YES Prep.

As a charter management organization, YES Prep does not receive government funding for buildings, so it is up to the organization to raise additional monies to cover these costs. YES has obtained funds through a host of foundations, numerous grants, individual donations, and in-house fundraising efforts such as the annual Oil and Gas Poker Tournament which raises hundreds of thousands of dollars. In September 2010, YES received a grant from Oprah Winfrey.

Four of the current eight campuses started as a string of portable buildings. This was almost a rite of passage in the first phase of YES's history. In the last three years, permanent buildings have been erected for three campuses and other buildings have been bought, gutted, and repurposed for two other campuses. With such humble beginnings, students and teachers are extremely gracious when these structures are ready for move-in. YES serves low-income communities, and as an organization, YES recognizes the importance of providing these students with the best instead of the worst facilities. I can still remember the day I stepped foot onto the YES Prep Revolution campus. Once a complex of medical offices, the building had been gutted and transformed into a mass of classrooms and much more. Tears flowed from my eyes. What a site! The students I worked so hard for finally had a beautiful place to learn and grow.

It is more than just the buildings that make YES such a successful organization. The sense of community is manifested in the frequent communication from school to home and vice versa which starts before a student even sets foot on a YES Prep campus. YES Prep provides a home visit to each incoming student prior to the start of summer school. I still remember the first home visit I participated in. A colleague and I arrived at the house and were welcomed by both parents and the two sons who would be attending YES. One would be a sixth grader and the other a seventh grader. The smiles on the parents' faces spoke volumes. Just like my parents, this mother and father had high expectations for their children and wanted to provide them with the best educational opportunities they could. The parents talked about wanting their sons to attend a university and work towards a career vs. just a job that paid hourly wages. These parents saw YES as a solid path to college acceptance and ultimately graduation.

The boys were both a bit timid during our conversation and rightfully so. At that point, they did not understand all that would be required to be YES Prep students. My colleague and I talked through the contract which delineated the roles and responsibilities of YES Prep teachers, students, and parents, and we all signed to indicate the partnership between the family and the school. Each boy received a pair of nails: one to hang his high school diploma and one to hang his college diploma. The family appreciated the fact that this home visit indicated entrance into a community of learners headed toward college graduation.

The home visit is just the beginning of the process. Another step towards nurturing the connection between home and school is cell phones for teachers provided by the school. Students and parents have the opportunity to call teachers until 8:00 or 9:00 PM with questions or concerns. While the phone calls begin with academic concerns, later in the year, students sometimes call their teachers just to talk. Though it takes some students longer than others, they begin to recognize that their teachers provide academically challenging work *and* care about them as people. YES alumni who come back to campus to visit or to speak at gatherings for staff always cite the relationships they had with their teachers as a major determining factor of their success. The cell phones are part of the school's outreach commitment. Teachers are required to make five positive phone calls to parents per week, as part of YES's core value of building and sustaining positive relationships.

YES teachers and administrators work hard to build and maintain relationships with parents as a collective part of the school community. Administrator Brenda Rangel involves parents through multiple avenues. When Brenda started at YES in the fall of 2010, she wanted to know more about what was on parents' minds. Conducting action research at three YES Prep campuses, she learned that parents overwhelmingly sought YES for their child because of the high expectations. Parents also shared that they continue to support YES because they feel comfortable talking with teachers and administrators and are pleased with the consistent communication. They appreciate the discipline system YES uses and the no-nonsense policy which holds both students and parents accountable. Lastly, the parents agreed that YES provides a safe environment with a clear focus on going to college.

In her current role as school director at YES Prep Brays Oaks, Brenda creates a family calendar at the beginning of every month which details events that are planned with the partnership of school and family in mind. The events feature topics that parents can utilize to make school-home connections and that equip parents for holding students accountable for assignments. In addition, Brays Oaks routinely hosts round table discussions and classroom walkthroughs for parents to ensure they are an integral part of the students' education.

Before moving to the Brays Oaks campus, Brenda helped to establish YES's first parent center at YES Prep North Central. She already has space set aside at her new campus to establish a parent center next year. The center serves as a place for parents to congregate and use resources the school can provide. Informal coffee talks with teachers facilitate two-way discussions. The new center will include several computers and a printer/fax provided by community partners, as well as a refrigerator, microwave, and coffee pot. The parent center will be open during promotion meetings and after school events with high school students providing childcare. The students will be able to earn service hours during this time.

This speaks to another aspect of YES Prep that excites me. YES strives to live up to its name, as YES stands for Youth Engaged in Service. Community service has been a priority for me since high school. I even remember asking whether or not I would be required to work on Saturdays when I interviewed to be an instructional coach because it would conflict with the foot washing ministry that I participate in with Houston's homeless. I actually had the opportunity to take students with me to serve on one occasion. Initially, they were shocked and did not know how to react. I remember them not wanting to get too close to the men and women. They watched from a distance, eventually warmed up, and began to get more involved.

Once per six weeks, every YES Prep student across the system takes part in community service. I believe this has a huge impact on the character of the students. They work hard toward a common goal and realize their collective effort makes a difference. Service learning opportunities range from planting trees at a local park to reading to elementary school students to painting the building at another YES Prep campus.

One teacher informed me that juniors from one campus didn't feel the sixth and seventh graders at one of the newer campuses were taking their education seriously enough. The older students expressed an interest in mentoring the younger students. This illustrates YES's emphasis on building a community that takes care of its members.

SEEING A BROADER WORLD

Students have opportunities to impact their community, just as *they* are impacted by annual Spring Trips. Parents pay a nominal activity fee at the beginning of the year, and the school covers the majority of the costs. Some trips focus more on teamwork and service while others (once students get to high school) focus almost solely on visiting colleges around the country. A student that starts at YES in 6th grade will have the opportunity to visit over 20 different colleges and universities by the time he or she graduates. The college counseling team at YES strategically involves parents in this process as these trips are often the first time that students spend time away from home. This is step one in the gradual process of preparing students and parents for what it means to leave home and go off to college.

Sophomores and juniors are also required to pursue summer opportunities. The experiences students have in the world outside of Houston provide valuable insights that influence their future decisions regarding college. Meetings with students and their parents about Summer Opportunities strategically take place in the fall because the programs are rather enticing and can motivate students to keep their grades up throughout the year.

Summer opportunities serve as a mini-crash course in applying to colleges as applications, financial aid, and deadlines are all essential components when students apply for these programs. The opportunities themselves can be challenging for families as this may be the first time their children have gone away for a significant amount of time without YES Prep teachers and students.

Sometimes faculty need to provide extra support for the families. One student opportunities coordinator shared stories about picking families up at their homes to take them to the airport. Sure, they had transportation available and could have driven themselves. However, she wanted to eliminate any barriers that may have existed regarding the student actually arriving at the program. On one occasion, a student walked beside her, several paces in front of the parents. The student was trying to maintain her cool and contain her excitement as they walked down the airport corridor. She turned to her student opportunities coordinator, tears welling up in her eyes, said, "Thank you," and then kept walking.

The process really comes full circle when "veteran" parents who were initially apprehensive about letting their children go away for a summer opportunity become the change agents convincing next year's parents to allow their children to pursue opportunities outside of Houston for the first time. Having seen their own children flourish after attending such programs, these veteran parents and the students themselves are the best advocates for the programs.

In the greater scheme of preparing students for college, Donald Kamentz, the senior director of college initiatives at YES, shared that parents want to be in the know about the path to college, and they rely heavily on YES to guide them and support them throughout the process. To provide a comfortable environment for the families YES serves, the college counseling team offers separate meetings, in English and in Spanish.

A crucial session offered in the spring of senior year called "Letting Go" ensures communication lines are really open between parents and their children. Parents and students are separated into two different rooms and then presented with the same general set of questions such as "How often do you expect your child to call home next year?" and "What do you plan to do with your child's room?" Interestingly, once the parents and students gather back together and share answers, the two groups realize that their answers are strikingly similar. Many students reveal that this session sparks heartfelt conversations with their parents.

I had the opportunity to see the value of the spring trips first-hand when I chaperoned a group of seventh graders a few years ago. In addition to exposing the students to the world beyond their school and home, students and teachers get to know one another in an academic setting that isn't a classroom. Little did I know sharing a cabin with a group of eight bubbly twelve and thirteen year olds would be such fun. My cabin mates reminded me how much time *must* be spent on primping in the morning. There was really no need for me to set my alarm clock. More importantly though, these students had only been at YES two years, and most of them were able to articulate where they wanted to go to college and why. The students that I accompanied, whether I bunked with them or not, are the ones who shout greetings down the hallway when I'm on their campus.

SUPPORTING TEACHERS FROM DAY ONE

I have truly enjoyed getting to know students across the YES Prep campuses; however, in my role as senior instructional coach, I work most closely with the teachers. While I sometimes miss being directly connected to and responsible for my own group of students, I thoroughly enjoy the challenges of training and supporting adults as they begin their journey in the educational reform movement. One of YES's core values is to "attract and develop high-caliber people as the source of our strength." Like our mission statement about sending low-income students to college, the organization lives and breathes the philosophy that the people make the difference. The energy, the enthusiasm, the desire to want more and therefore do more is what excites me about working for YES Prep.

YES Prep has a knack—actually it's more like a science—for recruiting and hiring passionate people who are eager to close the achievement gap. The vast majority of them are recent college graduates who want to ensure that our students are afforded the same educational opportunities they had. YES takes professional development very seriously—very few of our teachers have a degree in education, and even if they do, all first year teachers are a part of YES Prep's Teaching Excellence Program. This includes an intensive two-week induction during the summer, one-on-one coaching for the duration of their first year, and monthly professional learning sessions focused on classroom management, instructional strategies and pedagogy related to specific content areas. Additionally, YES Prep is the first charter management organization in Texas to house its own alternative certification program. Thus, teachers take two exams during the first year in addition to the development mentioned above in order to become certified teachers.

The one-on-one coaching is where I spend the vast majority of my time. Most of YES's students come in at least one grade level behind in math and English, so we can't afford to let teachers struggle through their first year to figure out what works and what doesn't. Having a quality teacher in every classroom is part of the "magic" that allows YES to achieve such dramatic results.

But what happens when a teacher isn't an all-star right out of the gate? As much as we try to select the right people and provide them with high quality training, sometimes there are barriers that keep well-intentioned individuals from being effective in the classroom. Our senior director of teacher development, my manager, often categorizes these barriers as knowledge, skill, or mindset issues. During our summer induction, we frontload the development we provide to impart the *knowledge* of best practices in the classroom. We engage teachers in role-plays, so they can hone the *skills* and technique to effectively manage a classroom and instruct students.

Once the school year begins, coaches are in new teachers' classrooms once every one and a half to two weeks. We continually aid the teachers in fine-tuning their skills and adding new skills to their teacher toolkit. And sometimes we coach teachers on struggles they are facing that are rooted in their *mindset* about teaching, learning, and what their students are capable of accomplishing.

Mindset, by far, is the hardest issue to tackle. Over the course of the last four years, I have coached about sixty teachers, and there are a handful I felt I just wasn't able to impact enough, to grow enough to reach and teach their students in the best way possible. All of them have one thing in common: a mindset that is not conducive to receiving feedback. They have a tendency to rely too heavily on their personal experiences rather than owning and appreciating the life stories of the students they teach.

One particular teacher comes to mind. She was a Teach For America corps member and came from a background of privilege. She attended a private Catholic school and believed that since she had received an excellent education in this setting, surely, her students would benefit from the same methodology. However, that wasn't the case.

She failed to truly connect with her students and seemed unaware or rather unwilling to aptly confront the misbehaviors taking place during her lessons. Time and time again, she was defensive rather than open to the feedback I offered. I felt like I was failing her, but more so, I was failing her students. I had to remind myself that I had tried every strategy of coaching I knew from model lessons to video-taping to co-observations of veteran teachers, but it came down to her lack of commitment in implementing the feedback and making a change. Ultimately, she didn't believe her students could do the work. She failed to make the connection that their lack of mastery stemmed from her poor performance as their teacher. At the end of the year, her administrators did not ask her to return for the following year.

A second teacher comes to mind in thinking about mindset impeding growth. However, his upbringing was in stark contrast to the first teacher I described. Even still, his own life experiences greatly influenced his views about what his students were capable of achieving.

His parents migrated to the United States and worked hard to provide for their family. Seeing the struggles his parents endured, he wanted to ensure their sacrifices were not in vain. He attended an Ivy League school and worked three jobs during college. Upon graduation, he joined Teach For America, passionate about providing rigorous instruction in upper level high school classes. From day one, two things were clear: his commitment to excellence was unwavering and he was easily able to develop strong relationships with students. Outside of the classroom, students often turned to him for support; however, during class, students struggled to keep up with the material and complained of too much homework.

On more than one occasion, he shared with me that the students weren't doing well because they were lazy. He explained that he was going above and beyond for his students, but they weren't pulling their weight. Being one of the most driven and hard-working people I have ever met, he yearned to improve, sought feedback, and almost immediately implemented strategies I suggested. However, his mindset about why students weren't doing their work was not something that a strategy could fix. He had always given 100% to his studies, really to every part of his life and couldn't figure out why his students weren't *willing* to do the same thing. He projected his life on his students, assuming the adversity he had faced paralleled the adversity his students were facing.

Through many difficult conversations initiated by his administrators and me, his views regarding his students' work ethic and fortitude have begun to shift. His students are performing well, and he is on track to finish his first year in the classroom strong.

LOOKING TO THE FUTURE

During the 2011–2012 school year, YES Prep will open its ninth and tenth
campuses. We will serve just over 5,000 students and twice as many will be
on our waiting list. We can't seem to construct schools fast enough to meet
the needs of the Houston community. Given a supportive environment and
rigorous instruction in every classroom, students succeed not in spite of their
low economic status or belonging to a minority group but rather because
YES fosters an environment of "100% every day," an environment where all
stakeholders — students, teachers, administrators, and parents — are held to the
highest of expectations.

Being a part of YES Prep inspires me as a teacher, from a family of
teachers, who knows how a good education can be life-changing. In helping
students of all backgrounds thrive, I am indeed able to thrive myself.

Note: All names in this chapter are pseudonyms.

ABOUT THE AUTHOR

Ashley Harris is the senior instructional coach at YES Prep Public Schools
in Houston, Texas. Her primary responsibilities include developing novice
teachers through one-on-one coaching and creating and facilitating sessions
on instructional strategies. As the senior coach, Harris is also responsible for
providing professional development opportunities for the other Instructional
Coaches. Harris began her career as an assistant buyer at a major retailer in
the D.C. area but quickly realized her heart was in education. After two years
in the private sector, she returned to Houston and joined Teach For America.
She taught in the Houston Independent School District for four years before
joining YES Prep as an instructional coach in 2007. Harris graduated from
The University of Texas at Austin in 2001 with a B.A. in Plan II Honors and
a B.S. in Marketing. She holds a master's degree in curriculum and instruction from The University of Houston. She lives in Houston, Texas, with her
husband and three children.

Courageous Leaders

Chapter 9

Serving Marginalized Children

A New Principal Fights for Equity in the Trenches

Stacie Stanley

"Human diversity makes tolerance more than a virtue; it makes it a require-ment for survival" (Renee Dubos). It is incumbent upon educators across the United States to see diversity as important as oxygen and as natural as every breath consumed. Then and only then will we move toward a more just and equitable education system in America. This commitment is a driving force in my work as a principal.

The shift in demographics across the United States has had a considerable impact on the education system and put pressure on school leaders to build the personal capacity to serve in schools with a significant number of his-torically marginalized children and families. While leadership for equity is certainly not a new topic—it has been nearly a decade since Michael Fullan challenged school leaders with a moral imperative (2003)—schools across the United States continue to produce dismal achievement for ethnically and linguistically diverse children. Serving as a new principal in a school with dismal achievement, I moved to examine systems, increase the capacity of teachers and *engage*—not just *involve*—families of marginalized students.

THE DRIVE TO BECOME A PRINCIPAL

After working in the medical field for more than a decade, I felt the personal drive to return to college and earn a teaching license. I secured a teaching position in an integration district that was established to minimize the learn-ing disparities that exist in racially isolated schools near St. Paul, Minnesota. In our case, state funding was appropriated to help fund magnet schools to attract students from urban and suburban communities. A criterion of school enrollment was equal distribution of white students and students of color. This was due to the long held belief that students of color benefit from learning in schools with white children.

The schools were newly built and equipped with the most recent technologies of the day. After five years of existence, an analysis of yearly test score data indicated that we had only pockets of success. Although students had *access* to the same learning environments found in most middle class neighborhoods, we found that achievement levels of our students of color were similar to that of their home districts.

I was intrigued and perplexed by this phenomenon and began to dig deeper into research related to learning disparities. I learned that there were many schools across the U.S. that had actually eliminated disparities. Some studies indicated that teacher expectations were indicative of student success, while others indicated an educator's instructional efficacy was a key ingredient to narrowing learning disparities. I was compelled to share my newly deepening understanding of the learning gaps with a greater population of educators. After serving as both a middle school math teacher and elementary classroom teacher, I moved into district leadership.

My work as a district leader focused on providing professional development and technical assistance to teachers and principals in the multi-district collaborative. The intermediate district provided support to ten school districts that serviced upwards of one hundred thousand students and five thousand educators. Nearly 95% of the teachers and school leaders we worked with were European American. The intent of the professional development was to better equip teachers and school leaders to serve students from varying ethnic backgrounds, with the ultimate intent of eliminating achievement disparities for racially and linguistically diverse students. While we received encouraging feedback related to *trainings*, shifts in personal practice were few and far between. I came to realize that many educators looked at students of color through a deficit lens. This was evidenced by comments received time and time again such as "*Those* people don't care about education" or "Is there an achievement gap or a *parent gap*." Perhaps the most incendiary comment I heard was when a teacher correlated low intellectual ability with students who lived in households with many siblings. He had apparently read an e-article about the topic and had used the information to justify the low performance of the Hmong and Somali students he served.

During my tenure in the position I administered the Intercultural Developmental Inventory to teachers and leaders. This standardized instrument provided baseline data that enabled me to guide departments in creating strategic and targeted professional development plans as they related to serving ethnically and linguistically diverse students. The plans included a detailed look into teaching and learning styles, intercultural conflict styles and studies of culturally responsive instruction. While the work at times appeared to be productive, I realized that the lack of ongoing, job-embedded experiences impacted the sustainability of the work.

My experiences in this work, coupled with my increasing understanding of effective professional development, led me to seek a school-based leadership position. I wanted the opportunity to work with *a singular* set of staff and students. I was moved by research conducted by Douglas Reeves related to 90-90-90 schools (2000). These are schools where 90% of students qualified for free or reduced priced meals, 90% of students were ethnically diverse, and 90% of the students demonstrated grade level proficiency as evidenced by state standardized assessment. This research reinforced my belief that a student's ethnic background or socioeconomic status was not and should not be a key indicator in determining whether or not a student learns.

I developed three search criteria to guide my job search: To serve (1) in a school that had a population where at least a third of the students were ethnically and linguistically diverse, (2) in a school with a significant number of students who qualified for free or reduced priced meals, and (3) in a school district that had demonstrated evidence of examining its systems through a critical equity lens. My search led me to a school in a first ring suburb and the on-going journey to assure that no child is left behind.

Contrary to popular belief, urban areas are not the only spaces where achievement disparities exist. My job search experience informed my understanding that schools in the suburbs are in need of leaders who possess the knowledge and skills to serve ethnically and linguistically diverse students; perhaps more so than within city boundaries, due to the greater disparity of access to social service resources. I would now serve in a school where 35% of the students were ethnically diverse. Over a four year period the percentage of students that qualified for free or reduced priced meals had increased by 16% and during the same time frame the number of linguistically diverse students had grown 1.5 times to 16%.

My experience as a school leader has reinforced my understanding of the power of the principalship. Leading for equity requires principals to analyze all systems for their efficacy in meeting the needs of all students, identify those systems that need modification and move toward cultural shifts (McKenzie et al., 2009; Theoharis, 2009). Historically our school had been successful serving upper middle class, multi-generational English speaking students and families. Upon entering my new role, I was given recent state test data that demonstrated the need for a change in the way we served Latinos, English learners and students who qualified for free or reduced priced meals.

TRUST AS A TOOL FOR EQUITY DRIVEN LEADERS

I knew as a new leader I needed to establish both trust and credibility. Establishing trust is a critical linchpin in the process of shifting culture. A strong sense of trust enables school leaders to guide staff through the decision-making and culture-shifting process in a collaborative and transparent manner. I wanted my staff to fundamentally understand the interdependence between instruction, assessment and student academic achievement. I also needed them to understand the interdependence between personal belief systems and student academic achievement.

My dilemma was to maintain trust while guiding everyone through the process of digging into our race-based achievement disparities. This coupled with the fact that I am a woman of color and my staff was 99% white would require an intentional and methodical process.

For the first few months I focused on our (my staff and my) similarities as opposed to our differences. I took advantage of every opportunity I had to discuss my experiences as an elementary school teacher. I spoke of my experience teaching the same math, health and science curricula. My strong background in data analysis and practical application was seen as an asset. Once a sense of affinity was established, I began the process of examining systems and using data to drive our accountability and feedback loops. It was also at this point that I began to shed light on our differences—not just between me and my primarily white faculty, but also within the ethnically homogenous teaching co-hort as well. We looked at our personal conflict styles, teaching style preferences, organizational styles and how those impacted the way we interacted with one another, students and families. This guided our faculty to a deeper understanding of a very important tenet—differing traditions, beliefs and practices within racially homogenous groups can often times be as disparate as the difference that exists between racially diverse individuals and groups (Lindsey et al., 2003).

EXAMINING SYSTEMS

I truly believe ineffective systems continue to exist because change seems to throw organizations into turmoil, and no one looks forward to turmoil. It is a common expectation for school leaders to be prepared to handle "chaos" that comes with a shift in organizational structure. However, a shift in culture to establish more equitable systems inherently means those who the current system has been working for will need to give up some of their privilege. Based on personal experience, the chaos that comes from this type of shift is more overwhelming than the typical resistance that comes during systems change and without the presence of a transparent and deliberate approach may cause community upheaval.

I began our quest to modify service structure by establishing a collaborative teaching model for our English language learners (ELLs). A benefit of working in a first ring suburb is that we are able to partner with and learn from educators in major urban centers. In the two years preceding my tenure, central office leadership had examined the instructional practices in a local urban school district. Information garnered had led to modifications in the job description and instructional delivery expectations for English as a Second Language (ESL) specialists. The most significant change in practice was the implementation of "push-in/collaborative teaching" structure vs. the traditional method of pull-out instruction.

This work allowed me to create a mainstream clustering program for many of our ELLs. The clustering method creates classroom rosters where four to six developmentally similar learners are placed together. This enables general educators and ESL specialists to establish schedules that allow for team teaching. My past experience as a content specialist guided my understanding of collaborative instruction and the need for intentional planning and professional development.

To ensure the new structure would succeed, I intentionally sought out classroom teachers who demonstrated the skills needed to work in a teaming environment. Although I didn't know teachers well, conversations about their past experiences with team planning and unit collaboration helped me to identify viable candidates. I also leaned on colleagues who are experts in the field to garner professional development resources that prepared teachers for the team teaching experience.

I began with an overview of the different approaches to team teaching and asked teachers to identify the approach they would use. I held monthly meetings to facilitate dialogue related to the nuances of team teaching. Teachers shared their successes and areas that they needed support in. As a team we collaborated to identify instructional resources, to make modifications in the schedule, or look at ways to modify the room layout to make the collaborative process workable.

My site-level ESL specialist and I partnered with our district literacy specialist to design monthly collaborative inquiry sessions that focused on best practice for teaching ELLs. Our study focused on intentionality. The staff I serve remain phenomenal educators for middle to upper class, multigenerational English speakers. As such, those instructional methods worked well—yielded high academic achievement—for most students in those demographic categories.

As aforementioned, our *clientele* has shifted, yet our faculty remains mainly white and female. Explicitly, this means that 65% of our student population has affinity with their educators. These students are able to learn from someone who looks like them and may have traditions, beliefs and practices that align with their own. We needed to ensure that the other 35% had the opportunity to experience that same sense of belonging and implicit self-esteem. This would inevitably have to come through "learning" about and then applying culturally and linguistically responsive instructional practices.

As we learned and tested instructional practices to better serve our ELLs, we also examined our personal belief systems. Did we *truly* believe that our linguistically diverse students were capable of learning at the same levels as our multi-generational English speakers? If the answer is yes, then how do we demonstrate that? What are the implicit messages we are sending that let students know this? This deep introspective inquiry yielded amazing results with nearly 85% of our ELLs meeting or exceeding their individual learning goals by the end of the school year—the highest level of performance across the entire school district.

Next, I established a system that would serve all of our students by adjusting our school schedule to build in common grade level collaborative planning time. Common planning time is a staple in schools that have successfully reduced or eliminated race-based achievement disparities. Educators need common planning time to examine classroom level performance data on an on-going basis, identify and monitor intervention plans, establish common assessments and develop a shared understanding for what constitutes proficient work (Reeves, 2010).

While our faculty had a history of dedicating time to examine personal practice, the experiences were limited to brief monthly meetings or district trainings. These s*cattershot learning episodes*, as Reeves refers to them, counteract collaborative inquiry and do not increase a teacher's ability to impact student learning (2010). The new schedule allowed for common learning times, which gave classroom teachers the flexibility to share students within their grade level. Another benefit of the schedule was that it allowed me to strategically utilize the instructional knowledge and skills of the paraprofessionals in our building.

I knew that the shift would impact internal stakeholders and as such facilitated transparent and open conversations about the shift with staff members. There were some staff members who expressed objection and demonstrated that through passive resistance, but overall most were committed to the process.

What I hadn't anticipated was the response from community stakeholders who questioned the change in scheduling. As a teacher I often personally modified my classroom schedule without notifying parents, and I sat on several school-wide scheduling committees that did not include community stakeholder voices. Months after we made the changes, I still don't know if this was a rookie administrator mistake or if something else prompted the community response. Either way the shift prompted incognito contacts with teachers on our staff. The question proffered to faculty members was, "Are you okay with this change? What do you think about the new schedule?" I was both perplexed and somewhat astounded that families believed they should be included in the process of developing a building schedule as this was not the norm I knew. After connecting with several of my veteran intra-district colleagues I learned that community voice related to scheduling changes was not a widely held district norm either. My attempts to explain the benefits of the new schedule were dismissed by some active community members as something that was only good for "those kids." In retrospect and like McClaren's experience described in a Kohn (1998) article, I now realize that my assumption that the adults in our school wanted *all* children to be successful was inaccurate (p. 569).

Fortunately, my intentional efforts to engage staff in open dialogue about the change was enough to avert the attempts to undermine the system shift. My takeaway from this experience is that leaders will not go wrong saturating the community with upcoming modifications and in the end leaders for equity must be prepared to handle extreme amounts of push back from community stakeholders.

Establishing the time and place for collaboration is only the first step to building a culture of collaborative inquiry. Collaboration is a skill that requires both a framework and time to practice, refine and re-engage in the process. Certainly, a positive collegial work environment sets the stage for collaborative work; however, Dufour's 2003 work to outline the characteristics of highly effective professional learning communities (PLC) indicated that deep learning (rather than glib collegiality) leads to higher levels of student academic success (p. 9). Setting the expectation for weekly collaboration may initially create a *rub* amongst staff; however, once educators are equipped with the skills and knowledge to effectively participate in collaborative inquiry you will find that educators embrace the process.

Leading for equity is not about being "right," it is about being "effective." As a result, those who lead for equity must be well read and prepared to model desired behaviors. For instance, asking for frequent examination of formative data requires the need for quick methods to garner reliable data. Leaders cannot and should not assume that faculty members are equipped to do this. Consequently, if the leader isn't familiar with the knowledge or skills they are attempting to build, she/he must bring in human resources to assist with this process. After observing several PLC processes throughout the district I chose to structure our PLC meetings with rotating weekly discussions related to three key areas—academic performance, behavior concerns, and curriculum and instructional practice. During this time we set specific goals for students who had specific learning needs and a six to eight week progress monitoring schedule to make certain the intervention plans were working. Leaders for equity must plan to build capacity in those that they serve.

TIME—THE ELUSIVE RESOURCE

I have learned to be relentless about instructional time. My experiences as a district administrator and later as a school leader led me to understand that I had to scrutinize building schedules to identify those areas where I might garner more time for educators to teach. Acquiring additional time may in turn be at the expense of historical traditions and practices. For instance, the practice of setting aside time for building-wide holiday celebrations has long been a practice in schools throughout the United States. Many practices were established well before the concept of standards based curricula became a key ingredient in student learning, before the information highway connected people across continents in unimaginable ways, and before the federal legislation of the No Child Left Behind Act shone a spotlight on the egregious learning disparities that existed throughout U.S. schools.

As I examined our community celebration practices I learned that the K-6 schedule would cost 42 hours (seven days) of lost learning over that period. Students performing in the lower percentiles could not afford losing a minute of instruction much less seven days. Leading for equity requires one to make tough decisions that will have dissenting views. Our move from a Halloween celebration to a more inclusive building-wide plan that consumed significantly less instructional time evoked intense dialogue amongst all members of our school community. As I negotiated an intense taskforce experience and later systems modification I learned as much about myself as I did about the students, families and educators I served. I also learned that leading for equity would at times—most times—be lonely and isolating.

Culture changes that impact traditions, beliefs and practices often times cause disequilibrium amongst faculty, students and community members. Thus, leading for equity requires steadfast mental stamina and the ability to take a firm and often times difficult stand, using the current organizational reality as a tool to guide the process (Cheesebrough, 2010). As I led our staff, families and students through this process, strong resistance surfaced. I relied daily on skills and much of the knowledge I had garnered while working in the integration collaborative. I drew on my knowledge of intercultural development. I knew that my word choice was critical depending upon who I was speaking with. I couldn't use language of adaptation and shifts with stakeholders who minimized the impact that difference had on our learning community. I also used my training with intercultural conflict, intently listening for language or observing behaviors related to different conflict styles. These tools helped me navigate fierce conversations.

Although I relied on processes established to foster transparency and trust, my motives were continually questioned by community stakeholders. During this period my religious beliefs and citizenship were questioned (I couldn't possibly be American or Christian if I was looking at modifying our Halloween celebration), and many attempts were made to discredit my ability to lead. Despite the extreme pressure, our faculty pulled together to establish a new plan for building-wide celebrations that allowed for greater instructional time and were aligned with learning initiatives as opposed to calendar holidays. Our faculty had a laser-like focus on our site goal and mission to provide instructional experiences that fostered high academic achievement for *all* of our students, and the plan that teacher leaders developed was aligned with our goal and mission. In addition, the new structures honor the pluralism that exists within our student population. When presented at a PTA meeting with strong faculty backing, the revised plan gained parent support as well.

ENGAGEMENT: AN ACT OF INTENTIONALITY

Engaging families in student learning has long been seen as pivotal to the academic success of children. Howard's (2010) summary of research on parental involvement indicates that it is important to forge substantive school-home relationships. In addition, Dietel (2006) outlined data from NAEP, the National Assessment of Educational Progress, which indicated that parental involvement had a significant impact on achievement. The important question that a leader for equity must ask is what constitutes parental involvement? Mainstream school norms would indicate that parental school involvement is represented by attending school conferences, concerts or volunteering in classrooms. However, many families of color demonstrate their involvement outside of the school's walls. For instance, in her research Gail Thompson (2007) found that African-American families stated they demonstrate involvement by encouraging their children to complete their homework and making certain they are fed and at school each day.

In speaking with Latino families I have heard many of the same declarations about their role at home. Members of the Latino community revere educators. As with many members of collectivist communities, Latino families believe school educators possess the expertise to teach their children and entrust this process to them.

I've learned from many African American, Latino and some underprivileged white parents that the school setting isn't always a welcoming place. Therefore, it is paramount that school leaders understand our schools can be intimidating for marginalized families. While it may not be intentional on the part of the school, parents have expressed feelings of inferiority related to socioeconomic status, personal English proficiency, level of education and personal K-12 experiences. To counteract this belief, school leaders need to create systems that are deliberately designed to provide a warm and welcoming experience.

My staff and I have made efforts to engage families by first meeting with parents in their neighborhoods. Hosting events in familiar surroundings ensures a greater sense of comfort for families, fosters authentic relationships, and enables educators to learn more about the communities where children reside. This additional information provides educators with the necessary background knowledge needed to infuse lessons with multiple perspectives and increase the likelihood that diverse student groups will be able to make direct connections to the school learning experience. Working in partnership with a local outreach agency, we hosted community cook-outs, family dialogue sessions related to topics chosen by parents and student/parent breakfasts. We provided transportation for those events held at school and worked to help parents get to know one another through low process activities related to what they had in common—a visceral desire for their children to succeed. The more we responded to the needs and requests of our historically marginalized families, the more we garnered their trust. I also took on the task of learning commonly used greetings and words of other languages. I found that this goes a long way to demonstrate my interest in a child's home environment and diminish the perception of superiority.

Those who seek to lead through an equity lens must be willing to network with the intent of garnering additional information to help the students and families in their communities. One summer we held a back-to-school event in a local community park. In speaking with many of our Latino families we learned that our school newsletter was not serving its purpose, as many parents weren't proficient readers of English. When asked how we might change to better meet family needs, they asked for an abbreviated version translated into Spanish. Through limited networking I learned that one of our parents was bilingual and more than willing to translate materials like the newsletter for the school.

Essential networking includes connecting with parents, students, colleagues and local businesses or social agencies. Forging partnerships with local businesses helps to identify community members who are interested in volunteering, may encompass in-kind donations such as space to hold tutoring groups and may provide greater access to members from communities of color—a human resource that is missing in most schools.

One such partnership was with our district high school. After meeting with a school counselor we identified several students of color who provided academic tutor support. In addition to helping students with math, writing and reading, they served as a sounding board about experiences related to racial isolation. I learned that many of our Latino and African American boys felt as though they were being singled out and disciplined for behaviors that White and Asian students displayed, but weren't reprimanded for. This was helpful to me as I used their words to guide a staff conversation about behavior referrals, how our mental models impact our interactions with students and how we can intentionally work to shift those mental models.

REFILLING THE WELL

In speaking with many administrators, a common thread is the number of hours dedicated to *the work*. The typical school principal works 50–60 hours per week. Those who choose to lead for equity can put in upwards of 80 hours per week (Theoharis, 2009). I can speak to this firsthand as I have frequently put in more than 80 hours. Leading for equity creates an experience where there is always something to work on. Whether it is checking in on the most recent progress monitoring data for target students or building community partnerships, the work is and will always be there. For this reason, it is very important to take time for yourself.

I recently surveyed several colleagues for advice for peers in the trenches. Three suggestions rose to the top. First, we strongly encourage school leaders to form collegial groups with other leaders in the trenches. The camaraderie you will form not only provides confidants, but also peers that will offer counsel when critical issues arise. Secondly, do not forget your family. Spouses and children need us just as much as the children, families and faculty in our schools. Learn when to talk "shop" with your significant other and when to "leave work at work." Never forget that your children's school events are just as important as the student's events at school. I have personally made the commitment to attend all of our son's sporting events. To do so, I've given myself the permission to *let go of the work*.

Finally, find a personal outlet that helps you to relax. For me that is power walking and my personal faith. I find that an outdoor walk helps me to clear my mind and keep a balance. Dealing with external pressures from families of dominant groups can at times be overpowering and drain all of one's energy. It is very important to find a way to *fill your well*. I rely on the tenets of my faith to provide the sustenance I need to keep going. My colleagues choose to read, exercise and listen to music. Others have taken up dancing or eagerly look forward to spending time with grandchildren. What matters is that you take the time to take care of yourself.

FINAL THOUGHTS

The children in our schools are the leaders of tomorrow. We have a moral imperative to, " . . . serve all children, not simply those with the loudest or most powerful advocates (Fullan, 2003)." Leading in the equity trenches will most likely not bring you popularity. It won't create harmony. Leading in the trenches certainly does not promote stability. What you will get is peace knowing that you are working to promote the true tenets of a democracy. You are working to establish a public school system that produces children who are equipped with the necessary literacy and mathematics skills to pursue *any* postsecondary endeavor. You are working to assure *every* child is prepared to give back to their local, national and global community regardless of their race, ethnicity or language spoken at home. These are the children who will one day serve in our schools as social workers, teachers and administrators; in our hospitals as nurses and physicians; and in our communities and nation as civic leaders and activists. These are our future leaders in the trenches.

REFERENCES

Atkinson, R. K., Derry, S. J., Renkl, A., and Wortham, D. (2000). "Learning from Examples: Instructional Principles from the Worked Examples Research." *Review of Educational Research, 70*(2), 181–214.

Cheesebrow, D. (2010). "Teamworks International Frameworks." www.teamwork-sintl.net.

Dietel, R. (2006). *Get Smart: Nine Ways to Help Your Child Succeed in School.* San Francisco: Jossey-Bass.

DuFour, R. (2004). "What is a 'Professional Learning Community'? Three Big Ideas Guide this School Reform Effort: Commitment to Student Learning, a Culture of Collaboration, and a Focus on Results." *Educational Leadership: Journal of the Department of Supervision and Curriculum Development, N.E.A., 61*(8), 6.

Fullan, M. (2003). *The Moral Imperative for School Leadership*. Thousand Oaks: Corwin Press.

Howard, T. C. (2010). *Why Race and Culture Matter in Schools: Closing the Achievement Gap in America's Classrooms*. New York: Teachers College Press.

Kohn, A. (1998). "Only for My Kid: How Privileged Parents Undermine School Reform." *Phi Delta Kappan, 569* (9).

Lindsey, R. B., Campbell Jones, F., and Roberts, L. M. (2005). *The Culturally Proficient School: An Implementation Guide for School Leaders*. Thousand Oaks, CA: Corwin Press.

Reeves, D. B. (2000). "90/90/90 Schools: A Case Study." *Advanced Learning Press In Accountability in Action: A Blueprint for Learning Organizations, 2nd edition*. Advanced Learning Press, pp.185–208.

Reeves, D. B., (2010). *Transforming Professional Development into Student Results*. Alexandria, VA: ASCD.

Skrla, L., McKenzie, K. B., and Scheurich, J. J. (2009). *Using Equity Audits to Create Equitable and Excellent Schools*. Thousand Oaks, CA: Corwin; National Association of Secondary School Principals; NSDC.

Theoharis, G. (2009). *The School Leaders Our Children Deserve: Seven Keys to Equity, Social Justice, and School Reform*. New York: Teachers College Press.

Thompson, G. L. (2007). *Through Ebony Eyes: What Teachers Need to Know, but Are Afraid to Ask about African American Students*. San Francisco: Jossey-Bass.

Thompson, G. L. (2007) *Up Where We Belong: Helping African American and Latino Students Rise in School and in Life*. San Francisco: Jossey-Bass.

ABOUT THE AUTHOR

Stacie Stanley is an elementary school principal in a suburban school district just outside of St. Paul, Minnesota. Stacie has earned an M.A. in Education, a postgraduate certificate in K-12 administration and recently is working on her dissertation to complete her doctorate degree. She has served in a variety of education roles including that of teacher, math specialist, curriculum and staff development specialist, and integration and equity program director. She also serves as an adjunct faculty member at Hamline University. Stacie's African-American heritage fuels her fervor for educational equity. She currently lives in the Twin Cities with her husband and college-age children.

Chapter 10

Forging Relationships with High School Students That Impact Learning and Achievement

Nardos E. King

I will never forget visiting a class and meeting a young lady name Lytia. After seeing her class state assessment data broken down by subgroups, she was disappointed that our black students were so far behind our white students, and she had some thoughts as to why that was happening. She said that many of her friends come from families in which no one had been to college. She also stated, "If no one ever talks to you about going, and you don't know how to get there, then why should we try our best to do what it takes to get there?" She ended her comments by saying that many students have no "HOPE."

I remember feeling an overwhelming sense of sadness. I told her that I would be her "HOPE" and that if she wanted to go to college and worked hard, I would help her get there.

Lytia's comments changed my thinking and impacted my decision-making process. I realized that there was a reason I was having this conversation with this student at this time. I decided that day that we needed to do something different at Mount Vernon to create the change we were looking for, and I knew that it would begin with the building of relationships between the adults and the students.

Two days later, I was working late reviewing first quarter grades. As I was scrolling through the grades of our students, I came across a student who earned all F's for the first quarter. Usually when I see grades like this, I also see a correlation in the number of discipline referrals and attendance problems. But when I clicked on the discipline atom for this student in our student information program, I was shocked to see that this young man only had two minor discipline infractions. His attendance record indicated that he attended school on a regular basis. That was not the norm for students who had failing grades, let alone all failing grades. After further investigation, I noted that this young man was a student who had an individualized education program (IEP). This meant he received special education services to meet his educational needs.

GAINING INSIGHT INTO THE DAY
IN THE LIFE OF A STUDENT

Recognizing that this student's achievement would have a direct impact on our school's report card, I wanted to know what a day in the school that I lead was like for a student who was failing all of his classes. I decided that evening that the next school day I would shadow this young man. I wanted to see first-hand how a student who attends school on a regular basis and has few minor discipline infractions could be failing all of his classes.

I will refer to the young man as John. The next day, I arrived to his first period Algebra class before the bell rang. I watched John walk into the room and take his seat. After the bell rang, his first period teacher called roll while the students watched the morning news show. Once the show was over, the teacher asked the students to begin working on a warm-up problem that was on the board. I observed John sitting at his desk with his head down. From where I was sitting, it appeared that he was not working on the warm-up problem but was doodling on a piece of paper. When his teacher began to go over the problem, John did not seem interested in the answer. The teacher began teaching a new lesson. As she asked her students questions, John never raised his hand to participate nor was he called on by his teacher. The teacher asked for volunteers to go to the board to do example problems, and John did not raise his hand. After a 45-minute lesson, the teacher assigned the students class work.

I got up from where I was sitting and wandered around the room to review student work. I did not want to make it obvious to anyone, including the teacher, why I was there, so I asked many students about their work. When I went to John's desk, he was not working on any problems. I asked him why he was not working on his class work, and he shrugged his shoulders. I went back to my seat until the end of the period. During the entire period, John was totally disengaged from the learning process. Because he was not disruptive, he did not stand out to his teacher, and it appeared to me that she did not notice that John was not doing any work.

Because his next period class met every day, the class time was much shorter. John had biology. Again, I arrived before John did and watched him walk into the class. He walked quietly to his desk and sat down. When the bell rang, the teacher asked the students to get out their homework from the night before.

I looked over to see if John had his homework, and he did not take anything out of his notebook or book bag as most of the other students did. The teacher began the lesson with a video she wanted the students to watch. The video was about 10 minutes long, and John's head was down on his desk; it appeared that he was not paying attention. When the video was over, John lifted his head. The teacher began to give notes on the board, and John again did not appear to be copying the notes as many of his classmates were doing. The teacher assigned silent reading and John again appeared to be daydreaming and not reading the assigned pages. He was not disruptive nor was he talking to his classmates. The bell rang and John got up from his seat and left the classroom.

John headed to the cafeteria and I did not follow him. After his 30-minute lunch break, I arrived in John's Spanish 1 class. The class was noisy. After the bell rang, the teacher called roll. When she called John's name, he responded. During this class period, students were presenting a project. When it was John's turn, he did not have anything to present. For the remainder of the class period, John sat quietly in the back of the classroom doodling. He was not disruptive, but he was totally disengaged from what was going on in the classroom.

After observing John during three of his classes, I could not bring myself to go to his last period class for the day. I felt acutely sad about what I had already observed. It appeared to me that John was almost invisible to his teachers and classmates. Other than calling his name during roll, no one talked to John. He was a student who was "falling through the cracks" at Mount Vernon High School. I wondered how many more *Johns* there were in my school. For the next few days, I thought about John. I kept asking myself, What can we do for all the *Johns* who walked the halls of Mount Vernon?

A COMMITMENT TO SERVE STUDENTS
FALLING THROUGH THE CRACKS

I became principal at Mount Vernon High School in Alexandria, Virginia, on July 25, 2006, after serving as the school's finance officer, instructional assistant, teacher, administrative intern, and assistant principal. My journey to this leadership challenge gave me a different perspective from that of many of my colleagues. I had the unique opportunity to see the same school from diverse vantage points through the different jobs I held over the last 15 years. Being African-American gives me an added perspective and often takes me back to childhood experiences. I never would have imagined that this journey would have brought me to this point.

I am the principal of a school that I love, and to which I am committed in spite of and because of its challenges. Mount Vernon High School is one of the most diverse schools in Fairfax County, Virginia. We have over 64 countries represented in our student body and 50 languages spoken. Our student body encompasses students from Ft. Belvoir Army Base, students from nations around the world, and students from every socio-economic status. We have students for whom English is their second language and students with disabilities. We embrace our differences and we believe it is why Mount Vernon is a wonderful place for children.

The challenge before me was to strengthen our school so that no child, like John, would fall through the cracks. I began having conversations with members of my administrative team and teachers with whom I had good relationships. I spoke with students in several classes, and I spoke with many parents including those in the Parent Teacher Student Association (PTSA) and the Academic Boosters Organization, Inc. I shared my story about John and expressed to them that we needed to find a way to make sure all students in this school were receiving the attention they needed. I shared with them my belief that we needed to come up with a schedule that would help us catch students before they fall.

With the support of the administrative team and the teacher leaders, I made the decision that we would implement a new bell schedule to better serve the needs of our students. I used my first year to talk to teachers, students, and parents about our new bell schedule. We had decided as a school to implement the FLEX program the previous year, which provided an extra flexible period every other day. During that period, only previously taught lessons could be reviewed. After shadowing John, I did not feel that doing more of the same thing was going to change the achievement of our students. At that point in time, I was not sure what kind of change we were going to make but I knew we had to do something different.

I became convinced that using our FLEX period solely for remediation was not the best way to address the needs of student like John. I thought we needed to find a way to provide time for the adults to build significant relationships with our students. We began as a staff to look for ways that we could build in the extra time to address failing students, give time for enrichment, and focus on some of our other academic goals. After months of meetings and debates, the concept of Major Time came to be.

CREATING TIME TO BUILD MENTORING RELATIONSHIPS

Major Time, named after our school nickname "The Majors," would be a full block class for every student in our school. Every student would now have eight class periods rather then the seven class periods they had the year before. We realigned our class periods and carved out a bell schedule that would give us four even blocks of time everyday. Students would attend periods 1, 3, 5, and 7 on what we call odd days and 2, 4, 6, and 8 on what we call even days and third period would be Major Time. We decided to divide students into classes by grade level and alphabetically by last name. Teachers would have between 15 to 18 students in this class, and the students would stay with their teachers for the four years that they attended Mount Vernon High School.

There were students counting on us—and the mission was critical. We knew we had to move quickly, but not carelessly. The thought here would not be unlike how a farmer prepares his field to yield the maximum number and highest quality crops. The farmer, our leadership team of administrators and teacher leaders, first has to plan. After all, a successful farmer does not just go out to an unprepared field, throw out seeds and hope for the best. There is the planning, described above, followed by the cultivating of the field, which in our case is the school environment composed of all stakeholders: teachers, students, parents, and support staff.

The importance of preparation or cultivating cannot be underestimated here. Time should be taken to carefully plan and prepare all stakeholders for implementation. Proper preparation will facilitate the growth and development of the relationships that support student achievement and student growth both academically and socially. However, the environment first has to be a safe place for students to expose their academic challenges. The critical element of relationship building must be well established before any progress can begin to be measured.

We were not able to implement a bell schedule change during the 2006–2007 school year, but we were able to begin the planning process for what I believe became the game changer at Mount Vernon High School. In order to successfully implement this new idea in the 2007-2008 school year, much work had to be done. We established a Major Time committee that consisted of administrators and teacher leaders. All academic departments had a representative from their department to keep all teachers informed about the direction we were going to take.

First we had to work on our bell schedule. We had to take a schedule that consisted of seven class periods that met every other day and one that met every day, and change it to a pure block schedule allowing for four periods to meet each day. In order to carve out time for four even blocks, four class periods each day, we needed to shave time from each of the previous periods and from the time allotted to pass between classes. We knew that shortening travel time was going to cause us attendance issues and heartache for some of our students who used much of that time to socialize with their classmates, but we also knew it would pay off in the long run.

After developing a bell schedule that we thought would work, we began the process of establishing how we wanted the Major Time period to look. We had 85 minutes of time to fill, and we wanted it to be meaningful and to foster academic success while building relationships between the Major Time teacher and the students.

Our school improvement plan goals included increasing student vocabulary and improving reading skills. We knew from formal data (state assessments, SAT, PSAT) and informal data (teacher observations of their students) that this was an area that we wanted to work on. Therefore, we decided that the first minutes of the class period would be used for sustained silent reading (SSR). Many of our students did not read unless they were mandated to do so through their academic classes. It was our hope that by establishing reading time during the school day, our students would develop a love of reading that would increase their vocabulary knowledge. The committee decided that everyone, including teachers, would read books of their choice. We thought it was important for our teachers to model reading to our students.

Next, we had to establish how we would use the remaining time to effectively address our goals for relationship building and maximizing student academic achievement. First, we decided that students could use this time after reading to visit teachers in whose classes they needed extra help. We wanted the process to be orderly and to make sure students were using their time wisely, making their choices based on a plan in which they took accountability for their own learning. To address the accountability piece, students would have to secure a pass from the teacher they wanted to see BEFORE arriving at their Major Time class. Major Time teachers would be prohibited from writing passes for students who said, "I forgot" or "I lost my pass."

For relationship building, we set aside Fridays as a "no passing" day. Students and teachers would be together for the entire class period for the purpose of getting to know each other, going over academic successes and challenges, and bonding as a class. This would prove to be the biggest challenge in the implementation and brought the most pushback from teachers.

We decided it was necessary to put together another committee that would come up with activities teachers could use on Fridays to cover a multitude of goals including facilitating relationship building. We called our final product the *Major Time Toolkit*. The 200+ page kit was provided to each teacher at the start of the 2007–2008 school year and included activities to support academics, study skills, character building and career exploration. We needed to provide the knowledge and supports for those students like Lytia, who, in her family, would be the first generation in college. This, in addition to relationship building strategies, met the needs of the whole child, and this was one of our goals.

BUILDING STAKEHOLDER SUPPORT

Now that the plan was in place, it was time to start introducing it to all stakeholders in order to implement it successfully in the 2007–2008 school year. First, I began speaking to our teachers during faculty meetings and department meetings. Initially, there was some pushback from a few. There were some teachers who saw this as something extra they had to do, and they wanted no part of it.

My message to the staff was sincere and consistent. I continued to speak about students like John. I asked teachers to commit to this mission or leave Mount Vernon. I knew that this was not going to be a popular message with some, but I believed in my heart that if we didn't began to build stronger relationships with our students, particularly ones who were at risk, all of our hard work towards academic achievement would be in vain. Too many students like John were not working to their potential, and they needed the help of a caring adult to ensure they would not fall through the cracks that already existed.

Still, some teachers complained that they did not want to be mentors to our students. Those who felt this way wanted to concentrate on teaching their curriculum. I stood my ground and again stated that I, and many others who helped create this program, believed that the students at Mount Vernon High School needed this program and that teachers had the option to transfer to other schools if they could not support our efforts. I reminded them that Mount Vernon is the school for our students, and we were going to give them what they needed.

After I spoke with the teachers, I then began speaking with parents. Every parent with whom I spoke thought that Major Time would be a great thing for their children. The only concern I received from a few parents initially related to how students would be placed with teachers. Some parents, whose students took our highest-level classes, wanted us to divide our students by academic levels. I was totally against this. For the most part, students attend their core classes with others students who perform at the same academic level as they do. This is especially true for our highest achievers and our lowest achievers. For Major Time, I wanted our students to be able to experience the rich diversity that our student body offers.

When explaining the process to students, most of the pushback came from having to read for thirty minutes. Again we knew from surveys and student feedback that reading was not a top priority for many of our students, and we wanted Major Time to help change this. The research on the value of sustained silent reading was encouraging. Evidence continues to show that those who do more recreational reading show better development in reading, writing, grammar, and vocabulary. These results hold for both first and second language acquisition (Krashen, 2004).

During the planning process, our students who are in our English for Speakers of Other Languages (ESOL) program brought a concern to my attention. At one of our student meetings, I pulled our ESOL students in with an interpreter to explain Major Time and the associated goals. I explained to the students that they would be staying with their base ESOL teachers during this time, because it was what the adults felt was best for them. Surprisingly, the students thought differently.

During the meeting a student named Daniel stood up and asked for the microphone. He said to me that all the ESOL classes are located on one side of the building, and they already feel segregated from the rest of the students. He continued by asking how they are supposed to improve their English and be seen as regular students at the high school if we don't treat them as such. I began to tear up. It took a student with limited English to make it clear to the adults that we were wrong in our thinking. After meeting with these students and hearing this student's voice as he spoke for his peers, we decided to include as many of the ESOL students into the mainstream Major Time classes as possible. Only the lowest level ESOL students who have very limited or no English language fluency would remain with their base teachers.

During the 2007–2008 school year, Major Time was implemented for the first time. We knew it would take time to collect and analyze data on the impact Major Time would have on the academic and reading achievement of our students. However, the overall program was implemented very successfully, and we immediately saw the benefits of the relationship-building piece. Within a short time, we began to see the connection between Major Time and the academic improvement of some of our students. Additionally, the data revealed that more students were reading more books. Our media center records showed that book checkouts increased substantially.

CREATING FURTHER STUDENT SUPPORTS

One of the strengths of our Major Time period is that it allows us to make adjustments when needed, so over the next three years we made some changes. One of the most significant changes was to begin the process of becoming a high functioning professional learning community. According to Richard and Becky DuFour, the originators of this concept, a professional learning community is a group of educators committed to working collaboratively in ongoing processes of collective inquiry and action research to achieve better results for the students they serve (DuFour et al., 2006).

As our school becomes this professional learning community, we are adapting best practices identified by this model as effective strategies to increase student achievement. One of these identified practices is to make remediation during the school day mandatory. To facilitate this, we established a program based on a model from another school in our district. We called our program Students on Academic Rise (SOAR) which mandates that students who are failing a class at interim time or the end of the quarter will have to follow a prescribed schedule for remediation of those classes during Major Time.

Because many of us believe that the relationships between the adults in our building and the students is crucial for the success of all students, particularly those at risk, we decided to carry our idea one step further. Although we were reaching students in every classroom through Major Time, we knew that there were some who were still struggling, our most underachieving students who had excessive discipline issues and poor attendance. It would not be an easy effort and with limited budget, I would need the involvement of the most passionate staff members to address this problem.

Out of the need to provide added assistance for these students, came the development of the 30/30 Program. The name 30/30 came from the idea of taking 30 of the most at-risk rising sophomores and working with them for the 30 months before their anticipated graduation date in June 2010. The vision for the 30/30 Program was to take our efforts beyond the school day to extracurricular opportunities in order to reach the whole child.

We began the 30/30 program with four staff members—one administrator, one teacher, the career counselor, one Spanish speaking parent liaison—and one dedicated community member, each committed to working with the program for the next 30 months to see if by building relationships with these students, we could keep them in school and help them graduate from high school on time. Students in the 30/30 program were placed in one Major Time class with a very caring and supportive teacher. The other 30/30 team members got to know each of the students very well, met with them regularly, visited them during Major Time, and engaged them in conversations about their lives both in school and out. The students were monitored in three areas: attendance, discipline, and grades.

As in the general Major Time classes, observable changes in data for grades take time to develop; however, we could get to work right away on attendance and discipline. Amazing things began to happen. One young lady we will call "Amelia" had more absences the previous year than she had days in school. Her attendance had resulted in multiple discipline referrals and began to make Amelia look like she was being intentionally defiant. As she entered her sophomore year, it was evident by week three that her attendance had greatly improved. Through discussions, we discovered that she wanted to do well in school but felt disengaged. She felt that since she had already failed some classes, there was no point in continuing to do her work. With encouragement, Amelia improved and was able to graduate on time with her class, something we thought was impossible three years earlier.

The program, though not without its challenges, further proved our theory that building relationships has a significant effect on student achievement. Sixteen of the 30 graduated on time. To some this may not seem like a huge thing, but for those of us who worked with this group of students this was a huge accomplishment for the students and for us. To us it means that for those 16 students, we changed generations to come. For those 16 students, graduation saved them from a confining future of limited opportunities bound by the stigma of being a dropout. Doors that were sure to be closed were once again opened, revealing unlimited possibilities for their future.

During the 2010-2011 school year, we implemented another program. The Men of Vision and Purpose (MVP) is a program designed specifically to change the perception of the African-American male in the high school setting. We opened the program to all students in the school but specifically targeted African-American males. Our data showed us that the African-American male student is more at risk and is underperforming more than any other student. This sub-group also has more discipline referrals than any other group.

Again, recognizing that something different needed to be done, we created a leadership class composed of a diversity of African-American males. We included those who are positive leaders and are earning good grades, with average students and students who are seen as negative leaders. The African-American male staff member chosen to lead this program and to teach the leadership class is the varsity basketball coach and a former counselor who is a strong role model for this group of students. Most importantly, he believes in the importance of mentoring, coaching and building relationships with students to show them how to be better academically, socially and emotionally. The class also teaches the students how to have a positive impact on our school and how they can begin now to prepare for a successful future. In the first semester of the programs existence, our data shows that this strategy is working. We are seeing positive changes in the academics, attendance, and behavior of this group of 62 males.

FOSTERING STUDENT SUCCESS FOR YEARS TO COME

At Mount Vernon High School we have implemented programs that forge meaningful adult and student relationships that have positively impacted learning and achievement. We believe that although the high school master schedule presents many constraints, schools can create opportunities for students and adults to make these important connections.

It is my hope that as I continue through this leadership journey, I can continue to develop and sustain programs that have a positive impact on the achievement of all students who attend Mount Vernon High School. When students enter the building in the morning, they are welcomed by a mural on the wall that contains a picture of our school crest and the words, "Through These Walls, The Sky is the Limit." It is my purpose to ensure that each student has the opportunity to realize that.

REFERENCES

Krashen, S.(April 2004). "Free Voluntary Reading: New Research, Applications, and Controversies." Singapore: RELC Conference
DuFour, R., DuFour, R., Eaker, R., and Many, T. (2006). *Learning by Doing*. Bloomington, Ind.: Solution Tree

ABOUT THE AUTHOR

Nardos E. King is the principal of Mount Vernon High School in Fairfax County, Virginia. In October 2007, she was honored as First-Year Principal of the Year in Fairfax County Public Schools. Nardos' career at Mount Vernon High School began in January of 1996 as the Finance Technician, then serving as an instructional assistant, teacher, administrative intern and sub-school principal until her appointment as principal in July 2006. She graduated from Virginia State with a B.S. in Business Information Systems. She holds a Master of Arts Degree in Special Education from George Washington University and a Masters of Education Degree in Educational Leadership from George Mason University. Nardos is currently working on her Doctorate Degree at Virginia Tech. Nardos and her husband Stan, a Lieutenant Colonel in the Army, are the proud parents of Chad and Tracy, both pursuing college degrees. She enjoys spending time with her family and friends, her book club and participating in community service through her sorority, Delta Sigma Theta, Inc.

Chapter 11

The Equitable Leader

Changing Beliefs and Actions

Roni Silverstein

In 2003, Clopper Mill Elementary was struggling. This diverse school of almost 500 students in an outer suburb of Montgomery County, Maryland, had not made Adequate Yearly Progress (AYP), and was trending even farther downward. Clopper Mill had 41.3% of its students receiving free and reduced price meals, and almost 15% of its students receiving services for English for Speakers of Other Languages (ESOL).

When I was chosen as the new principal, I was excited to lead Clopper Mill's dedicated staff and to help ensure that all of the students would experience the success they deserved and were capable of achieving. With more than 25 years of teaching experience and 3 years in the outstanding Montgomery County Public Schools (MCPS) leadership development program, I hoped I was ready for the challenge.

Schools must ensure the success of all students. The principal facilitates the development of a school vision that sustains a culture of high expectations, collaboration and continuous improvement that promotes student learning and professional growth. This was the most important task at hand when I began my tenure at Clopper Mill.

My experiences as a teacher, principal and later as a central office administrator have shown me that an effective equitable school leader has to keep two very different balls in the air in order to raise student achievement and close the achievement gap. The first is changing the beliefs and the teaching behaviors of the educators who come into direct contact with students, and the second is creating policies and procedures needed for effective change. While these changes are occurring, the leader must be cognizant of the difficult psychological challenges that these changes often bring, in order to support staff and encourage the challenging work that is necessary to ensure that every student reaches their full potential. Changing beliefs and changing policies and procedures lead to high student achievement.

I have found that these two distinct actions need to happen simultaneously in order for equitable and measurable student achievement to occur. These ideas are not new but are often separated as different theories of action. Many notable education researchers such as Schmoker (1999), Dufour (1998), Singleton (2005), Fullan (2006), Heifetz (2002), Collins (2005), Noguera (2006), and others have all talked about looking at data analysis, collaboration, antiracism, change theory, equitable culture, and high student achievement. However, I found through my work as principal and, subsequently, as MCPS director of elementary leadership development, that these theories must be put into practice all at once, simultaneously, to get the results we desire: raising achievement while eliminating the achievement gap!

STARTING WITH A VISION

An equitable school leader must understand this responsibility and champion the school's mission. Leading for equity starts with the vision that the principal's responsibility is to ensure that all students reach their full potential. This often involves changing beliefs and putting new actions, policies and procedures into play in order to make the progress we seek. What is the route a leader must take to reach this goal?

So often we think of leadership as a person, as a figurehead. The expectation is that the principal will make all the decisions and staff will carry out these programs. Principals, however, are not in the classrooms all day, every day. The challenge the leader faces is to create and sustain a school-wide culture of collaboration where leaders enable the staff to tackle the challenging work. When leaders develop this kind of culture consistent with their vision, a culture where risk taking is encouraged, and where there is a genuine commitment to rigorous instruction, then all students can grow. The principal must enable many to become leaders who are willing to take risks to effect change, if change is to be sustainable and effective.

CHANGE, BELIEFS AND EMOTIONS

When I became the new principal of Clopper Mill Elementary School, the summative data was very bleak. Due to illness, the principal had been on leave and at least two other administrators had served for short periods of time. This instability over several years had caused a lot of anxiety and lack of trust. As a new principal there certainly was a sense of urgency for change and improvement, but one really important consideration was the culture of the school and the psychological state of the staff. The staff was dedicated to helping our students achieve and believed they had done all they could to bring about the changes that were needed. However, because of poor student results, morale was low and often students and their families were blamed for poor test scores.

Meeting the challenges of leading a school is both difficult and risky and it takes time, sometimes years. Staff often looks for a strong leader who will take charge and make all the decisions. For some, that means they can blame administration when things don't go well. On the other hand, if the leader allows others to weigh in on decisions, staff will complain that the leader is weak. My school's staff was looking for stability and leadership, but many unforeseen land mines were in store as I began to make the needed changes. When I collaboratively made these changes, some teachers thought I didn't know what to do. When I unilaterally made decisions, some complained that I wasn't listening and didn't know their school. I knew then that I needed to help create a professional learning community that had a common vision and mission. The staff and I needed to focus our efforts on examining what our school stood for, look at the current reality, identify goals, and together determine how we would get there.

Dennis Sparks writes in *On Common Ground* that "profound change in schools, I believe, begins with profound change in leaders, which radiates out to others and into the 'system.' Structural change is almost always required, but it is not sufficient. New positions can be created, job descriptions rewritten, and teaching schedules modified—to name just a few structural changes—without deeply affecting teachers understanding of what they teach, the ways in which they teach it, or their relationships with one another and with their students" (Sparks, 2005, p. 157).

I needed to trust in my own vision for students and help others to believe in the students and themselves. We had the talent to make a profound difference in the lives of our students and I had to help the staff to see themselves as one team who could effectively engage in the kind of work that our students deserved. Together, the staff and I created a "Cycle of Success" that sustained us and helped give us a blueprint of sorts to follow as we worked to support all of our students (see Figure 11.1). This cycle began with changing the beliefs and confidence of our staff that they could make a profound difference in the academic and social success of our students.

There are critical beliefs that must exist in order for this kind of school-wide change to occur. My experiences as principal at Clopper Mill Elementary School and my recent work as director of the leadership development program with over 150 administrators has shown me that each belief is key to the changes we seek:

- Leadership is about developing relationships
- Equitable leadership is key to school improvement
- School improvement is an adaptive challenge
- Identifying root causes is crucial to making informed decisions—data is a tool, not an end
- All improvement involves change, new learning and new beliefs
- Collaboration is powerful and essential for sustainability
- Teachers are instructional decision-makers
- Effective problem solving and risk taking climate are cited as key elements in schools where needed change has been successful

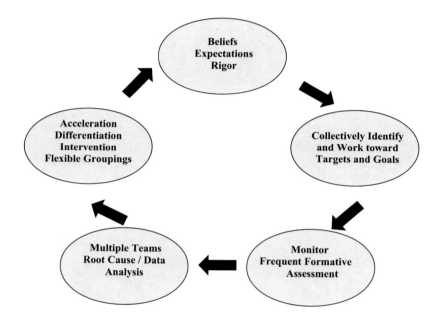

Figure 11.1.   Cycle of Success

LEADERSHIP IS ABOUT DEVELOPING RELATIONSHIPS

If we are to lead successfully, the principal must develop the trust of all the stakeholders who are in the school's sphere of influence. If we are to engage in the difficult work of school improvement, it will involve change and change causes disequilibrium to the organization. In order to rally the staff to do this challenging work, the leader must have the trust of the constituents. The principal must work on building trust and developing relationships constantly. This must extend to all groups if you want to succeed. "Starting with students, the idea of building trust should be foremost in your mind every waking moment. Never promise anything you cannot deliver. Never talk about confidential items with anyone who does not need to know. Always deliver when you say you will. Keep people informed. Tell the truth, always" (Schumaker and Sommers, 2001, p. 33) (DuFour and Eaker, 1998).

A leader must truly believe in their staff, believe in their ability to make the changes necessary to reach the school's goals, and believe that with the appropriate resources and staff development that equitable teaching can happen. This led me to create teams that focused on different aspects of the work. For instance, we developed an intervention committee that looked, each month, at students who were working below grade level. Teachers met to discuss the students' progress, their frustration with the lack of progress and to share ideas and strategies that might help each and every student who was struggling. This ensured that no child was forgotten, while at the same time, it gave staff a great deal of personal pride because of the trust and responsibility that was given to them.

As far as personal relationships, I took every opportunity to get to know and to speak to the staff on a personal level. Just like our students, teachers and staff members also come from different backgrounds and different cultures. They have families and lives outside of school that impact who they are and how they teach. Each morning, before school, I walked in and out of classrooms speaking to teachers about their students, but also their families, about their parents, and special or difficult events in their lives. I also shared stories about my family with them. As a result, I knew what was happening in the teachers' lives and how it might impact their work. The school is made up of real people with real lives and struggles. The leader cannot ignore this if they want to have each employee giving their best at work.

Another key responsibility of an equitable leader is welcoming and respecting the involvement and contributions of the students' parents and guardians. No school can be successful without this essential partnership! Over the years at Clopper Mill we worked very hard to make our school a warm and inviting place for our families. I started by redesigning our front hallway. I placed a donated sofa and chairs, plants and coffee table right up front so that our families could sit and chat each morning and afternoon.

No longer did we disallow parents to come into our school once class had begun. We hung giant sized data charts on the walls, put up framed photographs of students each quarter as they were awarded honor roll certificates, and advertised all of our school-wide activities in English and Spanish. All our important announcements were sent home in Spanish and English, as were on phone messages about upcoming events.

We tried to have events which eliminated any culture gap. Many parents who didn't grow up in the United States are hesitant to get involved in our schools. They incorrectly believe that they have nothing to contribute. To counterbalance these fears, we tried very hard to involve all of our families in activities that were comfortable for everyone. For instance, we had a family picnic the first week of school on our back field. Families came in droves to meet the staff, sit on blankets, eat their own food, and enjoy each other's company. We also had "Donuts with Dad" breakfasts so that dads who work in the morning could join their children in school—even for just a little while early in the morning. The students and dads loved this!

A warm environment is important, but we also needed parents to understand our work. We had study circles where parents could explore, through a MCPS program, each other's backgrounds, histories, struggles and hopes and dreams for our school. Parents were trained to be volunteers, they participated in a second grade reading program, helped in our classrooms and worked with our teachers to translate parent newsletters.

We developed a Hispanic parent group where parents could learn about our state testing, how to work on math at home with household items, how to teach their young children to read, how to encourage students to do their homework. We emphasized how much the school needed their participation. Parents crowded our library on these nights because the presentations were done in their home language and they felt needed and respected. Each and every parent event was translated by an MCPS translator.

Building trust and developing relationships is not an end but an ongoing process that is true and real. The relationships you build with staff, students and parents show that you care, and develop a professional learning community that respects one another and works for a common vision and collective purpose.

EQUITABLE LEADERSHIP IS KEY TO SCHOOL IMPROVEMENT

When asked what the criteria would be for a Nobel Prize for Leadership, Howard Gardner replied, "I define a leader as an individual who is able, without the use of force, to change the thoughts, feelings, beliefs and behaviors of other persons" (Gardner 2009).

My experiences have shown me that an equitable leader must use collaborative processes to define the current state, analyze all the data available, find root causes for the problems and then plan for action while at the same time changing the thoughts, beliefs and behaviors of the staff.

At Clopper Mill I saw firsthand that this school improvement process is not a quick fix to be accomplished in a few months or even a year. It must be done slowly, deliberately and with true understanding of the pain that uncovering the truth may cause. First my staff had to begin to understand what the current state was, where we needed to go and most importantly, why this was so important to the future of each of our students.

The first challenge was defining our goals. Naming the goals and having a common sense of purpose is one way to unite a staff. Developing a common vision was a place where everyone could agree. We needed to develop a professional learning community "in which teachers pursued a clear shared purpose for all students' learning, engaged in collaborative activity to achieve that purpose, and take collective responsibility for student learning" (Newmann and Wehlage, 1995, p. 30, as cited in Dufour and Eaker, 1998, p. 62). Our first few staff meetings were devoted to developing a common mission and vision for Clopper. What exactly did we believe? Who were we as a staff? Examining our hopes and dreams for the students helped to lay the ground work for the changes ahead.

Next we looked at our student data. What was the current state and how did it compare to our desired state? We used a root cause analysis protocol and we asked ourselves many questions about the data. Was the student data low across the grade level or was there one classroom where data was different? Did all students have access to higher level curriculum or was this available to only a selected few? What was our response when students weren't learning? These questions and the answers to them allowed us to take an objective look at ourselves and uncovered root causes for our poor student results. Our school needed to develop a process for data analysis, reteaching and retesting. We also needed to provide advanced curriculum and have high expectations for all our students. All of these strategies were part of our "cycle of success" that was not in place before.

During my second and third years at Clopper Mill Elementary, we engaged in an equity study to examine race, our own identities, our beliefs and how it impacted our teaching. Montgomery County Public Schools (MCPS), then led by superintendent Dr. Jerry Weast, had been nationally recognized for its focus on equity. MCPS "created an environment that encouraged schools to discuss the impact that beliefs about race have on expectations and student learning. The district's accountability systems include explicit goals for students of different races and ethnicities" (Childress, 2009, p. 18). Leaders and school teams, including my school, engaged in book studies about discussing race productively to increase individual and team capacity to examine how our own behaviors and beliefs are reflected in the structures of the school and might be contributing to achievement gaps.

At Clopper Mill, I saw that we needed to explore what true equity looked like. We needed to study together and learn how to have respect and high expectations for every student. We looked at what is often an "opportunity gap." We needed to be sure that each child had the opportunity to excel.

This process of learning about equity is a slow one. Long-held beliefs and assumptions about people don't change overnight. As a result, processes that allowed each student to have opportunities and access to rigorous instruction needed to be put in place simultaneously as we explored our beliefs and practices. For example, accelerated math lessons at every grade level became the rule. In order for students to reach the goal of math 6 by fifth grade, a county-wide benchmark which was linked to success later in high school on the SAT, acceleration needed to begin in the earliest grades. We created after-school sessions that filled in learning gaps so that students could access above grade level courses and we insisted on re-teaching and retesting when students didn't get it. We were dedicated to student learning, not just teaching.

At the same time we were learning about equitable practices and examining our teaching practices, we needed to examine our formative and summative data to see how it squared with the goals we had for our students. One crucial step in identifying the path to greatness is identifying the current state. Jim Collins calls it "confronting the brutal facts" (Collins, 2001, p. 88). My staff and I took the time during our summer leadership days to collaboratively look at each grade level's student summative data. We also looked at the data of similar schools. What schools were having success in the areas where we were struggling? We asked questions and looked deeply into the data to see if there were conclusions we could draw. A common mistake is to jump to conclusions and to develop interventions too quickly. This practice can lead to disappointing results because you often find you have not solved the problem at all. You attacked the wrong problem because the root cause was not found.

It is easier to put the blame somewhere other than your own actions. The equitable leader must help staff have courageous conversations about students so that all children can reach their potential. Are we providing rigorous instruction for everyone? Do we give students enough time to answer our questions or do we communicate that we don't believe they have the information? Do we have calling patterns that allow some children to shine and others to opt out? Do we allow students to work together and learn from each other or is instruction always teacher led? We need to have equitable classroom practices that lead to student achievement.

Often we have lower expectations for some students and these lower expectations create inequitable classrooms and low achievement for our Latino and African-American students. The leader must create a culture of respect and continuous improvement in the school in order to protect the staff members who are willing to open themselves to the scrutiny and self examination without blame. Classroom observation and staff development can help teachers to learn new ways of teaching that create rigorous classrooms for all children. Only then can we move the school forward.

SCHOOL IMPROVEMENT IS AN ADAPTIVE CHALLENGE

Ronald Heifetz has developed a very clear pathway to change. He first identifies what he calls "adaptive challenges." An adaptive challenge is a particular problem where the gap cannot be closed by the application of common sense or routine behavior. Most problems schools face are adaptive challenges. The solutions are often unique to that particular school at that particular time in history. A solution cannot be found quickly or by simply copying another school's actions. Solutions can span several years.

Heifetz warns against the classic error of "treating adaptive challenges as if they were technical solutions." The solution cannot be top down or solved by the head. The staffs' expectation of the authority figure is to solve the problem, provide direction. However, when principals face adaptive challenges, it is essential that we go "against the grain. Rather than fulfilling the expectations for answers, one provides questions; rather than protecting people from outside threat, one lets people feel the threat in order to stimulate adaptation; . . . instead of maintaining norms, one challenges them" (Heifetz, 1994, ch. 6) (Heifetz and Linsky, 2002).

The solution lies in the expertise and the knowledge of all of the stakeholders who own the problem. The teachers, support staff, and the community workers who all have direct contact with the students will have the answers-not necessarily the principal. Through root cause analysis, questioning and findings answers, the staff will find the best instructional route to take.

With this is mind, at Clopper Mill, we used our school leadership team as a vehicle to find the root causes for our student achievement needs. We used the summer leadership meetings to examine our data, ask the hard questions about our programs and to examine our work.

ALL IMPROVEMENT INVOLVES CHANGE, NEW LEARNING AND NEW BELIEFS

Adaptive challenges can get messy. Often by staff questioning their work, missteps can be uncovered, new insights come into view and we have to look at the root causes by looking at our own work. This is tough work and can cause anxiety and fear. The leader must allow honest open conversation and not allow any blaming to occur. The goal is what matters, not who or what caused the student need, but how can we move forward and fulfill our vision? As a result, a team of professionals and community members needs to be assembled to examine the data, develop goals for the students and begin to ask the deep probing questions about why there is a gap between our goals and where our students are currently. Once these questions are asked, the staff takes initiative to find the answers to these questions. The answers become what Heifetz calls the "findings." These findings are examined, prioritized and root causes emerge. Once you feel confident that there are no further questions about an issue, you can begin to tackle the instructional need based on this root cause.

At Clopper Mill we had several teams which met to examine student data and school practices. Our leadership team met monthly, as did the intervention team. It was at these monthly meetings that school-wide data and results were examined throughout the year. Grade level teams, however, met twice weekly: once a week to discuss reading and once a week to discuss mathematics. We developed a team processing form which helped teams to look at daily student work and to share best practices, as well as, to develop common lessons plans based on the student data. It also allowed each grade level to post their team meeting forms on line so that the other professionals in the building who work with the same students could see the updates and future lesson plans.

Before we engaged in root cause analysis, one action step on our school improvement plan was to accelerate the fifth grade math students into sixth grade math. However, there had been no attention paid to accelerating students from kindergarten through fourth grade. Acceleration could not occur in the fifth grade without building the students' capacity from their earliest grades. While this is so intuitive, when confronted with state testing, staff often ignore the big picture and concentrate only on the years that are tested. While acceleration in the early years did not solve the problem for our state testing immediately, it did build the students capacity over the next few years.

The low proficiency rate of our English Language Learners (ELL) was another challenge that needed our attention. We had to examine our beliefs and teaching behaviors first by looking at the number of "pull-out" lessons that our some of our students were receiving. We had not made AYP in the ELL subgroup. Over 40% of our students were from non-English speaking homes and 24.4% were receiving ESOL services. Some of these same children also had reading and math intervention time with paraprofessionals every day. When examining our ELL data, one question that our leadership team had was, "what percentage of the day are our ELL students missing the daily classroom instruction?" Another question we asked was, "do our ELL students receive on grade level instruction in math and reading or are they missing this due to their fractured instructional programs." We found answers to these questions to be one of the keys to our success. Students are tested on grade level curriculum; however, most of our ELL students were not receiving on-grade level instruction. Instead they were receiving interventions outside of their classrooms that were essentially causing them to fall further behind.

The logical changes resulting from this questioning made all the difference in the lives of our students. In four years, our ELL state math testing scores went from 10% proficient in 2003 to 70% proficient or above in 2006 and ELL reading scores went from 10% proficient to 75% proficient in the same time period. All NCLB subgroups, including special education and free and reduced-price meals had similar gains.

IDENTIFYING ROOT CAUSES IS CRUCIAL TO MAKING INFORMED DECISIONS

As one of the directors of leadership development for Montgomery County Public Schools, I have had the privilege of working with many administrators and school teams. One particularly important role has been revising and co-teaching the Data Driven Decision Making course. This course involves working with leadership teams from elementary and secondary schools who want to examine their school data and find root causes for their student achievement needs. The root cause analysis protocol involves looking at your current data and asking questions about the data rather than jumping to conclusions. This collaborative questioning of the current state helps staff to examine their own practices and to dig deeply to find solutions for their students' academic needs.

During the summer leadership week, I was asked to work with a middle school leadership team that was struggling with student achievement, particularly in the ELL subgroup. Using the root cause analysis protocol, the team discovered many things, but two important findings emerged. One had to do with the misconception that the Latino students couldn't or wouldn't attend the available remedial sessions after school because of family obligations or lack of motivation. When the team was encouraged to continue to ask questions about their data, new information emerged. It turned out that there was a competing, very popular, after-school program that involved going on trips into the community. Why would a student choose to attend a math resource session when they could go on a trip to see the local universities or go to a basketball game? This was not a cultural problem or a family support problem as originally thought. The solution was right under the school's roof.

Schedules simply needed to be coordinated between departments in order for the students to be available for the learning sessions.

The second revelation occurred when staff was able to question their successful data as well as their needs. The previous year, the sixth grade ELL students had made huge gains. When asked what they had done to achieve this great success, of course the sixth grade team had lots of answers. Why hadn't any teachers asked themselves this before? This happens a great deal in large schools. Often there is a gold mine of great ideas right under our noses. All we need to do is examine our work and share solutions. This wouldn't have happened without creating the safe haven for staff to examine their work and the questioning that begins the root cause analysis process.

Simply looking at the data could have resulted in making the wrong decisions. For example, dismissing the motivation and commitment of the Latino students allowed staff to assume, incorrectly, that there was nothing to do to improve student achievement. Finding the root cause, planning for more collaboration, creating effective communication among teams, and developing after school sessions that were targeted for success, was a plan that everyone could be excited about and could potentially change students' lives.

COLLABORATION IS POWERFUL AND
ESSENTIAL FOR SUSTAINABILITY

Collaboration is fundamental component of successful professional learning communities where the goal is school improvement. However, the term "professional learning communities" has been used to describe a myriad of things from committee work to effective meeting structures, and so on. Richard Dufour describes the three big ideas that characterize the true professional learning community. (Dufour et al., 2005, p. 33) They impact whether a staff can trust each other and their principal enough to engage in root cause analysis, whether their goals and vision involves every child achieving their potential and whether they can work together to have their collective knowledge solve the many adaptive challenges a school will face.

"School mission statements that promise 'learning for all' have become a cliché. But when a school staff takes that statement literally—when teachers view it as a pledge to ensure the success of each student rather than as politically correct hyperbole—profound changes begin to take place." (Dufour et al., 2005, p. 32) Every staff member must be committed to help create such a school. As my staff and I continued our study of professional learning communities and equity, our teaching changed, our expectations changed and as a result student achievement increased. Our confidence grew and our beliefs about children changed dramatically.

Judging our success on the basis of the data results is the only way we can measure what is truly happening in our classrooms. Simply assuming students are learning because we are teaching is not good enough if we are to have an equitable school. But data analysis alone is not enough. Are we using this data to analyze our students' needs and our own work and are we then taking this knowledge and making the necessary instructional changes to meet the challenge? Our school entrance had a huge banner above our school test scores which said, "Turn Data into Knowledge, Turn Knowledge in Action." Blindly solving student achievement challenges without examining data is not going to get you to your root causes. However, simply uncovering your needs without then changing beliefs, behavior and instruction is an exercise without possible new results.

TEACHERS ARE INSTRUCTIONAL DECISION-MAKERS

As stated earlier, the principal of a school must develop a culture where everyone takes on the role of leader. The principal and other administration cannot do the teaching. Therefore they must empower the staff to carry on the vision of the school.

In a culture of collaboration, teachers and staff examine not only summative test results, but also develop systematic processes to examine formative results together in order to improve their classroom practices. Sharing strategies, questions, frustrations, materials and results promotes team trust and collective learning. Teams can engage in developing common formative assessment, use root cause analysis, and ask questions of each other which will then lead to gains in student achievement. Root cause analysis is not only effective on the school leadership level, but at the grade level, team level and individual level as well. This is the way that we can focus on results, understand what success will look like and work together to attain this success. Everyone shares in the responsibility for the success of every child.

In order for teachers to carry on this important work, leaders must examine the data for gaps in their support of teachers. Staff development and policies and procedures put into effect by leadership must support the vision of the school and allow teachers to shine. The master schedule for instance, must support student achievement. At Clopper Mill, staff helped us to examine our school's practices for developing the master schedule. Previously, the arts team worked on the schedule alone. The needs of individual students and student data were not taken into consideration at all.

My second year at Clopper Mill, each grade level examined students' academic needs in order to collaboratively set the master schedule for the following year. Knowing which students will be able to accelerate in math next year will drive decisions about which grade levels will have math at the same time. If 10 third graders will be able to participate in fifth grade math next year, then the fifth and fourth grades need to have math at the same time in order for this to happen. If we have a large number of students that will need reading intervention, then reading must happen at different times of the day so that the reading specialist can support each grade level. These questions must be raised early in the spring and be brought to a collaborative leadership team of teachers. Together our leadership team designed a school master schedule that supported student achievement, not convenience or habit.

Another way leaders can support teachers is to align staff development with the school's mission, vision and with student achievement goals. If we are to encourage teachers to open their classrooms to examination of their beliefs and practices, then we must also ensure that we support continuous improvement through a strong staff development program. Staff meetings should be about student achievement and teaching, not administrative information. Gone are the days when we can take valuable time and waste it with mundane information sharing. We must turn each meeting into an opportunity for growth.

The same is true of team meetings. Again, combining processes with informing beliefs, I encouraged teachers, by providing templates for their team meetings, to use their team planning time to examine student work, to share teaching strategies and to form flexible reteaching groups based on formative data. The leader must model this effective use of time by using current communication tools to disseminate administrative information and utilizing valuable staff meeting time for staff development.

Effective problem solving and risk taking climate are cited as key elements in schools where needed change has been successful. A risk taking climate impacts the behaviors of both the leader and the staff. The leader has to risk sharing the baton. The leader has to allow the staff to examine the information available, make decisions and try out their ideas. This can be uncomfortable and scary, but allowing others to take on greater responsibility enhances and enriches the leader's power; it does not diminish it. The old saying goes, "two heads are better than one," and I contend that many heads are even better. Each member of the school team has a different perspective, different experiences and backgrounds and can bring vital information to the table.

Not only does the leader need to take risks, but the staff as well. This implies a great deal of comfort and faith in the leadership to allow them to experiment. The greatest compliment I received about school improvement was when staff would excitedly come to me with a new idea to try. This showed me that I had effectively created an environment which encouraged experimentation for the good of the school. It often involved more work for the teachers but was a genuine attempt at improving student achievement. It meant that we were one team working for a unified goal!

CONCLUSION

Raising expectations and eliminating the achievement gap is a complicated and multifaceted enterprise that must be done collaboratively with leaders, staff and community. We must change policies and procedures as well as engage in the study of race and equity in order to raise our own awareness and change beliefs and practices.

Leaders must create non-judgmental open professional learning communities where staff can openly examine student formative and summative data to identify successes and learning gaps. These gaps should be studied and questioned to identify root causes without blame and to determine new teaching strategies and interventions that can be put into place to address the issues. Schools must encourage all staff to become leaders in equity and provide effective targeted staff development which will address the unique student achievement needs of the school. Schools must work on changing teacher beliefs while creating policies and procedures that allow staff to examine their work and develop teaching strategies that have high expectations for all students.

The principalship is a complicated, challenging and most rewarding endeavor. What I have seen works best, through my own experiences and those of the assistant principals I have mentored, is a multifaceted approach that starts with the leader developing relationships and gaining the trust of all the stakeholders, including the students. The cycle of success begins by changing teachers' and staff beliefs and expectations about students; developing a common vision and shared goals; implementing and monitoring systematic accountability measures such as frequent summative and formative data collection and root cause analysis; involving stakeholder groups in the change process; and finally developing interventions, flexible groupings and acceleration based on the information gained through these collaborative processes. While a monumental task, it is truly possible to raise achievement while eliminating the achievement gap!

REFERENCES

Childress, S. M. (2009). "Six Lessons for Pursuing Excellence and Equity at Scale, Efforts in Montgomery County, Maryland, to 'Raise the Bar and Close the Gap' Depended on Deep Changes." *Kappan*, 13–17.

Collins, J. (2005). *Good To Great*. New York: HarperCollins Publishers.

DuFour, R., and Eaker, R. (1980 *Professional Learning Communities At Work, Best Practices for Enhancing Student Achievement*. Bloomington, IN: National Educational Services.

Fullan, M. (2006). *Turnaround Leadership*. San Francisco: Jossey-Bass, Inc.

Heifetz, R. A., and Linsky, M. (2002). *Leadership on the Line; Staying Alive through the Dangers of Leading.* Boston: Harvard Business School Press.
Noguera, P. A, and Wing, J. Y. (2006). *Unfinished Business: Closing the Racial Achievement Gap In Our Schools.* San Francisco, CA: John Wiley and Sons, Inc.
Schumaker, D. R., and Sommers, W. A. (2001). *Being a Successful Principal: Riding the Wave of Change Without Drowing.* Thousand Oaks, CA: Corwin Press, Inc.
Schmoker, M. (1999). *Results, The Key to Continuous School Improvement.* Alexandria, VA: Association for Supervision and Curriculum Development (ASCD).
Singleton, G. and Linton, C. (2005). *Courageous Conversations About Race: A Field Guide for Achieving Equity in Schools.* Thousand Oaks, CA: Corwin Press, Inc.
Sparks, D. (2005). "Leading for Transformation in Teaching, Learning, and Relationships." In *On Common Ground*, edited by R. DuFour, R. Eaker, and R. DuFour (pp. 155–175). Bloomington: National Educational Service.

ABOUT THE AUTHOR

Roni Silverstein is principal of Fallsmead Elementary School in Montgomery County Public Schools (MCPS), Maryland. She recently returned to school-based leadership after serving as the director of elementary leadership development for MCPS, coaching and designing professional development for over 275 aspiring MCPS administrators. In that role, she developed the spiraling curricula for assistant principals that include race and equity, professional growth systems and evaluations, and Baldrige processes. Prior to joining the central office, Roni served as principal of Clopper Mill Elementary School in Germantown, Maryland, for four years. During her more than thirty years of education experience, she has also served as special education coordinator and teacher. Her professional experiences include developing and conducting needs assessments and designing and delivering targeted staff development to teachers, assistant principals, elementary and secondary principals, directors and central services administrators. In addition, Roni has redesigned and taught the data-driven decision making course for MCPS administrators, presented "Are You Data Rich and Analysis Poor?" at the National Staff Development Conference, and presented at the U.S. Department of Education Office of English Language Acquisition (OELA) Summit V, "Turn Data into Knowledge, Knowledge into Action." Roni and her husband Robert live in Montgomery County where they raised their three children.

Community: The Village It Takes

Chapter 12

From Survivors to Leaders

*Stages of Immigrant Parent
Involvement in Schools*

Young-chan Han

My mother and four children immigrated to the United States in 1973 and joined our father who came to the country in 1971. For my parents, their American dream was their children's success. They wanted the best for their four children—the best education, the best career, and the best family. They worked six to seven days a week and 12–14 hours a day for many years while I was growing up. My parents came to school twice during my seven years of public school life from grades 6 to 12—the first time to enroll me in an elementary school and then seven years later, to attend my high school graduation.

As a parent who worked long hours, my mother was not physically present most of my teen life. She was not available to help with homework or to check for its completion, listen to my stories, attend parent-teacher conferences, sign school papers or volunteer at school. Even if she had been available to support her children, because of her limited English skills and lack of knowledge about American schools, she was not prepared to support her children academically. However, my mother did support us in the best way she could—she made sure that we had food on the table and a roof over our head. This was the extent of her parent involvement in schools—she was a survivor.

Today, almost 40 years later, as the immigrant populations continue to increase in our community, families with similar circumstances are found in many of our schools. Some like my mother are survivors, supporting education in their own way, although they are absent from school. But other immigrant families have different stories. They may have come to the United States with a stronger financial or education background, or with a large family already in the country; and with support and appropriate training, they are able to engage more in their children's school. Some immigrant parents are able to become leaders within their communities or advocate for families like themselves within the school district. They all require the support of schools, districts, and communities to assist them as they navigate American schools and to build their capacity as family and school leaders.

What is key is that educational stake holders not view all immigrants as a homogeneous group with similar needs. This leads to assumptions and poor planning to engage immigrant families. In order to support and engage all immigrant families through the various stages of involvement, schools, districts, and communities must first understand the unique needs and experiences of these families.

From my years of observational studies and experiences working directly with thousands of immigrant families from all over the world and from all walks of life, as well as my own background as part of an immigrant family, I came to see that immigrant families generally fall into four stages of parent involvement. These stages are *cultural survivor; cultural learner; cultural connector; and cultural leader* (see Figure 12.1, below).

The four stages serve as a dual framework. First, the framework provides information for understanding immigrant families' needs and their stages of involvement in education. Second, it provides valuable insight into how schools and communities can best support immigrant families through each stage of parent involvement in schools.

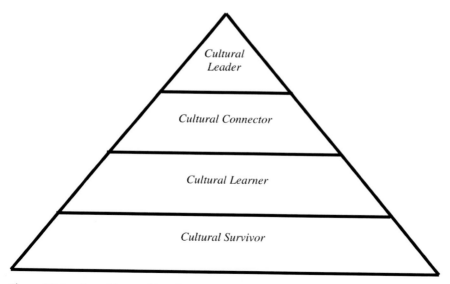

Figure 12.1. Four Stages of Immigrant Parent Involvement

The model (see Table 12.1) illustrates the extent to which some immigrant parents have gained the capacity to be engaged in their children's education. As parents learn to navigate the highly complex American school system, many, but not all, are able to move through the four stages of involvement. These stages are fluid due to various situations and circumstances that dictate the level or capacity of parent involvement. Parents struggling to meet basic family needs may have limited opportunity to be involved in their children's education while parents with greater resources and years of support and training have greater opportunities to be actively involved in children's education. The following provides a description of each of the four stages of school involvement for immigrant parents.

Stage 1—Cultural Survivor: The cultural survivor focuses on meeting the family's basic needs for survival. These parents are learning how to buy food and clothes, pay utility bills, locate affordable housing and access health care services, transportation, child care, etc. Parents at this stage require assistance navigating the essential paperwork for their children's schooling: registration; filling out emergency contact forms, including free and reduced-price meals application; purchasing school supplies; providing and updating health records; and understanding basic information such as bus rules, attendance policies, inclement weather procedures, etc. At the cultural survivor stage, the school staff often becomes the parent's primary source of contact for assistance in meeting their basic needs.

Stage 2—Cultural Learner: The cultural learner engages in learning about their children's education. They learn about American education by participating in parent programs and by attending parent-teacher conferences often using translated documents and foreign language interpreters. At this stage of involvement, the immigrant parent feels more comfortable networking within their language/culture specific groups.

Stage 3—Cultural Connector: The cultural connector continues to attend informational programs and gain knowledge of the American school system and learns how to navigate the system. They connect cultural survivors and cultural learners with resources and programs in their school and community. At this stage, cultural connectors expand their focus from their own child to the needs of other immigrant children and families.

Stage 4—Cultural Leader: The cultural leader is actively engaged in their child's education and has expanded his/her skills and knowledge to the level of advocacy for students and other parents. He/she takes on a leadership role in the decision-making process through opportunities such as Parent Teacher Associations (PTA) or other parent organizations, school improvement teams, advisory ommittees, and/or district's parent advisory council.

Table 12.1.   Stages of School Involvement of Immigrant Parents

Stages of School Involvement	Immigrant Parents
Cultural Survivor	Parents in this stage may be homeless, refugees, recent immigrants, illiterate in their native language, etc. • Focuses on meeting the basic survival needs of the family. • Enrolls their children in schools with the help of relatives, bilingual friends, community members, or school staff. • May work two or three labor-intensive jobs to support the family. • Physically absent at home. • Attends parent-teacher conference only if leave is granted from work and if an interpreter is available. • Does not know how to navigate the school/system.
Cultural Learner	Parents in this stage begin to attend school functions with the support of interpreters or bilingual liaisons. • Relies heavily on translated documents and foreign language interpreters or bilingual liaisons to gain knowledge about American schools. • Participates in parent-teacher conferences with the support of interpreters or bilingual liaisons. • Attends language specific parent programs and events. • Gains basic understanding of American school culture and how to navigate the school/system.
Cultural Connector	Parents in this stage continue to attend school functions and meetings and become a voice for cultural survivors and cultural learners. • Regularly attends school functions and meetings. • Seeks out more than basic information. • More easily navigates the school system. • Develops greater familiarity with the school system, educational terminologies, policies and procedures. • Feels comfortable with both the language specific programs/events and the English-only programs with the help of interpreters. • Encourages and empowers cultural survivors and cultural learners to become involved in their children's education.
Cultural Leader	Parents in this stage become an advocate for cultural survivors, cultural learners, and cultural connectors. • Participates in leadership programs and trainings. • Seeks and becomes involved in leadership opportunities in school and district: PTA or other parent-teacher organization, school improvement team, parent advisory council, district parent advisory committee, etc. • Communicates the immigrant families' needs to school staff, school district, community members and agencies/organizations. • Advocates for children of all families, especially the immigrant families.

By understanding the needs and roles of immigrant parents in each of the stages, schools, districts, and community partners can better understand factors that impact parent's capacity to be fully engaged in their children's education, as well as their potential for active engagement. Table 12.1 depicts examples of what involvement may look like at each of the four stages.

Understanding the stages of immigrant parent involvement in schools raises awareness of immigrant families' needs and experiences. This helps educators and community leaders to develop appropriate, intentional, and meaningful programs, services, and training to better assist families in becoming partners in their children's education. However, it is important to note the length of residency does not determine the stage of involvement. For example, a parent who has lived in the US for ten years and has a limited English proficiency but has not been exposed to an English-speaking environment may remain a cultural survivor for the rest of his/her life. On the other hand, a bilingual parent new to this country may begin as a cultural survivor, but with the appropriate and meaningful support from school, district, and community can become a cultural connector and a leader in a short period of time. The following stories portray immigrant parents at each stage and ways schools, districts and communities can support parents at these stages.

CULTURAL SURVIVOR: BURMESE REFUGEE FAMILY

A Burmese refugee family with five children ages six to 19 moved to the United States three years ago. In their home, there were few pieces of furniture, limited kitchen utensils, no pictures on the walls, no print materials (books, magazines, newspapers, etc.) and a refurbished computer but no printer. This family's main concern was to provide for basic needs such as food, clothing, shelter, and health care. Their immediate and basic needs superseded their children's academic and school life even though the parents wanted the best for their children. Their children's education, especially that of the 17 and 19 year-old teenagers, was sacrificed time and again because the children had a significant role to play in supporting their parents and family's needs.

When their father applied for the food stamp program, the 10th grade daughter had to miss school to serve as an interpreter. When their mother needed to go to a health clinic, it was the daughter, again, who had to miss school and accompany the parent. The teenage daughter's English was the most fluent in the family, although she still received English for Speakers of Other Languages (ESOL) support at school. She became the family's official interpreter for all family related matters.

The older brother dropped out of high school at age 19 when he realized how difficult it would be for him to graduate due to years of interrupted education while living in refugee camps in Malaysia. He started working at a local restaurant to help the family financially and was earning $7.00 an hour. Though this family believed in a good education, their life circumstances often became the barrier for their children's education. For this Burmese family, their basic need for food, housing, and health was their number one priority. They are cultural survivors.

WHAT CAN SCHOOLS, DISTRICTS, OR COMMUNITIES DO TO SUPPORT CULTURAL SURVIVORS?

1. *Refugee Youth Project, Baltimore City Community College in Baltimore, Maryland*
   Baltimore City Community College implements a Refugee Youth Project (RYP) for refugee children and youth in Baltimore City. This project is funded by a grant from the Maryland Office for Refugees and Asylees (MORA) to support refugee youths ages four through 21. Volunteers are paired with refugee students to spend two hours a day, twice a week at the home of refugees to receive academic tutoring and acculturation support from trained volunteers (Baltimore City Community College's Refugee Youth Project, 2010). These volunteer tutors become role models who can help with homework and practice speaking English. The volunteer and the refugee family's case worker also support the parents by helping them understand American school life and communicating about their children's educational successes. During the 2010–2011 school year, the RYP served 160 refugee youth in Baltimore City schools (Baltimore City Refugee Office, 2010).

2. *English Speaking Partner Lunch Series: School and Business Partnership in Laurel, Maryland (*Howard County Public School System, 2011*)*
   Bollman Bridge Elementary School (BBES) in Jessup, Maryland, and Coastal Sunbelt Produce in Savage, Maryland, collaborated to provide an informal English lunchtime conversation for Burmese employees at the company. This program was initiated when a staff member from Coastal Sunbelt Produce, also an active parent at BBES, realized a large number of Burmese parents from BBES were employed at the company. Together, the school administration, ESOL teachers, and the management of Coastal Sunbelt Produce collaborated on a partnership that brought the English- and Burmese-speaking employees together for six weekly lunch time conversations during the employees' lunch break.

In order to facilitate English conversations, the ESOL teacher and the BBES parent provided simple lessons every week that included a variety of topics such as American holidays, favorite foods, how to access the county library and apply for a library card, words used for shopping, American schools, how to get involved in their children's education, and more. The program was so successful that some employees continued to meet even after the program was over. This partnership created a win-win situation for employees, the company, and the school. Most importantly, for everyone involved, this program helped cultivate a cross-cultural understanding between the English and Burmese speaking employees.

CULTURAL LEARNER: MARLENY'S FAMILY

In 2003, a family of six migrated to America from El Salvador. No one spoke English, no one knew anything about American schools nor had any social network. They were cultural survivors. They had to make sure all the family's basic needs were met first before they could become involved in their children's education. With the help from a bilingual Spanish speaking liaison, the mother, Marleny, came to understand the expectations American schools hold for parents and the importance of her involvement in her children's education. Gradually, she began to attend school events and parent-teacher conferences. A bilingual liaison provided the support that Marleny needed for this involvement.

The liaison served as the interpreter during the parent-teacher conferences, and connected Marleny with other community resources. If any communication was sent home from school, the liaison made sure that Marleny understood it in her native language. She began to feel comfortable coming to school when the liaison was working at the school. With the support of the school administrator, ESOL staff, a guidance counselor and the school psychologist, the Hispanic liaison started a monthly program called "Coffee with the Principal" and invited Marleny and other Hispanic parents. Marleny faithfully attended every month, taking along her two-year-old daughter to every meeting.

During this monthly meeting, the school provided information and materials about the curriculum, instruction, assessment, and also shared specific suggestions with the parents about how to support the children at home. Everything that was said during this meeting was interpreted for the parents. With time, the parents could comfortably ask questions and freely speak what was on their mind. Parents attending "Coffee with the Principal" began to feel welcome and connected to the school. Though Marleny's comfort level has increased, she still preferred to be with her own language group. She has become a cultural learner.

WHAT CAN SCHOOLS, SCHOOL DISTRICTS AND
COMMUNITIES DO TO SUPPORT CULTURAL LEARNERS?

Anne Arundel County Public Schools (AACPS), Maryland: Hispanic Education Forum (Anne Arundel County Public School System, 2010).

Anne Arundel County Public School System in Maryland understands the cultural learners paradigm and has created an ESOL Family Outreach Office to ensure that all immigrant parents have equal opportunity to fully participate in their children's education. The district employs bilingual facilitators to work with LEP families, particularly at schools with large number of Hispanic families. These facilitators are able to provide support for parents like Marleny to help navigate the school.

In October 2010, Germantown Elementary School in Anne Arundel County offered an Hispanic Education Forum to provide information about how families can better support their children's academic and social achievement. Information was provided to parents in their native language on data including high school graduation rates, attendance, math and reading scores, as well as breakout sessions on *Helping Children With Homework, Mental Health, School Safety, and Career and College Readiness.* This event brought more than 200 families into the school. Light dinner, child care, and transportation were provided by the school and district.

Germantown Elementary School and the school district are committed to providing support to families to increase parent involvement for student success. These families are actively engaged in learning within their specific language group. This creates a safe environment for families who may not have developed a comfort level yet to be with predominantly English-speaking families. Through the Hispanic Education Forum, Spanish-speaking parents become informed, empowered and engaged in their children's education. As they begin to feel more comfortable and connected with the American education system and school culture, their journey of parent involvement in school begins. These families move into the cultural learner stage of involvement in their children's education.

CULTURAL CONNECTOR: MARLENY'S JOURNEY

Marleny's parent involvement journey continued to flourish for the next several years from a cultural survivor to a cultural learner. She was able to participate and learn from the Coffee with the Principal meetings about how to support her children at home whether it was helping with homework, checking academic progress, asking questions, praising good work or giving guidance to her four children. She also attended several educational workshops throughout the year. Of course, she regularly attended the fall and spring parent-teacher conferences with the help of a bilingual liaison.

She began to network with other Spanish-speaking parents and felt more comfortable sharing her concerns with other parents and school staff. After being in the United States for six years, Marleny began to take on a role as a cultural connector for other new Hispanic families in her school. During the first week of school, a "form-filling" day was held for Hispanic families to assist in the completion of the many school forms that need to be completed at the beginning of the year—free and reduced price meal application, emergency form, field trip form, grade policy form, etc. Having completed all the forms for the past several years, Marleny volunteered to help new families that day. Marleny is now taking on the role of a cultural connector.

Marleny encouraged other new families to participate and become members of the school's PTA to support their children. She began to communicate the needs of the LEP Spanish speaking families to the school staff. Marleny also realized that new immigrant parents were not aware of the variety of children's extra curricular activities sponsored by the school and the county. As she signed up for sport activities for her own children, she wanted to make sure that other new immigrant families in her school knew about the opportunities for sports teams and actually guided them on how to register their children. Not only was she focused on her own children, but she was now assisting other immigrant families to support their children. She had become a cultural connector who connects Spanish speaking new immigrant families with the resources and programs in the school and the community.

Parents like Marleny who are motivated to active involvement need more than just basic information about American schools. At the cultural connector stage, the parent is willing and able to go beyond the basics of helping children at home, attending parent-teacher conferences, and signing up for extra curricular activities. The cultural connector can provide insights for school officials that help the school develop more effective outreach programs to the families. It is incumbent upon the school and the district to build Marleny's leadership capacity. Marleny and her peers could learn from more intentional programs and training that are geared to encourage and equip parents to become actively involved in their children's education.

WHAT CAN SCHOOLS, SCHOOL DISTRICTS AND COMMUNITIES DO TO SUPPORT CULTURAL CONNECTORS?

Montgomery County Public School System, Maryland: Conquista Tus Sueños—Hispanic Leadership Program (Montgomery County Public School System, 2008).

Conquista Tus Sueños ("Realize Your Dreams") is a Hispanic parent program in Montgomery County, Maryland that empowers parents to become advocates for their children, and to gain skills and knowledge to become leaders in their children's school. Training sessions conducted in Spanish are offered through the Parent Academy in three week increments in the evening for parents. The first session focuses on learning about American schools—curriculum at all school levels, county and state assessments, academic programs, the attendance policy. The second session focuses on instructional programs and school system and county support services available to families. The last session focuses on developing leadership among Hispanic parents. Topics include advocating for academic success, addressing concerns with schools, and ways to get involved in school parent groups. The program is held at selected schools throughout the county providing opportunities for greater systemwide representation.

Empowering and equipping cultural connectors opens many opportunities for schools and the school system to increase diverse representation in school groups and organizations. Parents like Marleny are the voices that speak for cultural learners and cultural survivors. As of 2009, a total of 30 Conquista sessions, all presented in Spanish, were held in selected Montgomery County schools (Maryland State Department of Education, 2010).

CULTURAL LEADER: BECOMING A PARENT LEADER

When I first started working at the district's office at the Howard County Public School System in Maryland, I received a phone call from the supervisor of elementary education asking me to identify and recruit a minority parent to join the Elementary Advisory Committee. She wanted either a Hispanic or a Korean parent since Spanish and Korean were the leading languages in the county's schools. I attempted to recruit from among my many bilingual friends who have lived in the United States for over 20 years and who have children in public schools. They all asked me the same question, "What is an advisory committee?" When I explained what the committee did and what their role would be, I heard the same response—"I don't have enough knowledge about the school system to be involved in a committee like that." "I don't think I can do it." Soon, I ran out of people to ask.

These experiences illustrate the challenges the schools and districts face as they try to engage immigrant families in leadership roles. As schools become more diverse, the composition of parent leadership also needs to reflect the diverse student population. Often times, community leaders, districts, and schools seek minority parents to join various groups or committees. Just because groups want to diversify their profile and be inclusive does not mean that the immigrant parent leaders will suddenly appear and feel comfortable for the task at hand. Schools, districts, and the community partners must be very intentional about building parent leadership capacity.

Many immigrant parents like Marleny want to expand their knowledge about the American school system and gain confidence to be involved in leadership capacity. Even if these parents have lived in America for decades, immigrant parents are puzzled by school culture, policies, roles of school boards, and how decisions are made that impact children's education. A story from a colleague summarizes needs felt by parents like Marleny. "When I taught immigrant parent leadership classes, most of the parents told me that before that class, they didn't even pay attention to programs aimed at immigrants because they are always at a basic level. While programs such as basic computer classes did draw a large group of immigrant parents, the parents in my class also needed and deserved programming geared to their level of knowledge and experience."

WHAT CAN SCHOOLS, SCHOOL DISTRICTS AND COMMUNITIES DO TO SUPPORT CULTURAL LEADERS?

Howard County Public School System: International Parent Leadership Program (IPLP) (Howard County Public School System, 2010).

To develop leaders among immigrant parents, the Howard County Public School System in Maryland launched the International Parent Leadership Program (IPLP) in 2006. The mission of the IPLP is to develop parent leaders to ensure a diversified pool of parent leadership at the school and district level to improve student achievement for all children. The participants meet six times for 2.5 to 3 hours per session to learn about the district's school board, parent-teacher organizations, school policies, elementary and secondary curriculum, academic programs including special education, gifted and talented, and ESOL, county and state assessments, and instruction and in general how to navigate the school system. The speakers include the superintendent, high-ranking administrators, school principals and other experts from various education fields.

In the Fall of 2006, Ania and Teresa both participated in the IPLP. Teresa, a bilingual mother from Argentina, moved to the US in 2000 with her husband and two children. Ania, also a bilingual parent, moved from Poland to the US over 15 years ago. They both had children in high school. As part of their leadership training, Ania and Teresa testified before the school board to share the value added benefit of the leadership program for immigrant parents.

In Teresa's testimony, she stated, "The IPLP training gave me the confidence that I needed to go a step further helping in the school system and gave me the opportunity to get a deeper understanding of the public school system" (T. Norman, personal communication. December, 2006). Ania also spoke about what she had gained through this six week leadership training. "We were introduced to the ins and outs of assessments and now we are able to decipher the mysterious acronyms like MSA, BCR and ECR. We became familiar with the work of the School Improvement Team, PTA, and Booster Clubs and learned about the responsibilities of the Board of Education" (A. Szczepaniec-Bialas, personal communication, December, 2006).

The following year, three Nigerian parents participated in the IPLP. Even though they came from a country where English was their native language, because of the differences in culture, these women faced barriers in parent involvement. They wanted to participate in a leadership program to learn about how American schools educate their children. They were very interested in understanding grade promotion, county and state assessments, and gifted and talented programs. The high school course selection was also new information to them. These parents questioned why the students and parents had to make these decisions and not the schools. For these parents, it was the differences in the educational system that became a barrier in their involvement in education and not their language.

IPLP in Howard County, Maryland, exists to support parents like Ania, Teresa, and Marleny. Through programs like this, the school system is focused on increasing parent leadership among first generation immigrant parents. The program provides opportunities for parents to gain knowledge about the intricacies of American schools and to increase their confidence in their leadership ability to make a difference in the lives of their own children and the children of others. As of 2010, IPLP has graduated 112 international parents representing over 15 languages and 20 countries (H. Mesias, personal communication, December 7, 2010). Many of these parents have gone back to their schools to participate in leadership opportunities through school's PTA or School Improvement Team. Ania joined the School Improvement Team at her son's high school and also became a member of the International Outreach Committee at the district level.

WHAT CAN SCHOOLS, SCHOOL DISTRICTS, AND COMMUNITIES DO TO SUPPORT IMMIGRANT PARENTS FROM ALL STAGES OF SCHOOL INVOLVEMENT?

Office of International Student and Family Service, Howard County Public School System Model (Howard County Public School System, 2010).

Howard County Public School System (HCPSS) in Maryland is a diverse school system with students and families that come from 87 countries and speak 77 languages (Howard County Public School System, 2011). The school system created the Office of International Student and Family Services (OISFS) to provide educational services to international students and to students and families who do not speak English proficiently. This office ensures that LEP communities have equal access to information and resources about school system services, policies, programs, and academics. One of the goals of this office is to actively engage all immigrant parents in their children's education.

There are a number of critical services and programs offered through this office that support parent engagement for all immigrant families. They are: interpreting and translation services; school-based bilingual liaisons; district-based bilingual liaisons; International Student Registration Center (ISRC); professional development for educators; and workshops and training for international parents. The OISFS supports over 3000 families in any given year (Howard County Public School System, 2010).

Having an infrastructure at the district level makes it easier to identify cultural survivors, cultural learners, cultural connectors, and cultural leaders in order to provide critically needed services and programs to immigrant families. With the support of the OISFS, immigrant families are able to engage in the education of their children even if they do not speak the language or understand the American education system.

The work of OISFS goes beyond traditional parent outreach that often leaves many parents disconnected. For example, a Haitian interpreter in middle school assisted a family when she learned that a new 8th grade student from Haiti did not return the required signed field trip permission form by a specified date. The school had no way of contacting the single mother who worked long hours at a nearby nursing home. The interpreter contacted the nursing home and found out the break time for their workers. She then visited the mother during her 15-minute break, explained to the mother about the overnight field trip for her son, and returned to school with the signed permission slip. Without the support from this interpreter, the student would not have been able to participate in a two-day field trip and would have missed out on the valuable learning experience.

The OISFS also provides support for the cultural learners. Throughout the year, the school system holds a number of language specific outreach programs. In 2004 and 2005, the OISFS provided targeted outreach to parents who spoke Korean, Spanish, Urdu, Arabic, and Chinese. For parents with limited English skills and the parents who may not have the comfort level of being involved in school, this type of outreach plays an important role in helping parents learn about American education. Parents are able to take small steps toward more meaningful engagement in their children's lives while learning about the American school system in their native language.

CONCLUSION: MEETING THE NEEDS OF
A DIVERSE IMMIGRANT POPULATION

While immigrant families bring unique challenges to schools and districts, the families themselves face their own unique set of challenges. Research affirms that when parents are involved in their children's education, the children are more successful in school (Henderson and Mapp, 2002). However, there are circumstances specific to the immigrant experience that present barriers to parent involvement, such as language, unfamiliarity with the American school system, cultural difference or long work hours, precluding parents from full participation in the schools. It therefore behooves the schools, districts, and community to create and implement more culturally relevant and appropriate parent programs and supports.

Cultural survivors, whose focus is centered around daily survival, require more intensive support for their children. Schools and community organizations need to connect parents with social services and community agencies to meet the needs of the families. Families need basic information about American schools such as how to fill out school forms, buy school lunch, use school bus services, purchase school supplies, etc. Effective home-school communication is essential at this stage. In-person meetings with interpreters arranged through personal phone calls are more effective than written notices. Instead of holding meetings in the school building, school staff can take the meeting to a location where the cultural survivors frequently visit such as their place of worship, ethnic grocery stores, public library, public meeting house, or even the parent's work place. This may require school staff to step out of their comfort zone in order to meet parents in their comfort zone. In order to support these families, it is necessary for schools to provide foreign language interpreters and translate vital documents. Often these services become lifelines for parents.

Cultural learners and cultural connectors continue to need language support through effective communication such as in-person meetings and workshops, translated fliers and written communication, and for some, school websites and e-mails. The school websites and Internet become more readily accessible to cultural connectors. At this stage, parents need more than basic information, which may include information about assessments, curriculum, academic programs and school and district policies. Cultural learners and cultural connectors gradually become more involved in their children's education beyond parenting at home. Even though these parents still feel comfortable networking within their specific language group, the schools begin to notice emerging leaders among cultural connectors.

Cultural leaders include limited English proficient, bilingual speaking, and English only speaking parents from countries that speak English.

Communication at this stage expands to electronic communications via e-mails, school and district websites and personal phone calls. Parents at this stage need opportunities to attend workshops and training to expand their knowledge about American schools and to refine their leadership skills in order to advocate for their children as well as for the children of other immigrant parents. However, there are few programs and training opportunities that are created to develop parent leaders among immigrants who represent a wide variety of languages and culture.

Many schools and districts have exemplary programs, workshops, and services to support cultural learners and cultural connectors, but there are far fewer opportunities targeting cultural survivors and cultural leaders. In order to support all immigrant families effectively and to increase student achievement of all children of immigrants, schools and education stakeholders must first understand how parents integrate through the stages of parent involvement so they can strategically support the educational needs of all children. Programs, services, and training must be *intentional, meaningful, and purposeful* to meet the needs and experiences of all immigrant families as identified through the four stages of school involvement for immigrant parents.

MARLENY IN 2011

It has been over eight years since Marleny's family arrived in the United States. Since then, Marleny's involvement in her children's education has evolved from Cultural Survivor to Cultural Connector. In 2008, Marleny successfully completed her Graduate Record Examination (GRE), a huge step toward achieving her American dream. Her oldest son is now a student at a local community college; her second daughter is working, and her two youngest children are attending middle and elementary school. While working full time, Marleny volunteers at her children's schools as much as she can. She is a PTA member and also helps with the school's PTA membership drive. With the help of the school's bilingual liaison, Marleny has truly connected with both the English-speaking parent groups and Spanish-only-speaking parents. Like parenting, school involvement of immigrant parents is a process and a journey.

REFERENCES

Baltimore City Community College's Refugee Youth Project (2010). Baltimore, MD: Refugee Youth Project.

"*Conquista Tus Sueños*" (2008). Montgomery County Public Schools. Rockville, MD. March, 2008.

Henderson, Anne T. and Mapp, Karen L. (2002). *A New Wave of Evidence: The Impact of School, Family and Community Connections on Student Achievement.* Austin, TX: Southwest Educational Development Laboratory.

"Hispanic Education Forum." (2010). Anne Arundel County Public Schools. Annapolis, MD.

"International Student and Family Services." Retrieved October 7, 2010 from www.hcpss.org/ schools/international.shtml#iplp.

"Lunch Series Connects English, Non-English Speakers" (2011). *Howard County Public School System January Newsletter.* Ellicott City, MD: Howard County Public School System.

"Maryland Schools Outreach to Parents." Retrieved October 7, 2010 from www.marylandpublicschools.org/MSDE/programs/titleI/pit.

ABOUT THE AUTHOR

Young-chan Han immigrated to the United States from South Korea as a child with her family in 1973. Her career in education began in 1999 as an international student and family outreach specialist for the Howard County Public School System in Maryland. There, she worked closely with over 3000 immigrant families and refugees, developed a parent leadership institute for immigrant parents, and created services and programs benefiting immigrant students and families. In November 2007, Young-chan expanded her local focus to the state level where she currently works as a family involvement specialist for the Maryland State Department of Education providing leadership, coordination and assistance to local school systems and schools on programs, projects, and activities that promote family engagement in schools. In her spare time, Young-chan serves as the president on the board of directors for a local non-profit, FIRN (Foreign-born Information Referral Network), teaches kindergarten class and serves as a children's ministry advisor for her church. She lives with her husband of more than 25 years and three children in Columbia, Maryland.

Chapter 13

Ready to Learn

The Benefits of a Neighborhood School Readiness Team

Debra Fulcher and Andrea Sobel

The kindergarten teacher met Juan at the door and asked him to find his nametag on the table. He selected a nametag and stuck it on his shirt. Throughout the morning, the teacher continued to identify him by the name on his nametag, at times asking him if that was his name, to which he nodded. There was one remaining nametag on the table. When the kindergarten teacher reported a child absent, the school office called the parents to find out why the child was not in class on the first day of school. The astonished parent said that he sent his child to school that morning. The police were immediately notified that there was a missing child. Police helicopters were dispatched and the police combed the school grounds and community hoping to find the missing child. The alarmed father rushed to school and straight to the kindergarten classroom to find his child with the wrong nametag attached to his shirt. His child's nametag was the one left on the table—unclaimed!

Could this unsettling and frightening scene have been avoided? Could this child have transitioned to kindergarten on the first day of school successfully with support from not only his family but also with support from the community and the school? The answer is a resounding yes!

One multicultural community in a Northern Virginia suburb accepted the challenge, by developing Neighborhood School Readiness Teams. Fairfax County, Virginia is a diverse community where over 44% of the population represent ethnic or racial minorities. The creation of the Neighborhood School Readiness Teams was a collaboration between the County's Office for Children and the Fairfax County Public School system to ensure that all children begin school ready to learn, particularly children who do not speak English and those growing up in poor households. This project was funded, in part, through the work of Fairfax Futures,[1] a community non-profit, whose mission is to support young children so that they will be successful in school and life. When there is shared commitment and responsibility, amazing things can happen.

WHAT ARE SOME OF THE CHALLENGES FOR FAMILIES, SCHOOLS AND COMMUNITIES?

Schools are working to respond to changing demographics, which include a rise in the number of immigrant families, as well as an increase in the number of children who are eligible for free and reduced-price school lunches, an indicator of financial need. Because social class often overlaps with race and immigrant status, this increase in diversity potentially means that economic disparities will adversely affect larger numbers of children than may have been anticipated (Capps et al., 2004). Challenges resulting from a lack of financial resources for families, the increased number of children who are homeless, and the rise of children from families new to the country can often interfere with early and important connections between families, schools and communities.

Language, cultural norms and values, as well as early experiences greatly influence how a five-year-old child will feel and respond when entering a kindergarten classroom for the first time. Children begin school with huge differences in those early experiences. Some children attend pre-school, full-day center-based or family childcare programs. Other children spend their first few years at home or cared for by a friend or neighbor. Differences in pre-kindergarten experiences range from rich and healthy environments that support the development of young children, to situations that may actually hinder the child's optimal development, leading to a stressful start to school.

Sending young children off to school can be traumatic for parents and even more so for parents new to American schools. A parent's fear that their child won't be understood and cared for can be a source of stress and worry. When families do not speak English, schools are often ill equipped to support them through the transition process, or to connect with them before their child begins school.

Paperwork is often a barrier for parents trying to understand what is required for their child to begin school, particularly when information is available only in English. Navigating where, how and when a parent should begin the school registration process can impact their readiness to start school on the first day, ready to learn. Families often expect that the start of school will be similar to their own experiences with schools. Principals described situations where families brought their child to school on the first day, assuming they would begin that day, without any prior registration or paperwork completed.

Additional challenges exist for families and communities without available resources to provide needed health, social and educational experiences for young children before beginning formal schooling. Some families do not have the financial resources needed to access health care. Others are not aware of the available community resources. Immigrant families may face additional challenges in accessing services of any kind due to language, cultural norms, expectations, and in some cases, fear of contacting community agencies.

Principals reported that some children did not begin school on the first day due to the lack of a current health physical or the required immunizations. Starting school late puts stress on everyone. Some families were confused as to what needed to be done for their children to begin school, and were frustrated if they had to take time off of work with little notice to complete needed health requirements for their children. Schools were impacted by not knowing how many children will be attending kindergarten in advance so they could hire teachers based on anticipated class size. Children starting late were placed at a disadvantage by starting school after their peers had already adjusted to school, particularly for children without prior group experiences.

WHY DO EARLY EXPERIENCES MATTER?

A child's preschool experience and initial transition to school is directly related to that child's later success in school and in life. Without quality experiences and opportunities before beginning school (whether with family at home, or in a preschool program), and effective transitions, children may experience greater difficulties with peer relationships, acquiring academic knowledge and skills, and may have a greater chance of school adjustment problems (Schulting, Malone and Dodge, 2005). High quality early education experiences for young children may benefit the child's early development and their transition from home to school (Belsky et al., 2007). They may be even more beneficial to children of immigrants in supporting them while adapting to a new culture and language, as well as helping families to become more familiar with what American schools expect of families. Children of immigrants typically have fewer early experiences in group care outside of the home (Capps et al., 2004).

A family's experiences and connections with their child's school from before the child enters kindergarten until graduation are also linked to success as the student progresses through school and life (Henderson et al., 2007). These relationships and opportunities for families to work as partners with schools, supporting their child's development and learning, are strongest in the early years. Some families have not experienced this type of school-family involvement, and some schools do not take steps to develop and encourage these partnerships.

Schools cannot create sustainable partnerships solely by reaching out. Families cannot create needed partnerships by just reaching in. Communities cannot change school and family expectations of transition on their own. Together, however, change can occur. Young children's development is intricately linked and dependent on their relationships and experiences in many different settings—with their family, in preschool, school and the broader community.

WHAT IS SCHOOL READINESS?

School readiness has changed throughout the decades. Forty to fifty years ago parent co-ops and other high quality preschools, serving primarily children whose families had economic resources available to them, focused mainly on play and social-emotional development. Teachers observed children, responded to their behavior and created an appropriate environment to support children's development and learning. There was little emphasis on standardized curriculum and academic skills were not a primary focus, as that was the work of kindergarten, not nursery school. Families were often able to support the language and literacy development of their children through books and other learning materials at home.

However with the rise of Head Start came the recognition that children from poor families were starting school behind their more affluent peers. Head Start pre-school programs were developed to offer a focused curriculum that included intentional support in language, early literacy and other academic topics so that children attending these programs will start school with skills equal to their peers with greater resources at home. Head Start programs continued to support children's development through play based experiences.

Over the years a focus on closing the achievement gap has resulted in a greater emphasis on assessment and academic skills in all preschool programs, even though early childhood research continues to emphasize that young children learn best through hands-on explorations and play experiences. There has been an increasingly "pushed down" elementary curriculum into kindergarten in a misguided attempt to help children pass federally mandated tests.

Today, "school readiness" has many varied interpretations. For families new to American schools, perceptions and understandings of what constitutes school readiness are even more varied, due to differing priorities and experiences with school expectations for young children. In 2006, a multidimensional view of school readiness set the context for a three year, seventeen state initiative supported by the David and Lucile Packard Foundation, the Kauffman Foundation and the Ford Foundation. The National School Readiness Indicators Initiative: Making Progress for Young Children was tasked with developing sets of indicators at the state level to track results for children from birth through age eight. The goal was for states to use the school readiness indicators to inform public policy decisions and track progress in meeting key goals for young children. Virginia was one of the seventeen states involved in this initiative to create a common understanding of school readiness (Rhode Island KIDS COUNT, 2005). A later outgrowth was the development of Virginia's definition of school readiness:

> *School readiness* describes the capabilities of children, their families, schools, and communities that will best promote student success in kindergarten and beyond. Each component; children, families, schools and communities—plays an essential role in the development of school readiness. No one component can stand on it's own. (Virginia's Definition of School Readiness, 2008, para 1)

Looking at readiness from a wider angle than the child provides an ecological point of view. Every child, as part of a family, is unique in development, dispositions and culture. As they enter a formal group schooling situation, these differences may become more pronounced in the eyes of the school and teachers. It is therefore, imperative that each school and community collaboratively address expectations and strategies to ensure that all children have a successful start to school.

WHAT WAS THE PROCESS FOR BUILDING COMMUNITY SCHOOL READINESS TEAMS?

Collaboration was the operative word in the development of a school readiness neighborhood team model in Fairfax County, Virginia, a suburb of Washington, D.C. County and school administrators identified elementary schools that were currently serving a diverse population and with large numbers of families qualifying for free and reduced-price lunch. If the principal believed the project was a good match for their school program, a team was initiated. Team members were identified to represent the school community as well as county resources relevant to families in that community. The teams were brought together at each participating school on a monthly basis to develop shared goals to ensure that all children in their community, regardless of socio-economics, English proficiency or immigrant status, begin school ready to learn.

Four school communities created school readiness teams in the first year of the project, growing to nine by the fourth year. School demographics among the nine schools vary. The number of children who are proficient in English ranged from 31% to 76% and the trend over the past few years shows an increase in children for whom English is not their home language. The numbers of children needing financial assistance has also grown. In one school, 87% of the children attending the school were eligible for free or reduced-price meals.

This collaborative model depends on stakeholders representing diverse perspectives, effective relationships, and strong leadership support in the schools, communities and early education programs. Stakeholders as defined in the Virginia definition of school readiness are inclusive and varied. Bringing stakeholders together to support a school community is complicated. Each community has a unique culture and personality, requiring different connections and relationships with families, schools and children. Teams often included the following stakeholder roles.

Early education center directors provide a perspective of how their program supports children and families before they begin kindergarten.

Preschool teachers include community preschool teachers and school based preschool teachers as part of the pre-k program within the school system.

Family childcare providers provide their unique perspective of both teacher and administrator, working closely with families while caring for their children before they begin school.

Childcare supervisors work for the county government and support early education professionals in child care centers and family childcare homes.

Childcare assistance and referral experts work for the county government and support families in accessing financial assistance to pay for childcare.

Healthy families professionals provide support for overburdened families with infants and young children, through a nationally recognized home visiting model.

Kindergarten teachers connect with children and families when they first begin school.

School administrators provide the wider school perspective and often serve as leaders within the team.

Social workers support children and families and include those who work for the county government, school and Head Start.

School-based Head Start teachers provide the prekindergarten perspective from within the school.

Families provide perspectives on the transition process before and after their children begin kindergarten. The family perspective may include a PTA representative.

Special educators provide information related to the unique transition needs for children who are suspected of or identified with a disability.

An example of stakeholders for one team shows the personalization of teams to address specific resources and needs within a school community.

One school principal and other key community and school representatives invited the following stakeholders to join this team.

- Community preschool directors, faith-based and for-profit
- Special education preschool teachers serving incoming children from neighboring centers
- Local university child care center director
- Family child care providers caring for children in their homes
- Parent of an incoming preschooler or a former kindergarten parent
- Head Start and kindergarten teachers
- School principal
- School parent liaison
- School registrar
- School technology specialist

In order for a school with a diverse community to connect with families, it was imperative that they include as many perspectives as possible in the collaboration process. Many of the community members, such as preschool directors and family childcare providers reported that they had never been to the school although parents often asked for information about the school. Was it a good school? Was it effective in supporting families who had children with special needs or were just beginning to learn English? Would they send their own child to the school? Information and relationships gained through the collaborative team increased the ability of early childhood programs to support families in the transition process.

HOW DID TEAMS CREATE COMMUNITY GOALS?

Teams developed their unique vision of what they believed school readiness could look like in their community. They developed goals to address identified issues that interfered with a successful start to school. Many of the issues highlighted specific challenges for immigrant families and for families with limited financial resources. The work of the teams was to develop strategies that addressed the issues or concerns specific to their community, using the framework provided by the Virginia school readiness definition that included the following components:

Ready Children

Ready children are prepared socially, personally, physically and intellectually within all developmental domains. Ready children, as described in the Virginia definition of school readiness are:

- Comfortable in a group setting
- Excited about learning
- Curious
- Aware of and understands what "school" is about
- Comfortable and familiar with the school before they begin in September

Teams identified issues of concern that may be interfering with children starting school ready to learn. Some of the skills students were missing included: self help skills; vocabulary development; ability to participate in group settings; knowledge of English; following directions and separating from parents.

Integrating diverse stakeholder perspectives provided a unique opportunity to develop strategies for addressing some of these issues and for moving the team closer towards their school readiness goals.

> As a preschool teacher, I believed that the schools wanted children who could walk in a straight line, follow directions, and write their names. I always worried that perhaps I wasn't doing enough to prepare my preschoolers for kindergarten but I wasn't really sure what the kindergarten teachers wanted their students to know or be able to do. So I often made assumptions that reflected what I heard from parents or that I thought was right.

Following this preschool teacher's visit to a kindergarten classroom with a follow-up visit by the kindergarten teacher to her preschool, both teachers experienced a sense of enlightenment. The preschool teacher gained a better understanding of the kindergarten program. Seeing the preschoolers in action in the classroom helped the kindergarten teacher see where her students were coming from.

The kindergarten teacher noticed at the kindergarten orientation that some children she met when visiting the preschool program were not present. Because of the relationship nurtured through the school readiness team, the kindergarten teacher contacted the preschool teacher to develop a contingency plan for the preschoolers and families to visit a kindergarten classroom.

School and community relationships such as these help to bridge meaningful connections for all children and their families as they transition from preschool to kindergarten.

Ready Families

Ready families have adults who understand their role as their child's first and most important teacher. According to the Virginia definition, ready families:

- Provide safe, healthy and nurturing early experiences for their children
- Understand expectations for children when they enter school
- Access information needed so children begin school on time
- Understand their role in the transition process
- Understand their important role in connecting with the school

Reaching families to share school readiness expectations and registration requirements was identified as an important issue for many teams. Goals specific to the needs of immigrant families and those in financial difficulty were developed. Reaching and supporting this population became a focus for many of the teams, as they addressed the following issues:

- Some families may not be aware of importance of early experiences as related to American school expectations.
- Families may not be aware of resources available related to early experiences for children.
- Families may not have access to immunizations and physicals required for school registration.
- Families may not have information about school registration. They may not understand information if is not available in their home language.

Some families do not register their child for school early enough to become familiar with school policies and procedures, and for the school to know who will be starting in September.

Teams were most concerned in identifying strategies to reach families who were not involved with community early care and education programs. As teams began discussions about family readiness, barriers emerged specific to reaching immigrant families. Teams became more aware of the many documents that were currently not being translated for families. A renewed understanding that written communication may not be the best strategy to reach all families became apparent.

One principal shared a strategy she implemented after the second year with a neighborhood school readiness team. She wanted to make sure that families had the information they needed so that children were able to start school on time. She was particularly sensitive to different strategies for communication. Because of the large Spanish speaking population in the school, bilingual school staff called families to ask if they were registered for school this year and if they knew of families with young children who may be sending children to school for the first time. Parents were eager to share this information and in some cases, called a neighbor to tell them that they should come and talk to the teacher from the school. Families who were not previously registered came to visit the school and receive assistance, if needed, in completing the required paperwork.

Ready Schools

Ready schools accept all children and provide a seamless transition to a high-quality learning environment by engaging the whole community. Virginia's definition states that ready schools:

• Know who will be coming to school before they begin
• Integrate the diverse cultures within the school community
• Accommodate the language needs of families
• Welcome all families as partners

Few team strategies identified specific changes for individual schools. The majority of discussion related to the school's need to know who will be attending school, as well as concerns about the early connections between families and schools. Most kindergarten teachers do not have information from preschool programs and families to better understand the children who will be in their classrooms.

As a "Kick-Off" to the 2010–2011 school year, the Freedom Hill Elementary School staff boarded two Fairfax County school buses for a ride that would take over 70 staff members through the neighborhoods where our students live. Reaching out to our families is a critical part of our mission. Freedom Hill draws over a quarter of its students from two large apartment complexes that are adjacent to each other. The administrative team had posted flyers throughout these two complexes inviting the children and families to greet their teachers. We did not tell the staff that we had informed the community.

Early on during our ride we passed a bus stop where two families stood waving to the staff. As the buses drove into the two large apartment complexes we pointed out the bus stop that serves over 180 students. There was no one to be seen. Then we turned the corner and suddenly the sidewalks were lined with children and parents. Older children and former students were coming down the hillsides to greet their elementary school teachers. Younger children were waiting to hug their teachers from previous years and to wonder who would be their teacher this year. Mothers pushing babies in strollers came with their other children in tow. Fathers stood hand-in-hand with their sons and daughters. As the buses came to a stop the teachers clamored off to be hugged, greeted and welcomed to the children's neighborhood. Popsicles were given to the children as everyone enjoyed the fellowship and the unique relationship that exists between families and teachers.

—Tim Stanley, Principal Freedom Hill Elementary School

This school was able to increase their readiness by initiating important relationships between the school and families. Immigrant families increased their belief in the message that the school really wanted to partner with them.

Kindergarten teachers are at a disadvantage when it comes to advanced knowledge about their students. Teachers at other grade levels have access to student test results, reading levels, knowledge of any special needs a child may have and other relevant information passed on by previous teachers. However, kindergarteners begin school basically unknown except for children transitioning from a Head Start preschool program within the public school. These preschool teachers complete a transition form for each student going to kindergarten that identifies the child's strengths, strategies that work well for the child and other pertinent information. The neighborhood school readiness teams adopted the practice of using this same transition form for the family childcare providers and preschool teachers on the team. Preschool families were provided the completed transition forms prior to their child starting kindergarten and were asked to share the transition form with their school principal to assist the kindergarten teacher in planning for their child.

One kindergarten teacher reported that she had tried a number of strategies to assist a child who was having significant problems adjusting to school, but was not successful. She remembered the transition form, re-read it and implemented a strategy suggested by the child's preschool teacher: "He enjoys being a leader. Assign him a leadership role, such as materials manager and allow him to pass out the needed supplies to others." Instant success: the child put his energy to work and became a contributor rather than a distraction in the class!

Schools that are ready for all children actively strive to connect with families, before their children begin school. They are respectful of each family's home language and culture, and are enthusiastic about fostering a partnership that builds on the child's strengths to support their success in school.

Ready Communities

Ready communities work together to promote the children's school and long-term success by providing families affordable access to information, services, high quality childcare, and early learning opportunities. Ready communities, described in Virginia's school readiness definition:

- Provide needed information for families, and access to health, housing and child care resources

- Know who is in the community including civic groups, church groups, early education programs, and health care services
- Work together to support families

Reaching families new to the country presented multiple challenges for the teams. Focusing efforts on increasing their connections with immigrant families before their children started kindergarten, teams addressed issues related to language and culture. The team identified two overarching issues. Communities are not always aware of families with young children within their boundaries and may not have integrated resources available to and easily accessible for families.

For many of the teams, the ready community became a focus for developing outcomes and strategies. With diverse representation on the team, each member could identify individual connections with the larger community and their specific professional roles in supporting change.

Several neighborhood school readiness teams identified a need for children and families to have greater access to health care, specifically health clinics, that could provide physicals and immunizations required for entrance into kindergarten. The few clinics that were available were overwhelmed with the large numbers of children needing their services. Through discussions with county health care providers and directors, two additional health clinics were created to serve children entering school for the first time in need of physicals and immunizations. Notices were sent out through community school readiness teams in English and Spanish. Personal connections helped to spread the word. As a result, no child in Fairfax County was denied entry into kindergarten for that school year because they did not have a completed physical or their required immunizations!

Family childcare providers were identified as important stakeholders in communities. Understanding that many of the families in the community, particularly immigrant families, utilized family childcare, three school readiness teams collaborated to support family childcare providers in their work with children and families. Licensed family providers who cared for children in the school community were invited to a school transition workshop. Team members shared information at these well-attended sessions, relative to their role in the transition process, so that family childcare providers could enhance their program and provide valuable information about school registration requirements with families. Family childcare providers in Fairfax County represented many of the cultures found within the community. Their strong relationships with families of the children in their care provided a link to reaching immigrant families. Family childcare providers felt empowered in their role supporting families through the transition and requested more meetings to discuss school transition. As a result, many teams included a continuation of these meetings in their yearly goals.

The school readiness teams provided opportunities for communities to connect families with schools with other resources. Additionally, the connections each member had with the wider community were invaluable in expanding resources for families. The intricate web of community programs and resources was capitalized on in these communities.

WHAT WERE SOME MUTUAL LESSONS LEARNED?

As the project entered it's third year, trends began to emerge. It was becoming more evident that key components are critical to the success of integrated school readiness teams in providing smooth and successful transitions for all of the children within a community.

Leadership and Encouragement of School Principals

The leader signifies the importance of the task at hand. The principal was seen as a leader not only for the school but also for the entire collaborative team. When leaders value a project as a part of their mission and role, the team is more likely to give the work a higher priority.

Principals were aware of the changing nature of their school population and the impact on school readiness. Through team discussions, and shared information from community stakeholders, some principals were able to work with the community to increase the school's awareness of family perspectives and needs around school readiness. One principal arranged for his teachers to visit a large apartment complex to connect with children and families who would be attending that school, and to send a message to families that they are welcome. Another principal instituted home visits for all teachers in the school, using grant money to fund this important connection between school and families. This same school opened a family resource center and made efforts to establish a safe, welcoming environment for immigrant families new to the school. Another school with a long time, highly effective, parent center invited rising kindergarten families to participate in their weekly parent coffees.

Some principals expressed their belief in the value of the project, but because of other commitments, were unable to provide active leadership on the teams. New principals were particularly stretched in many directions, which made it challenging to add this collaborative project to their already overloaded schedules.

Commitment to Shared Goals by All Stakeholders

Bringing a diverse group of individuals together does not necessarily ensure a shared focus on school readiness and transition. There must be ongoing commitment and buy-in from all stakeholders if the team's goals are to be achieved. In effective teams, stakeholders contributed their perspective to the group, as well as made changes in their work around school readiness.

One community program, Healthy Families,[2] that supports low-income families, added a new focus to their work with families as a result of participation in the school readiness teams. Healthy Families professionals, understanding the value of group play and learning experiences prior to kindergarten, worked with families to identify community early childhood programs that might be available for their children. Some recent immigrants did know about programs such as Early Head Start and Head Start. Understanding what those programs were, why they could be a great resource, and how families could access them, became an added focus for Healthy Families professionals.

Family childcare providers were empowered with new information to support the children and families in their programs, so both children and families were ready for the transition to kindergarten. Visits to schools, integrating transition activities into the preschool classroom, and developing transition portfolios were a few of the strategies these stakeholders implemented to support identified goals.

Prior to children's first visits to their new elementary schools, I talk with families about how to ensure a successful and positive experience for their children. Over the past few years, as a result of discussions on the neighborhood school readiness team, I began to ask families to take photos of the school their child will attend for Kindergarten. I suggested that they take photos of the classroom, teachers, cafeteria, library, and other spaces their child was interested in. Together, I made a transition book with each child, which contained the photos of their new school and thoughts from the child. We talked about the book often using it to create discussions about expectations, fears, excitement, and things to look forward to in kindergarten. When the time came for the child and family to move on to Kindergarten, I gave the transition book and work samples from throughout the year to the family. I also completed a transition form, provided to me through the neighborhood teams, describing the child's strengths and successful strategies I used to support their learning in my class. Families were asked to share these items with the kindergarten teacher to help him or her learn more about their child.

—Tonya Nolan, Pre-Kindergarten Teacher

This teacher integrated lessons from the team into strategies to increase: (1) the child's excitement and comfort with his impending transition to kindergarten; (2) the family's understanding of the child's progress; and (3) the kindergarten teacher's understanding of the children who would be entering his or her class.

Through collaborative workshops, family childcare providers were empowered with information to support the children and families in their programs, so both children and families were ready for the transition to kindergarten. Visits to schools, changing the dramatic play center to a "school cafeteria," and developing transition portfolios are some of the strategies they implemented to support transition goals.

Value of Relationships

Relationships are critical to the success of any collaborative endeavor. They are also essential for children's success in schools. At times, surprising outcomes emerged simply from a connection between two organizations, while at other times these relationships required nurturing and support. Recognizing the need for enhancing connections between immigrant families and schools, teams used the strong relationships being fostered on the neighborhood teams as leverage to help foster family-school relationships.

Schools became more connected with early childhood resources in the community. One school community illustrated this new connection through their support of a family in need. Building on the strong relationship the school already had with the family, as well as community relationships developed through the school readiness team, the school parent liaison was able to connect this family with a team member who was a director of a preschool program. The director, understanding the needs of this family, was then able to convince her board to find money to provide a scholarship so that the child could have a positive early childhood experience, and the mother was able to keep her job.

Schools began seeing more children registered for school in the spring before they begin kindergarten than in previous years. Team relationships enabled programs and schools to get the word out to more families, sooner. Immigrant families received information through their childcare providers as well as county childcare specialists. Families were reached through relationships among team members and invited to school events before their children began school. More families attended kindergarten orientation, where they were provided assistance, often in multiple languages, to complete the needed paperwork. At one school, the school readiness team collaborated to share resources with families at the kindergarten orientation, as well as provide additional language supports to families who needed them.

NEXT STEPS?

It is common knowledge that change is difficult and at this level requires multiple years to achieve. Combining perspectives and systems increases the complexity of this task. Individuals come to the team with an established system perspective, which can often impede the ability to integrate beliefs and ideas across the team. As the project entered the fourth year, teams continued to focus on connecting with the increasing number of children from immigrant families and children living in poor homes. Efforts included: providing shared professional development opportunities; increasing the number of school/community collaborative programs, such as kindergarten orientation, and transition workshops for family childcare providers and community preschool teachers; and enhancing the available information on transition and school readiness. With a growing interest in the program by principals throughout the county in the face of decreasing resources, the project team is looking more deeply at different levels of support that teams might need to create a community infrastructure around individual schools.

The current school readiness teams continue to strategize on how they can better use the collaboration to build a supportive community-wide foundation to ensure children succeed in school. As a result, through closer examination of the school readiness team goals, a renewed focus on the following emerged:

Increasing the awareness of families with young children living within the community so that no child arrives at school without the social and emotional, language and other skills needed to begin a successful year in kindergarten. When businesses, agencies, physicians, health clinics, libraries and other community members are aware of these families and the importance of school readiness, they are better able to share information and resources with families.

Schools cannot do it alone. As schools continue to become stretched for resources and encumbered by increased testing requirements, their abilities to reach out to families and communities before children begin school is decreased, particularly with a growing number immigrant families and poor families. Forming strong partnerships with families and the community will better enable schools to know and understand the families and children in their community, build on their strengths, and understand their culture so they are ready to receive the children in kindergarten. Additionally, partnerships between county government early childhood programs, schools, businesses and community non-profits can work to address financial needs of families in accessing health and education services.

Aligning curriculum between early childhood programs and schools can lead to more children entering kindergarten with the needed abilities, dispositions and knowledge for success. In Virginia, curriculum guidelines have been developed at both the state and county levels. These guidelines are in alignment with kindergarten standards. The school readiness teams provide a venue for exploring these guidelines to develop a common understanding of curriculum that will provide a foundation for children to begin kindergarten ready to learn. The diverse stakeholders of the school readiness team can assist in increasing access to this information as well as developing strategies to support children, families, and early education professionals.

Community school readiness teams are one strategy to enhance the likelihood that all children begin school ready to learn. They provide a window into the community so that schools can better understand and address changing needs of families. If every school community was connected around the idea of school readiness, what might the rewards be for children, families, schools and communities?

Children would have opportunities during their early development, to participate in quality learning experiences, whether at home, in preschool programs or in family child care settings. Children would be nurtured and supported by caring adults who foster a sense of excitement and curiosity for learning. They would visit their school many times before beginning kindergarten, so when the first day of school arrives, they would eagerly enter the classroom, ready for new adventures.

Families would understand their role as "first teacher" beginning with their child's birth. Understanding the importance of language and early literacy, parents would talk with their child and read to them in their home language. They would have connections with community resources to support that role. Families would have access to health care and nutrition education. They will know where their child will be starting school well before they begin, and will visit the school with their child. On the first day of school, parents will say good-by to their children, knowing that the school is ready to welcome all children and the children are excited about starting school.

Schools would know the children and families who will arrive each year. They would have invited them to the school for family events, visits and other family programs. Schools would readily welcome information from preschool teachers, families or family childcare providers, about a child's early experiences and transition information. Increased connections with early education programs in the community would assist kindergarten teachers in meeting the needs of the children. Family culture and language will be embedded within the school culture, so that the school was truly reflective of its population. Schools would reach out to families, in their own languages to build connections and a sense of belonging.

Communities would provide access to resources for families, such as health care, nutrition information, and early literacy exposure. Quality early care and education programs would be available to families in their community. Financial resources would be available to those who need assistance. Flyers about kindergarten orientation would appear in multiple languages in grocery stores, doctor's offices and fast food restaurants. The early childhood community will be united in efforts to support all children.

All children WILL start school. Millions of children began kindergarten in the United States every year. Communities will continue to change. With the knowledge that children of immigrants are the fastest growing component of the child population it is imperative that communities and schools collaborate to support all children and families to succeed in school and life.

NOTES

1. Fairfax Futures collaborates with school, community and business partners in Fairfax County, VA. Their mission is to ensure that young children in the county are well prepared to succeed in school and in life. For more information about Fairfax Futures visit www.fairfax-futures.org.

2. Healthy Families America is a national home visiting program model. It is designed to support families who may be at-risk for adverse childhood experiences. For more information about Healthy Families and the program in Fairfax County, VA, see www.healthyfamiliesamerica.org/home/index.shtml and www.fairfaxcounty.gov/dfs/factsheets/healthyfamilies.htm.

REFERENCES

Belsky, J., Burchinal, M., McCartney, K., Vandell, D., Clarke-Steward, K., Owen, M., (2007). Are there long-term effects of early child care? *Child Development 78* (2). 681–701.

Capps. R., Fix, M., Ost, J., Reardon-Anderson, J., and Passel, J. (2004). *The health and well-being of young children of immigrants.* Retrieved from Urban Institute website: www.urban.org/publications/311139.html.

Executive Summary: National School Readiness Indicators Initiative: A 17 state partnership. (2005, February). Retrieved from the initiative website: www.GettingReady .org. Prepared by Rhode Island KIDS COUNT.

Henderson, A., Mapp, K., Johnson, V., and Davies, D. (2007*). Beyond the bake sale: The essential guide to family-school partnership*s. New York: The New Press.

Schulting, A., Malone, P., and Dodge, K. (2005). The effects of school-based kindergarten transition policies on child academic outcomes. *Developmental Psychology, 41*(6), 860–871.

Virginia's Definition of School Readiness (2008). Retrieved from Virginia Department of Education website: www.doe.virginia.gov/instruction/early_childhood/school_readiness/index.shtml.

ABOUT THE AUTHORS

Debra Fulcher is an educational consultant for the Office for Children where she co-coordinates the School Readiness Teams in Fairfax County at eight elementary schools. As co-coordinator, Debra is involved in the creation of the collaborative model, as well as facilitating and documenting the work of the teams. Debra serves as the local coordinator for the Virginia Star Quality Initiative in the Fairfax Coalition. Debra is a part-time faculty member in the Gradate School of Education at George Mason University where she teaches early literacy and assessment and supervises interns working toward a Master's of Education and/or licensure in Pk-3. She serves as an advisor to early childhood education and special education graduate students. Debra worked for more than 30 years in Fairfax County Public Schools as an early childhood teacher and administrator. She served as the coordinator of the Early Childhood and Family Services department where she served as the director of Early Head Start in addition to developing early childhood curriculum, assessments and staff development for teachers and schools. Debra and her husband, Terry, live in Herndon where they raised their daughter, Lindsay and continue to remain active in the community.

Andrea Sobel, Ed.D. is an educational consultant and co-director of National Educational Consulting Services, LLC. Andrea consults with Office for Children where she co-coordinates the School Readiness Teams in eight school communities in Fairfax, Virginia, Andrea is involved in the creation of the collaborative model, as well as facilitating and documenting the work of the teams. Andrea is a part-time faculty member in the Graduate School of Education at George Mason University where she teaches curriculum, assessment and family courses for early childhood and early childhood special education candidates. She coordinates the field-based university support for the *Teach for America* early childhood cohort through George Mason. Andrea serves as a "master trainer" for the state of Virginia's Quality Initiative. She trains raters and mentors around the state in the quality improvement system. Finally, Andrea continues to provide professional development training in the Washington DC metro area that supports the creation of high-quality programs with an emphasis on enhancing diverse learning communities and promoting strong, effective family-school partnerships. Andrea currently lives in Annandale, Virginia, with her husband Mike, where they raised their two children, Gina and Eric.

Chapter 14

The Power of Family Aspirational Values on Student Academic Success

Jesse Bethke Gomez

Throughout the world, the family is the primary human social organization that prepares the next generation to become members of society. In many ways, where goes the family, so goes the society. Most importantly, parents play the central role in the socialization of their children in regard to family, language, culture, community and education.

John Adams, the second President of the United States of America, in a May 12, 1780 letter to his wife Abigail Adams, articulates his hopes and dreams for their children. He wrote " . . . Our sons ought to study mathematics and philosophy, geography, natural history and naval architecture, navigation, commerce and agriculture in order to give their children a right to study painting, poetry, music, architecture, statuary, tapestry and porcelain" (Butterfield and Friedlander, 1973). As our nation becomes more diverse, educators need to further advance the emerging best practices in language-appropriate and culturally-competent parent engagement skills, in order for all parents to fully realize their own hopes and dreams for their children's future—just like our second president did so long ago.

Years past, I had the opportunity to train with Dr. W. Edwards Deming, on his work entitled "A System of Profound Knowledge." His work provides meaningful insights for us as we examine achievement gaps and how best to address them in America. Deming was a consultant in statistical studies who helped to rebuild Japan after World War II. He is recognized as among the inventors of the Quality Improvement Movement worldwide.

His work was far reaching and vastly encompassing and addressed quality, appreciation for a system, knowledge of variation, theory of knowledge, the psychology of people and optimization. Sub-optimization, from his view causes loss to everyone in a system. Equally important in his view is that measurement can aide us in advancing optimization. While competition can lead to a win-lose structure, he believed that cooperation can lead to optimization. Deming believed that "One is born with a natural inclination to learn and to be innovative" (1990).

As educators we must begin with the assumption that achievement gaps are not limitations to learning by any sub-population group in the United States. I have met leaders in education who mistakenly have looked at achievement gaps as the limitations of learning by an entire racial or ethnic population. Achievement gaps can be understood as indicators of sub-optimization of the true productive potential of our schools, our community and our society. Any effort to eliminate achievement gaps requires two powerful truths that all stakeholders need to contemplate, namely (1) All children, adults and populations have the need and infinite potential to learn; and (2) the family system is the primary human social organization that prepares the next generation of people who become members of society.

In order to eliminate achievement gaps, we need to do two things very well. (1) We need to nurture within our academic institutions, community and society a more cooperative environment for learning through the value of universal commonality—namely that all people have the common need and unlimited potential to learn; and (2) we need to better help parents and families succeed through language-appropriate and culturally-competent parent engagement skills, in order to efficaciously engage and support parents in their role as the primary means of nurturing the value of education with their children. If we do both of these well, all children can better internalize aspirational values of learning from their parents as their own, and find affirmation of these values for themselves at their schools and in their communities.

It seems self-evident that parents play the primary means of socialization for their children. Certainly our schools can't play this role. Yet, if schools do not acknowledge, involve and understand how to engage parents in their children's education, those schools will sub-optimize learning for children. School board members, superintendents, principals, teachers and school support staff have to recognize and support this unique parent role. First and foremost, parents are the means by which the importance of learning as an aspirational value as part of the child's belief system can become internalized by their children.

But even if parents want their children to have education as an aspirational value, their children may not necessarily incorporate this value as part of their belief system. Children are more likely to adopt the aspirational values of their parents when they are treated and cared for with positive supportive parenting skills. Parenting with love, care and sensitivity is essential for children to be more likely to incorporate aspirational values from their parents. The children of parents who are supportive are more likely to conform to parental desires than the children of non-supportive parents, because these children are more likely to adopt parental standards as their own (Lee and Reiss, 1988).

Furthermore, aspirational values and beliefs operate at the unconscious. A person's belief system tends to be the source of inner strength that helps them overcome barriers, and which drives them toward success. This is important when you consider that by age three, the brain is 90% adult size and the emotional, behavioral, cognitive and social foundation for the rest of life is in place (Perry, n.d.). The early childhood years provide for the greatest amount of learning an individual will ever experience and parenting becomes ever more important for the child, the family and the next generation of members of society.

Clearly, parent engagement must be among the areas of innovation in education. This idea is supported by U.S. Secretary of Education Arne Duncan, who has called on educators to learn more about effective parent engagement. He recognizes that parents must be involved if our students are to achieve at greater levels enabling the United States to regain our lead in the highly competitive global economy. Our continual fall as a country in international standings of student achievement is as much a crisis facing our families as it is a crisis facing our educational system in the United States.

Thus there is a critical need for the development of language-appropriate and culturally-competent parent engagement best practices for all families in America. Effective parent engagement holds much promise in helping accelerate academic achievement for all U.S. students and for us to regain the number one standing in all academic areas of achievement in international academic standings.

What are ways we can look at the power of working with parents in their great hopes for their children's future success? The following examples of a Latino family, a community-based organization, the business council of a major corporation and a school district shed light on how we can engage parents at a critical time in our country's history.

1. The Elidio and Carmen Cervantes family, whose educational hopes and dreams for their children to pursue education played a major role in their children's academic achievement and long-term educational success.
2. The Learning Together Program of *Comunidades Latinas Unidas En Servicio* (CLUES) which provides expertise in language appropriate and culturally competent parent engagement skills, volunteers and community resources that facilitate schools' effective partnerships with Latino families to advance their children's educational success.

3. The Hispanic Business Council of Target Stores Inc. which exemplifies innovation and creativity in helping Latino families aspire toward long-term academic success.
4. The St. Paul Public Schools, led by Superintendent Valeria S. Silva, which is strongly committed to engaging families in advancing student achievement.

MR. AND MRS. ELIDIO AND CARMEN CERVANTES

Elidio Cervantes and his wife Carmen came from Mexico to Minnesota many years ago. Elidio worked as a laborer in agriculture in Blue Earth Minnesota. Elidio and Carmen, like so many who immigrate to the U.S., did not graduate from high school. From Blue Earth, the family moved to St. Paul so their seven children could attend school in the metropolitan area.

Education was a strong value for Elidio and he expressed this value to his children as a means for them to achieve a better life. Carmen also held this belief and played a strong, supportive, nurturing role with her children in the daily preparations she made for her children to go to school. When the seven children ranged in ages from one to ten, Elidio passed away. Afterwards, Carmen, as a single parent, worked many jobs and was able to maintain their home.

By the time the older siblings Manuel and Raquel attended high school, they were able to attend a supplemental pre-college educational program. They were both accepted to Macalester College in St. Paul. The remaining five children, Ramona, Jose, Guadalupe, Juan and Ricardo followed Manuel and Raquel to Macalester College. In 1999, TRIO, which refers to three separate federally funded college-related opportunity programs for disadvantaged students, gave their national award, for the first time in their history, to an entire family, the Cervantes family, in recognition that all seven children had graduated from Macalester College. Furthermore, five of the seven siblings continued their education and obtained advanced degrees.

Manuel went on to law school and now serves as an Administrative Law Judge with the State of Minnesota Office of Administrative Hearings. Judge Manuel J. Cervantes, the oldest of the seven children, recalls from the earliest years of his childhood that his father's greatest desire for him and his brothers and sisters was that they pursue education so they could live better lives.

Honorable Judge Cervantes states, "I do remember when I was three or four years old, a very powerful experience with my Dad about going to school. I stood between my Dad's knees and he had very heavy calluses on his hands. I remember holding his hands, which I will never forget were so worn. As I stood there I remember telling my father, 'Dad, I want to have hands just like yours when I grow up.' My Dad looked at me and said 'Son, I don't want you to work so painfully hard with your hands your whole life like I did: I want you to use your mind and get an education.'"

By the time Manuel was nine years old, his father passed away. Judge Cervantes remembers the early years when his mom Carmen was the sole parent. He remembers his mother's role and influence on him about the importance of education: "My Mom would require all of us to do our homework. When it came to the new math and the new division, I remember my Mom crying because she did not know how to help me. Mom could not go to our events after my father died because she was always working. But she did provide the moral support at home about the importance of education for us."

The role that Elidio and Carmen played in the socialization of their children is clear. The aspirations of parents become the aspirations of their children through love and nurturing. In the journey of the Cervantes family, both Elidio and Carmen consistently nurtured their children around the value of education. When Carmen was a single mom, the older siblings helped to support the value of education within the family through their example. The family itself was the sole source for their dream of seeking a better life. These aspirational values became real and internalized means for each sibling to open the door to discover their own potential of attaining a better life. Schools can help all families with such a discovery, but it is the family itself that is the primary and most powerful means by which this human potential is released.

To pursue education so the children could attain a better life was the aspirational value that Elidio and Carmen nurtured within their family system. This value, this aspiration, was expressed day-in, day-out by the parents with their children. These expectations to pursue education became new values within their family and also internalized by their children. Within one generation, this family of new immigrants was able to see their dreams for their children lived out, as each child attained a college education.

THE LEARNING TOGETHER PROGRAM OF CLUES

Since 1995 I have served as President of CLUES which is ranked among the Top 25 Hispanic Non-profit Agencies in America (Hispanic Business Magazine, 2007). The agency is located in Minnesota. Our headquarters in St. Paul includes a training room fittingly named after Carmen Cervantes. We have a major service site in Minneapolis and our Aging Well Center in another location in the City of West St. Paul.

The mission of CLUES is "To enhance the quality of life of Minnesota's Latino community." The agency touches the lives of over 38,000 people with a professional and dedicated staff through a family-centric coordinated-care service delivery model. The agency serves people speaking over 14 languages who come from all over the world to Minnesota seeking a better life. The agency began in 1981 and provides services in behavioral health, aging well, family centric community health promotion, educational, financial literacy, employment and other related economic advancement services. There are over 9,000 volunteer hours annually provided by a mosaic of volunteers who help our newest English language learners become proficient in English as a second language. The Consulate of Mexico in St. Paul is located at our headquarters.

Among our newest services, the Learning Together Program is an educational program designed to help families do better in school and prepare for long-term educational success. The program began as a proactive way to help families prepare for success in academics and in society. I led the research and development phase of this program in examining the multi-generational pattern of acculturation to society made by immigrant Latino families. We examined primary and secondary research on families who evidenced academic accelerated performance within one generation of residing in the United States, such as the Cervantes family. We also looked at the circumstances around families when they were not successful.

Our work led to the discovery that helping parents express and nurture their aspirational values—that encompass education as a major value—with their children can lead to those values becoming internalized by the child.

As we began to research and develop the program, we were struck by a client situation at our agency that typified the need for the Learning Together Program. Many years ago a local county requested that CLUES help a mother whose child was placed into child protective services. An assigned case manager from the Family Services Department of CLUES went to meet with the mother who was from a country in South America. The mother had taken her nine-year-old son out of the Minneapolis Public Schools. The case manager asked the mother why she took her son out school, given that to do so was against the law. The mother replied that when she was a nine-year-old child in her home country, her parents took her out of school in order for her to work to help contribute financially to the family. The mom mentioned that she took her son out of school because she was expecting him to go to work to help their family financially too, just as she had done at nine years old.

I recall, when I was first told of this client situation, thinking that family systems theory would aid us in understanding what was happening at an inter-generational level. We began to see more clearly how values are transferred from generation to generation through the arc of their lives.

We recognized we had to go farther upstream to make a difference for families. We began to think about the significance of learning during the early childhood. We kept reminding ourselves that parents are the primary means of socialization for children. We recognized that we could not play that role as an agency and that schools could not play that role either. By adolescence, children start to formulate ideas about what they would like to do in life both in terms of education and career. These values, once learned, become part of the belief system in the family and are transferred from one generation to the next.

In this light, language-appropriate and culturally-competent family engagement skills take on increasing importance. It is essential that schools, community organizations and the community help parents clarify their aspirational values for their children. We have found parents are more than willing to learn of new ways to better nurture their children's success.

We were able to look back with greater understanding on the situation of the mother who took her son out of school in Minneapolis. Perhaps she didn't know that she was breaking the law. Most likely she was simply operating from what she learned from her parents when she was a child at age nine. Now as an adult those beliefs come to the fore. Her family as a human social organization, and her parents in particular, were the means of preparing her in a societal context of cultural norms that were the means of survival for families in the agrarian sector in her country of origin.

This essential construct of how people become prepared for society, namely through the family, is the cornerstone of the Learning Together Program. Through the development of the program, we began to formalize the essence of language appropriate and culturally competent parent engagement skills for educators in working with Latino families.

The Learning Together Program was created to help newcomer Latino families accelerate student academic success in America. Newcomer families who come to the United States from agrarian and cash-based third-world societies are often confronted by the complexities of first-world society of the United States. The Learning Together Program centers upon a question which we call "the universal question," which arises from the inalienable rights of humanity. The question is one which all families seek to answer: *"What are your hopes and dreams for your children's future?"* When parents are asked this question, they often express deeply personal aspirational hopes for their children's future, notably that their children have a better life.

The Learning Together Program recognizes that language appropriate and culturally competent parent engagement skills in working with the Latino community include:

1. Universal commonality of learning: All parents and children have the need and infinite potential to learn.

2. Universality of aspirations: All parents have hopes and dreams for their children.
3. All parents seek to answer the universal question as best they can in raising their children.
4. Family designed activities at school can help parents learn specific family educational skills as a powerful means to nurture the value of education with their children.
5. Specific teaching on positive, supportive and rewarding parenting skills can help parents nurture healthy child development.
6. Principals and educators can support parents by creating a welcoming school environment where parents can find support from one another in creating community connectedness, knowledge, empowerment and parenting skills that nurture healthy child development.
7. Engaging in school-based educational activities can build bridges between school officials and the Latino community, enabling them to work together to advance long term educational success of Latino children.

Kendall Bruhl, Strategic Planning Project Manager, Education Services for CLUES, who manages the Learning Together Program, sees this program helping to change the dynamics between Latino parents and schools, as schools become a place of support for Latino children and their families. Newcomer Latino families often place their children in schools without any knowledge of available support or community resources. It is important for the schools to reach out to Latino parents with respect and warmth and invite them to learn how the school system works and how to access available resources in the community for themselves and their children. The Learning Together Program works to empower parents so that they can support the educational efforts of their children, establish high expectations for their children, and access community resources for their children's success.

The Learning Together Program is able to replace isolation with community connectedness as parents develop close ties with other parents. They find care, support, community resources and information in the school. In this community of parents supporting one another, they come to feel empowered and valued. Kendall described the progress in a pilot of the Learning Together Program in a school district north of the Twin Cities in the Fall of 2010. This pilot drew 22 parents to the first session. The room was full, and when Kendall first entered the room, there was total silence. There were no conversations among the parents as they did not know one another. To me, this is an indicator of isolation that parents had felt at that time. By the eighth session of the program, the parents were standing with one another in lively conversation. They took the initiative and organized a potluck supper by themselves to take place at the end of the program. The parents developed friendships and they have continued to meet on Friday nights at the school.

Kendall saw the impact on the participants of the program. One father thanked Kendall at the end of program, telling her she initially was not sure he could read to his children in English since he was just beginning to learn to read in English himself. His children were reading from English-language books, and began to bring these books home from school. He further stated that sitting together with his child, he began to try to sound out words that he saw on the page. His child also read to him the words that he did not know. This was a collaborative experience. This father was grateful for participating in the Learning Together Program because it brought him to work directly with his children educationally and helped him to realize that language does not have to be a barrier to that work.

Kendall has witnessed how parents have responded favorably to the program because it helps them attain their hopes and dreams. When asked about their aspirations for their child's future during the first session, most parents respond that they want their child to attend college. Yet they don't know how to help their children to realize that dream. The parents want their children to become successful contributors to society and are grateful for the Learning Together Program for helping them attain the skills to support their children's success.

Kendall talks with parents on areas that they want to learn about supporting them through the program. The program is comprised of eight sessions, generally one session per week. One of the topics covered in a session is on "Behavior and Discipline" in which parents are encouraged to reflect upon their upbringing, how they were disciplined as children, and what the effects of this discipline have been on their lives. Parents are provided with training on the conscious connection of how the discipline they use is related to how they were raised as children. Parents are provided constructive, supportive and nurturing parenting skills they can encourage and better guide their children while increasing their child's self-worth.

Kendall notes that parents are enthusiastic in using community resources to help them help their families. During this particular session, a representative from the local library is invited to come and speak to parents. Kendall has found that public libraries are an untapped resource for Latino families. Parents are able to obtain a library card and check out free resources such as books, tapes, and DVDs to help them reinforce their children's literacy and development. Many libraries have a "homework help" service and a tutoring service through the libraries.

Kendall also sees another topic area that is making a difference for families is "Family Health." She has found that newcomer Latino parents want information on nutrition and exercise to combat the increasing rates of obesity and diabetes they see occurring in their children. The program teaches parents how to develop healthy habits, pursue regular exercise and how to incorporate fresh foods into their family diet. Parents are asked to complete an analysis of how much exercise they get and of the foods that they eat. They then compare their diets to the Food Pyramid. Many families lack sufficient servings of fruits, vegetables and dairy products. They are taught about exercise and a wholesome diet to maintain a healthy weight.

Kendall sees how happy children are that their parents are with them in school. The Learning Together Program provides a session for parents and a related one for their children at the same time. The children see that their parents are engaged at school to support them academically. This leads to enhanced parent involvement at home, and pursuing activities together as a family.

At one session, parents were asked about their hopes and dreams for their children and the children were asked to draw pictures of what they wanted to be when they grow up. The children were so excited that they went running into their parents' session holding up their drawings shouting, "Look, this is me; I'm a doctor!" or, "Here's me as a vet working with animals!" or "Look at me, I'm an astronaut with my own spaceship!" Parents learn to encourage their children to dream. Parents see the power children begin to have in nurturing their own hopes and dreams for themselves, too.

THE HISPANIC BUSINESS COUNCIL OF TARGET CORPORATION

The Hispanic Business Council of Target Corporation exemplifies innovation and ingenuity. Liz Brennhofer, Senior Manager of Community Relations with Target, is also the Chairperson of the Council. The Hispanic Business Council has the aim of fostering career growth and providing role models, offering on-site opportunities for professional development and networking. Ms. Brennhofer shared with me that education is important to Target and to their team members.

The Council is committed to supporting Latino parents as they prepare their children for future academic success. The Council organizes various programs including Saturday events that bring families together to gain information, inspiration and support. One event hosted by the Council in Minneapolis included Team Members serving as volunteer hosts to provide role models for the Latino community. CLUES acted as a liaison to the community, encouraging family participation and helping to plan the day. This fun filled Saturday included a performance by local theater group *Teatro del Pueblo*.

Target's Council also partnered with CLUES on a Book Fiesta for the entire community, held at CLUES sites in Minneapolis and St. Paul. Hundreds of families participated in the program that included story time, interactive learning games, free books in different languages, as well as refreshments.

The Council looks for opportunities to serve as volunteers in helping families, notably parents, aspire toward success, so that their children become even more motivated to do well in school. In this way Target shows how corporate America in encouraging and supporting the engagement of parents in their children's academic and educational success.

THE ST. PAUL PUBLIC SCHOOLS

Many parents like the Cervantes' have high aspirations for their children, but some are simply not able to overcome the obstacles they face—from financial concerns to lack of information—without support. Imagine if all school board members, school administrators, principals, teachers and assistants understood language-appropriate and culturally-competent parent engagement skills, valuing the parents' aspirations and helping them achieve these goals. We need to look at emerging and innovative efforts that employ language appropriate and culturally competent parent engagement within the school system. Such a commitment requires informed leadership, strategic focus and constancy of learning by a school district. St. Paul Public Schools in St. Paul Minnesota is an emerging example.

Valeria S. Silva was selected as the Superintendent of the St. Paul Public Schools (SPPS) in 2009. Her leadership is focused on best practices in a strategic framework that recognizes all children have the unlimited potential to learn. Valeria Silva recognizes the important role that parents play in the education of their children and how schools can best engage families.

The St. Paul Public Schools budget serves nearly 40,000 students, making them the second largest school district in Minnesota. There are over 103 languages and dialects spoken by school families. The vision statement for the St. Paul Public Schools includes the following: *Imagine your family welcomed, respected and valued by exceptional schools.*

Superintendent Valeria Silva believes that throughout her experience as an educator, she has come to know that all parents want the best for their kids. When parents see that the St. Paul Public Schools cares about them and their children, parents are more likely to become involved with their children. She believes that engaging parents is among the most important requirements for academic success (Silva, 2010).

Superintendent Silva recognizes that in order for all children to work toward improved academic performance, schools need the right teachers, need to be energized and those schools need to be engaged with parents. She sees this last requirement as the hardest to achieve as a community. Yet in her view, the St. Paul Public Schools has the responsibility to reach out, to invite, to engage and to work with parents toward the academic and educational success of their children.

Superintendent Silva recalled from her days as a teacher the difference that involved parents made in the lives and academic performance of their children. As a principal, she saw how parents involved on an ongoing basis provided insightful input to the school. Her direct experience with parents has given her the insights needed to increase involvement of families in the district.

Superintendent Silva sees that schools in the United States can play an important role through greater partnership and engagement with parents to help families have the needed conversation about educational expectations for academic success. She sees that schools can play an important role with the family in helping parents making better informed decisions about education related matters.

The Office of Family Engagement and Community Partnership at the St. Paul Public Schools (SPPS) was created as part of Superintendent Valeria Silva's vision of facilitating greater involvement with families by the SPPS. Valeria looks for opportunities to directly reach out to parents meeting with parents from all parts of the District. Valeria has discovered that by regular voice mail messages to the home telephones of SPPS families, she has become a familiar voice to many. She notes that she is pleasantly surprised by the number of times she is stopped by parents who personally thank her for caring about them and their children. As Superintendent, Valeria sets a leadership style, tone and commitment for the District to engage parents in a mindful and welcoming manner; in this way, more parents feel safe and respected by the local schools which educate their children.

Superintendent Silva sees challenges facing families such as the use of text messaging replacing face-to-face communication between parent and child. She is concerned that parents sometimes find out more about their children from their children's social media web sites than through the direct conversations.

Superintendent Silva wants all teachers to better engage parents of their students and learn more about their home life. She sees that, for example, the teacher needs to know if the family is homeless and might be staying at a shelter. Her renewed efforts are leveraging the many years that the St. Paul Public Schools has invested with parents.

Pablo Matamoros is a District Liaison with the SPPS The Office of Family Engagement and Community Partnership. Pablo, who is a licensed teacher, meets each month with Latino parents at monthly Latino Parent Advisory Committee meetings.

The parent involvement in these District-wide monthly meetings has increased dramatically in recent years, to 1,726 in 2009–2010—a 90% increase over 2006–2007 (St. Paul Public Schools, 2010). Pablo believes the increased participation is because the meetings have an educational focus on topics that matter greatly to Latino parents. Pablo and his staff provide an evening dinner and create a welcoming, safe and respectful environment for families. Another key factor is that the leaders of the meetings talk in the language of parents. They see their parents as their customers and they treat parents with respect. They constantly ask parents to help them do better.

Pablo also believes that community collaboration with organizations such as *Comunidades Latinas Unidas En Servicio*, the Consulate of Mexico in St. Paul and others have helped Latino families considerably at the St. Paul Public Schools. Pablo is grateful that the CLUES' Learning Together Program helps Latino parents at the local school level. For Pablo, the program provides the social emotional support parents need in supporting their children at school.

CONCLUSION

We need to nurture within our academic institutions, communities and society a more cooperative environment for learning through the value of universal commonality—namely that all people have the common need and unlimited potential to learn and grow. We need to better support parent and family success through language appropriate and culturally competent family engagement skills. We must recognize that parents are the primary means of nurturing the value of education with their children. If we do these things well, all children can better internalize these aspirational values of learning as their own in their homes, and find affirmation of these values for themselves at their schools and in their communities.

We have only begun as a society to discover the power that parents can play in nurturing aspirational values with their children. Education of America's children with greater involvement by parents who express their hopes and dreams in supportive and loving ways can lead to more children who internalize these hopes and dreams as their own. A journey in which all parents are able to fully realize their aspirations for their children's educational success in schools, a journey in which communities and a society recognize the need and unlimited potential all people have for learning, can allow us to advance a more just, civil and prosperous America.

REFERENCES

Butterfield, L.H. and Friedlander, Marc, eds. (1973). *Adams Family Correspondence.* Vol. 3; *April 1778—September 1780*, Cambridge: Harvard University Press, Belknap Press.

Deming, W. Edwards. (1990). A System of Profound Knowledge, *The North Central Deming Management Forum*, p. 10.

Lee, Gary R., and Reiss, Ira L. (1988). *Family Systems in America* (4th Edition). Holt, Rinehart and Winston, p. 339.

Perry, B. (n.d.). *Biological Relativity.* Teacher: Scholastic. www.teacher.scholastic.com/professional/bruceperry/biological_relativity.htm.

Silva, V., personal communication, December 3, 2010.

St. Paul Public Schools (2010). Latino Consent Decree/Parent Advisory Committee Attendance Report 2006–2010.

St. Paul Public Schools. (n.d.) Vision Statement. boe.spps.org/Mission_and_Ends.html.

Target Corp. (n.d.). Diversity Business Councils, Encouraging communication and education. www.target.com/diversity.

Top Twenty-Five Non-profit Hispanic Agencies in America (2007). *Hispanic Business Magazine.*

ABOUT THE AUTHOR

Jesse Bethke Gomez is president of *Comunidades Latinas Unidas En Servicio* (CLUES), a leading provider of behavioral health and human services for Minnesota's Latino population and among the Top 25 Hispanic non-profit agencies in America (*Hispanic Business Magazine* 2007). Jesse's professional experience includes clinical system redesign for healthcare, business consultancy for international business, government, education, non-profit and private companies, advanced executive leadership development, international relations, health and human service administration, and fundraising, where he has raised over $50,000,000. Jesse is among the "100 Most Influential Healthcare Leaders in Minnesota" (MN Physicians Publication Sept, 2008), and the first Minnesota recipient of the Reconocimiento Ohtli Recognition from the country of Mexico (2006). He is a national Kellogg Fellow, an alumnus from the University of North Carolina–Chapel Hill as an Emerging

Leader in Public Health, an alumnus from the Minnesota Executive Program for Advance Strategic Leadership from the Carlson School of Management, University of Minnesota, and a Presidential Scholar Recipient from Elizabeth Dole, then president of the American National Red Cross. Jesse trained with international leaders Tor Dahl, chairman emeritus of the World Confederation of the Productivity Sciences, and Dr. Edwards Deming. He holds a Masters of Management and Administration degree from Metropolitan State University, where he was Alumnus of the Year in 2008, and a Bachelor of Arts degree from the University of Minnesota. He serves on the board of trustees of the University of Minnesota Amplatz Children's Hospital and has served on numerous boards of directors, including The Minneapolis Foundation and Blue Plus of Blue Cross and Blue Shield of Minnesota. Jesse also has composed and arranged a music score for orchestra entitled "Mi Vida Amor!" Jesse lives with his wife Raquel in Woodbury, Minnesota.

Global Perspectives

Chapter 15

Healing a World of "Terror" by "Valuing Diversity"

A New Curriculum to Encourage Deeper Understanding and Mutual Respect

Amineh Ahmed Hoti

I was traveling from the place of my birth, Pakistan, where I had been conducting fieldwork for my research on Muslim Pukhtun women. I landed in
Washington, D.C., to visit my parents before I returned to the United Kingdom, to finish work on my PhD thesis at Cambridge University. Then the
world, from where I stood, changed. My husband called me from Pakistan to
tell me about the horrific events of 9/11. Switching on the news and watching television that day was like watching a dramatic blockbuster movie such
as *The End of Time* or *Armageddon*—the images were unbelievable and
although it felt like fiction, my heart sank at the horror and impact of what
was happening—could this actually be reality?

News started pouring in pointing to Muslim names and links and the then-
President of the United States of America was using dangerous and explosive
mediaeval terms such as "a crusade" and "war" against the "axis of evil."
The next few weeks, months and even years were witness to news headlines
such as: WAR ON TERROR or more regularly: RED ALERT. Sensationalist
headlines had the effect of scaring both the Western public from people with
Muslim names and cultures and successfully alienating many Muslims from
mainstream society, thus making even peace-loving Muslims feel threatened
and defensive about their identity and cultures.

As a Muslim living in the U.K. and visiting the U.S. regularly, I had not
experienced racism but in subtle ways. I was often asked questions like, "where
are you from? France?" and when I would say "Pakistan" this would be the
end of our conversation on the part of the person who had asked the question.
I wasn't surprised, as Muslims in general and Pakistan in particular received
negative press in a regular almost systematic way in the media. My husband

who has coloured eyes and looks European (or "Italian," as he has been told) always received a cordial welcome from strangers who did not know that he was a Pukhtun from Pakistan, but when once when he told an elderly retired British officer whom he took care of in his carehome that he went to Pakistan during the Christmas break, he replied: "Did you bring back a bomb!"

Anxiety and general distrust heightened after 9/11. There was widespread confusion about "The Other" and other cultures in general and about Muslims in particular. As an educator, I knew that schools had a responsibility to help students learn the value of respecting "Others." In a post 9/11 world, schools and teachers worldwide wishing to convey to their pupils the values of good citizenship needed to introduce new and cutting-edge curricula, encouraging mutual respect and understanding through a study of other cultures from their own perspective.

To support this educational effort, I prompted Dr. Edward Kessler—a pioneer in education and interfaith dialogue, and whom I worked with in Cambridge then—to create and print a second edition of a learning resource for teachers and students called *Valuing Diversity: Towards Mutual Respect and Understanding*. Although the idea of understanding and respecting other cultures and peoples is a common theme in this learning resource, this edition began with a focus on the three Abrahamic faiths of Islam, Christianity and Judaism, adding Islam to the initial 2002 edition which focused on only two religions. The book was distributed to more than 2000 (out of 5200) schools in the UK; in addition, copies have been requested and distributed to schools in the United States and South Asia.

Valuing Diversity is aimed at pupils aged 11-16, a key time when children begin to understand the concept of respect for "The Other" and just before college when students may encounter fellow students and staff from other cultures and faiths. It contains a range of innovative and stimulating classroom activities which encourage good citizenship, dialogue, and understanding. Dr. Kessler, the founder of two successful interfaith centers in Cambridge, emphasizes:

> Teachers today have a huge impact on childrens' lives not only in providing a first-class education but in their personal and social development as citizens. Ours is a multicultural, multireligious society and it is vital that teachers are handed the resources to guide children in this development.

Valuing Diversity explores encounters between people of different faith and cultural groups. "It is based on the principle that we are all uniquely different as individuals and communities, but we are also all connected and have shared values. Our lives are shaped by those whom we meet. Although we remain essentially ourselves, our encounters with others change us. An encounter requires that there is willingness on each side to participate. The process involves an exchange and, hopefully, a dialogue. It involves listening as well as speaking" (*Valuing Diversity*, 2).

The book aims to equip pupils for "fruitful encounters" between individuals from different communities, "Pupils are encouraged to understand others on their own terms, as they wish to be understood." This is a constructive and positive attitude I aimed to promote in my teaching at Cambridge and study of Islam and Muslim societies and I called this approach looking at culture from "the inside out."

FROM "THE INSIDE OUT": A PERSONAL REFLECTION ON MY JOURNEY TO VALUING DIVERSE CULTURES

My subjects at school and university—sociology and anthropology—encouraged me to value one of the important tools of dialogue that we teach in *Valuing Diversity*—i.e. how to "foster the development of positive attitudes towards the religious beliefs and cultural identity of others" (p. 4). I, therefore, approach my work from the point of view of an anthropologist. Anthropology, in a nutshell, is the study of different cultures. The very subject of anthropology has gone through a great deal of refinement and change which is significant for the purposes of understanding and respecting cultures today. It began as a subject used by early Europeans—sometimes colonialists—to analyse and deconstruct society, often so-called "primitive" societies. Although these societies were described in great detail they were said to be "savage" and other derogatory terms and phrases were commonly used to describe the peoples of different cultures—the most notable example in anthropology is Bronislaw Malinowski's extensive book *The Sexual Life of Savages* (1929).

Later anthropologists, especially those studying their own societies, argued that it is important to see a society and its people from their own perspective and not impose on it the values and ideas of other (dominant) cultures. This way of *seeing* gave the people studied a greater degree of respect. These scholars were often indigenous anthropologists who introduced a more empathetic and, more importantly, "insider's perspective."

MY "INSIDER'S PERSPECTIVE"

My subject and personal background helped shape my ideas about the importance of valuing diversity and respecting people different from myself. As a Muslim woman studying my own society for my PhD research, I was able to interview an exceptionally large number of men, women and children to attain insight into an often misunderstood and sometimes misrepresented society: Pukhtuns from northern Pakistan, specifically, and Pakistan in general. Earlier anthropologists (often male and European) had argued that women were "invisible," "marginal" and "ghost-like" in this society—known as one of the largest tribal societies of the world—and that men played a key role in almost all aspects of political life.

Yet when I undertook fieldwork and research on the Pukhtuns for nearly a decade, I found that women played the most essential role by maintaining the very fabric of society—political and social networking—in their key dealings with other people by giving and receiving money during *gham-khadi* (events of *rites de passage*, such as funerals and weddings). Women, the Pukhtuns told me, are the key players in *zeest-rozgaar* which translates as "The work of life" or "The employment of life." If women determined who to maintain social relations with and who to drop relations with, they were active agents in their choice of maintaining a pattern in their social network which impacted directly on their husbands' or fathers' political standing and votes. In some current cases women decided to maintain relations with their own family (kin) and avoid relations with their husband's family (affines). So then, how, I wondered, did European male anthropologists describe Pukhtun Muslim women as "marginal"?

The problem was obvious to me after research and reading on the area: it was a question of methodology—in a strictly segregated society, "outsiders" were given little if any access to women and the women's section of the house. Male guests were often entertained in the men's house called the *hujra,* which is very clearly a male environment and not an appropriate space for "respectable" women. It was, therefore, a question of perspective: whereas male European anthropologists saw and defined Pukhtun society for the last three to four decades as political and male-dominated, an insiders' perspective gave me (and through my work,[1] readers on this area) a completely different picture of the very same society—where women were dominant, vocal and active deciders in their own social and political environment.

There was always another side to old accepted facts and stories. This was a valuable lesson that was reinforced in my mind.

LESSONS FROM MY OWN BACKGROUND

The association of Islam with violence in the West after 9/11 was something deeply disturbing for me; I understood and saw the gentler face of Islam through the love and compassion of my own Muslim parents, and heard the kind and lovingly parental voice of God in the Quran and other revealed books (Hebrew Bible and the New Testament). God says that He loves us 99 times more than our mother, and the Prophet of Islam is said to be "a mercy to all mankind." Jesus, another key figure in Islam, stood out as a role model for his mercy and compassion—a theme of God commonly emphasized in all three Abrahamic faiths: Judaism, Christianity and Islam.

My father, in his early youth, witnessed the partition of India and Pakistan in 1947—the senseless and brutal killings of Muslims, Hindus and the diverse people of the area did not make sense to a small boy who had lived side-by-side with people of different colours and cultures in a vast land called "the Indian Sub-Continent." His local friends, house and land had changed for other friends and land, amidst the change, my father learnt to hold on to his own values of respecting and loving people even those different to him as he learned to see them all as God's creation. Being a mother myself, I know that the best way a child can learn is through watching their own parents: for many years after partition, when some people had no home to live in or food to eat, they would turn up at my father's parents' home in Karachi. My father says, "Our rather large official Karachi house was shared by dozens of strangers who would turn up shattered and dazed sometimes with chits in their hands saying, 'We were told to go to Ahmed Sahib and he will help you!' My mother personally made sure they had food and a place to sleep. We had two tennis courts with tent-like structures for them."

Such altruistic acts of compassion were something keenly observed by my father as a young boy and impacted his attitude towards others for the rest of his life. With that foundation, my father, Akbar Ahmed, has spent more than three decades building relations in the public arena between people of different cultures and faiths. He currently holds the Ibn Khaldun Chair of Islamic Studies at the American University and has won many global awards for his interfaith efforts. The lesson he passed on to us in more than one hundred ways during the course of his enlightened *shamma*-like life is: hatred and violence continually create further circles of destruction; but the values of love and compassion are far higher, and the only way to heal our fractured world.

The importance of respecting diversity came from our families' personal encounters with different peoples from the world while living in South Asia, Europe and America. (My father was a professor at numerous institutions including Princeton, Harvard and Cambridge Universities—I thus made friends with the children of my parents' colleagues from diverse cultures and countries and value my friendships.) This helped us to learn to respect diversity and not take for granted the wonderful colours of the world and nuances of cultures and peoples. We began to see this as something that is an essential component of making our shared world a richer place—after all the variety in our world (in, for example, animals, fish, plants, humans and so forth) is something to marvel and wonder at.

Growing up in South Asia—home to more than several hundred languages—was one more wonder. After all, for me as an anthropologist, language was essential to understanding culture. While we grew up learning fluent English in a post-colonial context in South Asia, our own mother and national tongues were so varied and multiple. I began to appreciate this further when I went for higher studies to the U.K. While most local people in the U.K. spoke English and had some exposure, at school, to at least one more foreign language, in South Asia, by contrast, we grew up with a background of being exposed to multiple languages (in my case more than six to seven languages: English, Urdu, Pashto, Persian/Farsi, Arabic, French and recently even some Hebrew).

INSIGHT FROM THE U.K.: DECONSTRUCTING STEREOTYPES, CONNECTING PEOPLE AND BUILDING UNDERSTANDING

The U.K. in general is a rich and diverse society. Although it benefits from being labelled as cosmopolitan, multi-cultural and multi-religious, officially it is a "secular" society. Hence, when I held one of my first major conferences at the Guild Hall with senior members of the three Abrahamic faiths and senior professors from the faculty of divinity at the University of Cambridge, the Lord Mayor, Councillor John Hipkins, our host, insisted I continue with this "excellent and good" project. He said he gave the project his full support, but I should avoid using any term such as "religion" in my invitation so as not to give the impression that the Mayor—a representative of the secular government—was hosting a religious event.

Yet, with the influx and migration of people from all over the world, especially from the Abrahamic cultures, there are now many Muslims, Christians and Jews living side-by-side in the U.K. After the terror attacks on public areas and innocent citizens on 9/11 in the U.S. and 7/7 in the U.K., many interfaith organizations have mushroomed from amongst these groups overnight. Meeting people from these faiths with so many similarities and yet differences, to make each unique, was a means of building relations and healing a multi-cultural society. There was no better way to do this, I thought, than to engage in learning about "Others" through scholarship, personal encounter and teaching the subject. This inspired the development of the 2008 edition of *Valuing Diversity*. The lessons encouraged in *Valuing Diversity* of deeper understanding, constructive dialogue and critical reading of certain problematic texts and the media were regularly implemented in my teaching at schools and university in the U.K.

Over the last decade, I have had the opportunity to lecture to and teach various levels of students at Cambridge, both at the University and outside, from the private and public sectors of education, and from nursery schools to senior students at the University. At Lucy Cavendish College, the only college for women over 21 at the University of Cambridge, I set up the Society for Dialogue and Action with the support of many whom I would call "interfaith ambassadors." From here we worked at the grass-roots with the general public, women from diverse classes and young people at schools. We offered courses, published teaching material for schools and held major conferences with the blessings of the Queen of England, the Archbishop of Canterbury, Sir Rowan Williams, HRH Prince Hassan of Jordan, Professor Akbar Ahmed and the Chief Rabbi, Sir Jonathan Sacks. All of these figures have spent a lifetime connecting diverse people and different cultures in an attempt to increase mutual respect and deepen understanding between different peoples and cultures of our shared world.

The Archbishop of Canterbury launched *Valuing Diversity* at Michaelhouse in Cambridge in 2008, stating, "Its theme of mutual respect and understanding is an important one and in offering practical and thought provoking material for use by teachers, it meets a real need. Because it is rooted in the experience of Christian, Jews and Muslims, it has a realism which is of particular value." The event was hosted by the three interfaith centres in Cambridge which sponsored the learning resource book.

Among the sponsors was the first-ever Centre for the Study of Muslim-Jewish Relations (CMJR). Working with this Centre as the Director was one of the most notable educational projects I have engaged in. I had the opportunity to set up a Cambridge University diploma course at the new Centre, outlining it and then teaching relevant parts of it for three years. The students in "Islam and Muslim Perceptions of 'The Other'" ranged from young teenagers to imams and rabbis. After the first term, the Centre offered the second module, "Judaism and Jewish Perceptions of 'The Other'" and the third term was about finding solutions to conflict and the way forward.

As I was one of the tutors on the first course, in line with *Valuing Diversity's* critical reading of problematic texts, I argued that it is important to study the historical relationship between Muslims and "Others" and examine the perception of each about the "Other" by examining scholarly literature (and the media). It is important to confront the ghosts of the past which defined the image of "The Other" from our different points of view, deal with them and put them aside to begin afresh in a positive constructive way to avoid the same mistakes.

This principle is an important element of *Valuing Diversity* and is the foundation of Activity 7: "Looking at stereotypes in literature." The learning resource looks at excerpts from two books: *The Merchant of Venice* by William Shakespeare and *Does My Head Look Big in This?* by Randa Abdel-Fattah. Both are highly sensitive topics for the faith communities concerned and illustrate for students how to critically discuss and evaluate problematic texts in class. One teacher in an international school in Pakistan who used the learning resource notes how the book helped students confront their own stereotypes and negative perceptions of "The Other":

> In exploring ways to integrate literature, history, and the study of stereotypes, I implemented a lesson from the *Valuing Diversity* Teachers' Handbook concerning how Jews and Muslims are portrayed in classic and modern literature. One of my male Muslim students stuttered and giggled when reading aloud "I am a Jew" from Shakespeare's *The Merchant of Venice*. Other male students giggled with him. I asked him to proceed with the reading. After he finished the passage, we talked about the response from the students and why they thought that happened. I then asked if they knew students in our school who would have refused to even read the line, and they all agreed they could name some. We then discussed the issues behind the struggle and misunderstandings between Jews, Muslims and Christians, and how three faiths from the same background could grow apart in such drastic ways. This provided a forum for understanding the similarities among the three faiths and how the role of extremism in any ideology can affect the views and perceptions of the whole.

TEACHING FROM AN "INSIDE OUT" PERSPECTIVE

Personal encounter is another key factor in helping break down stereotypes. This moves beyond studying media and texts to interpersonal dialogue. In my own experiences, I've learned that not just students, but senior teachers can harbour stereotypes. In a post 9/11 context in Cambridge, I met the English mother of my son's friend—a senior school English teacher with a Catholic background and a Protestant husband who is a priest. When I invited her in for green tea to my kitchen the first questions she asked me, if I did not mind, were, "Is Islam a moon religion? And are Muslims terrorists?" Although her questions seemed to confirm stereotypes about Islam, I was glad that she had been so directly honest and brought out all the ghosts from the cupboard, rather than walk around with them; now we could begin to deconstruct these stereotypes and overcome them step-by-step, question-by-question—a way that would lead us to better understanding of our different cultures and consequently becoming good friends. I explained that the core belief was in the

One and Only God (of Abraham) and working good deeds or righteousness. The term "Islam" is from *salaam* meaning "peace" and a Muslim is one who submits to God as did Abraham, Moses and many others. Some people who we hear about in the media, who happen to be Muslim, were violent due to political reasons and lack of broad good-quality education in their homelands causing extreme poverty and multiple deep frustrations combined with ignorance of their own sacred texts.

We spent more than three hours and many more days discussing this topic and my friend soaked up everything I had to say about Islam and perceptions of "The Other," at one point saying with several nods, "Jesus said that too." Her keenness in asking all problematic questions created a space for dialogue and discussion and a willingness to learn. Her willingness to listen and learn about "The Other," in this case, me and my kind, allowed her to become deeply understanding and sympathetic to my perspective. We have become the best of friends and I value our friendship deeply. The initial encounter between us had led us on the road to true Socratic dialogue, deeper understanding, mutual respect and finally true friendship across cultures.

As my friend's husband is a priest at Ridley Hall at the University of Cambridge, he had asked her to send me an invitation to teach a course to Christian youth workers on Islam at the Centre for Youth Ministry (CYM). The Muslim tutor on Islam had to withdrew at the last minute and there were few, if any, articulate and experienced teachers on Islam available to teach. I accepted with some reluctance as I was seven months pregnant and on leave from work, but I did not want to leave a gap in the teaching on Islam for these students.

The teaching room was packed with an array of young students aged 21 and above during a bright English summer day. I began by briefly introducing myself and our topic of Islam and then asked students to write on the board anything that comes to mind when thinking about Islam, whether positive or negative. Each student was encouraged to participate. Some of the positive points about Islam in their minds were: "devotion," "respect and fear of God," "modesty," "hospitality," "community" and "inclusion"; and the negative points were: "*Jihad* (Holy War)" (which they put right at the top of the list), "Terrorism," "honour killings," and "gender oppression." The negative were all clearly stereotypes of Islam which I had heard time and again and reflected in some writings on Islam, the media, and other general reporting on Islam and Muslim societies.

During the course of the class, we discussed the important difference between the religion of Islam and the diversity of Muslim cultures and human behaviours, which the media often failed to point out when flashing fast images of incidents in the Muslim world. We examined different books including passages from the Quran about the Abrahamic faiths or the *ahl-e-kitaab* (People of the Book). Few of them had seen the Quran and none had ever heard of the following passages: "Those who believe and those who follow the Jewish (scriptures), and the Christians and the Sabians, any who believe in Allah[2] and the Last Day and work righteousness, shall have their reward with their Lord, on them shall be no fear, nor shall they grieve." (Quran, Surah 2; Verse 62); "And dispute ye not with the People of the Book [i.e. Christians, Jews, etc], except in the best way, unless it be with those of them who do wrong . . . (V)erily this Ummah (body of people/community) of yours is a single Ummah and I am your Lord and Cherisher . . ." (Quran, Surah 23; Verses 51-52).

These verses were an eye-opener to many of my Christian students who were training to be youth workers in the community—whom I saw as the healers of society. They, like my friend, had thought of Islam as a separate inexplicable religion and as Christians they told me they thought the only way to salvation, in their concept of religion, was through Christianity. Yet here was the Quran in which a just and loving God accepted not just Muslims, but good believing Jews, Christians, Sabians and others by rewarding them and keeping them safe and free from fear and grief (Quran, Surah 2; Verse 62). Step-by-step, we tackled each stereotype and caricature of Islam and Muslims and it gave the students a safe and open environment to ask all the deep-seated questions that had troubled them but never before been answered for them.

For the exercise examining stereotypes in literature (similar exercises are found in activity 7 in *Valuing Diversity*, page 19), I divided the students from the Youth Ministry into four groups and we examined texts on Islam particularly those that had come to be seen as classic and used as reference material on Islam. After a long period of cross-comparisons of these works and in-depth discussion, one of the most important books the students chose as their favourites to challenge their own stereotypes of Islam was by Bauben on the *The Image of the Prophet Muhammad in the West* (1996). In this PhD thesis, the author argues that the most eminent Arabic scholars of Islam who were said to know more about the 'Moslims" and were more "knowledgeable on Islamic matters than most Arab scholars" (*The New Encyclopaedia Britannica*, 1974, p. 615)— were mainly from a Judeo-Christian background. David Samuel Margoliouth, William Muir and William Montgomery Watt were the flag bearers of defining their version of Islam which became the accepted version of Islam in the West. Sir William Muir's extensive work in the 19th century became the classic reference material on Islam and was acclaimed in the West for its "objectivity" and "sobriety of judgement" yet uses "insulting language" such as his implication that the Prophet used negative tactics including "plunder" which the "wild Arabs" found irresistible (Bauben: 26). Margoliouth, Chair of Arabic at the University of Oxford, in the second half of the 19th century describes the Quran (which Muslims see as "the sacred word of God," the complexity, beauty, and compassionate language of which is beyond ordinary human comprehension) as "imperfect, self-contradictory and destitute in order." Montgomery Watt, in the 20th century, points out that " . . . on every frontier of Christiandom where there was inhabited land, Islam was dominant. Is it surprising that Islam came to be thought of as the great enemy?"(Bauben, 1996, p. 176). And "In deadly fear Christiandom had to bolster confidence by placing the enemy in the most unfavourable light possible . . . [t]he image created in the twelfth and thirteenth centuries continued to dominate European thinking about Islam" (Bauben, p. 185). It continues to do so till present.

Watt argued that at the end of the day selection of material, interpretation of data and the evaluation of their acceptability or importance would have been due to the particular orientation of a particular scholar and his own faith background and beliefs (Bauben, p. 176). Although Watt emphasized the importance of a shift in attitude (away from deep-seated prejudice of "war propaganda"), when examining faiths other than the scholars' own, he "accuses Muslim scholars of making dubious conjectures in their explanations" (Bauben, p. 181).

This picture of Islam "left [a] deep and permanent mark on Oriental studies" and continues to be the root of Islamophobia (note when President Bush, as mentioned in the beginning of the chapter, used medieval crusader war terms after 9/11). These authors were defining and shaping the image of Islam for their audiences not only in the West (Daniel, 1980) but beyond; the irony and problem was that students from South Asian, Middle Eastern and other Muslim lands, due to lack of good-quality higher education, were flocking to the West to study this version and image of Islam—hence the pervasive presence of Western-educated "confused *desis*" in Muslim lands.[3] Of course, there are many good scholars, both Western and Eastern, who engaged with existing literature on the subject and began to question it in order to mend fractured relations between cultures. This we hoped to do by reexamining and challenging stereotypes in literature through activities like this one in *Valuing Diversity*.

The students' responses after the session were extremely positive, with comments such as "the day was very insightful and helped clear up some common misconceptions." The director noted that the students were very challenged by what I said. "This is the first time many of them will have spent extended time with people of other faiths and you certainly went a long way towards dispelling some of the myths and caricatures." The students said they respected your depth of knowledge and faith.

MOVING TO PAKISTAN TO INCREASE OPPORTUNITIES
FOR WOMEN IN HIGHER EDUCATION

I have had rich experiences of teaching and learning about Islam and other faiths at Cambridge in different schools, colleges and Universities. Walking down the halls of the "UL" or University Library at the University of Cambridge or LSE (London School of Economics and Political Sciences) or Madingley Hall in Cambridge made me think that these old established and well-maintained institutes are a brilliant metaphor for the West—knowledge was sacred and its value well understood in society; therefore, society was thriving and well balanced and its people, I found, were generally positive and constructive as most were mentally and physically occupied with various forms of work.

I wanted to offer the same educational opportunities to women in South Asia in general and Pakistan in particular. It was important to educate society through its women especially in a largely patriarchal culture that practices segregation. "Give me educated mothers and I will give you an educated nation" said Quaid-e-Azam Muhammad Ali Jinnah, the founder of Pakistan. Yet since the creation of Pakistan—one of the largest Muslim countries— almost 65 years ago, there is not a single all-women's non-government university in four of the five provinces of Pakistan. My husband and I have started to lay the grounds for such a university, with, we hope, branches in the capital, in the Khyber Pukhtunkhwa, and elsewhere.

Although knowledge is highly valued in Islam and *ilm* (the word for knowledge) developed to the highest level amongst Muslims, Christians, Jews and other faith cultures under Muslim rule at different periods of history in Andalusian Spain, Morocco and elsewhere—giving it the name of "The Golden Age"—present people in Muslim societies (post-colonialism) have suffered due to lack of good-quality education that keeps a balance between Eastern and Western wisdom and knowledge. Having worked at some of the top universities in the U.K. and seeing how education under the social welfare system benefits all citizens, it is my dream to set up a new cutting-edge shorter curriculum based on *Valuing Diversity* to educate the estimated 180 million people of my country of origin, Pakistan.

Pakistan—a land of great cultural diversity and breath-taking natural beauty—is sadly often overshadowed in the media by its political instability, paradoxes and lack of widely available good-quality education and poor social services. Most people I encountered were "based at home" and few occupied with professional work outside the domestic space. Education has one of the lowest records and there are few top-quality schools, yet paradoxically there is an abundance of schools, with home-made schools in old residential houses on every corner of a sector in Islamabad with the most profound and grand names such as "School of Excellence," "The Oxford and Cambridge School," and "Vision School."

As I retuned to Islamabad in Pakistan recently, I found good education and the love of knowledge almost absent due to the over-stringency of schools and the lack of interest of students. In many schools, students are over-worked and some, I am told, must work till 4 am to complete their assignments. Some students are given exams on each subject at the end of every month and in some cases refused entrance to school and sent back home in the morning if they are even five minutes late. With one of the lowest education records, a country cannot afford to send school children home for being late.

I see that in most cases knowledge is sought not so much for the love of learning but as an opportunity to escape to a foreign country and then perhaps acquire a well-paid job. Parents who can afford it send their children (in the past it was only sons, but now more parents choose to send their girls, as well) to universities in the U.K., U.S., Canada and Australia. At university most Pakistanis study accountancy or medicine and one asked me why I wanted to do anthropology when "there was nothing in it." I aim to re-shape certain subjects so that students strive towards learning to widen their knowledge as well as to utilize it in their lives.

"I do not read. Full stop!" said one young elite woman to me. Although this lack of interest in reading may be the case anywhere else in the world, in this particular case it points to a crisis in present-day Muslim cultures where illiteracy is widespread, education opportunities minimal and many of the elite invest little time in reading and writing. I aim to encourage learning through reading. There are only a handful of libraries in Pakistan today and some under lock and key, although new initiatives which include accessible and additional libraries have started opening with centres for dialogue like *Kuch Khaas*. The key, in this context, I thought, as the founder of Pakistan said, was to educate mothers in order to educate society.

I have been told that setting up a non-government university for women in Pakistan is a great challenge. But I think that the challenge is well worth it if our subjects—based on ideas from the model of the learning resource *Valuing Diversity*—can help break down negative perceptions of the other and help people respect each other through understanding and knowledge. Through cutting-edge education, I want to challenge the misinformation and stereotypes amongst some of the present people I encountered: one lady wrote to me in an email "not to trust the Jews." I replied that in the Charter of Medina, the Prophet Muhammad (pbuh[4]) dealt with the People of the Book peacefully and gently yet firmly and both he and God in the Quran mention the People of the Book as "one *Ummah*" (community). It was because the Prophet was inclusive of "Others" that he asked the first group of Muslims to seek refuge with a Christian king, and some of the Jews, including a rabbi, fought beside the Prophet in the battle of Uhud. By any standard, it is not right to label an entire community as, for example, terrorist or immoral and the cause of "all the mischief on earth." During my stay abroad, I met many good Christians and Jews who engaged in a lot of good charity and worked tirelessly to build relations with Muslims and people of other faiths and cultures. In my reply I emailed the lady above that, "Only God, not us, can be the final and best judge of who is good and who is not. God is constantly talking about mercy, compassion and forgiveness. I feel it is important to revive this spirit of compassion in the *ummah* and for the world to see this side of Muslims. In reverse, it is also not fair and inaccurate when, as a Muslim living in the West, I see Islam and Muslims being categorized as 'fundamentalists,' 'extremists,' 'Islamists,' etc. A much more sophisticated and complex approach will reveal that Muslim cultures are so diverse and that Islam is not a monolith as is often portrayed in literature and the media. Once we—on both sides—begin to study, understand, respect and help 'The Other,' the world for our children will be a better and more peaceful place to cohabit."

It is important to support educational projects in countries like Pakistan to help people understand and appreciate others and other cultures—I met many who did this already and a few who we needed to do more work with. For instance, A woman whom we may call Spongmai (pseudonym) prided herself on being "racist": "I am racist," she said. "So what! And the Quran says you should *not* befriend them." Having studied the people in Pakistan for more than ten years through anthropology, I knew that there was a great need amongst people to read the Quran for its true meaning, as some people misquote the Quran. I replied that God is fair and merciful and He cannot say that, but His words are often taken out of context, misunderstood and misrepresented. Using the learning tools of *Valuing Diversity* in which we analyse a certain text and then challenge peoples' perceptions of the other, and having recently read the Quran in meaning for the 14th time, and the extended biographies of the Prophet, and the Caliphs: Abu Bakr, Umar, Uthman and Ali, I replied: The people of the book are given special respect and protection by God in the Quran and by his Prophet and the Caliphs (each Caliph stressed to his heir to take special care of the *ahl-al-kitab*—Jews, Christians and other minorities). The Prophet of Islam (pbuh) said that the person who wrongs a person from the *ahl-e-kitab*/or a *mu'ahid* "or imposes a greater burden on him than he can bear, or detracts from his rights, or takes anything from him without his consent, I will be his opponent on the Day of Resurrection" (As-Sallabi 2007: 172). Based on these instructions, Umar in his advice to the next Caliph of Islam said: "I urge the Caliph who comes after me to treat *ahl-al-dimmah*

[Jews, Christians and other minorities living in Muslim lands] well and to fulfill the covenant with them, to protect (and defend) them against their enemies and not burden them with more than they can bear" (See Sallabi 2007:88 and 172).[5] In his first letter to the tax collectors Caliph Uthman pointed out two types of people who are to be protected and treated with kindness as they are the weakest in the *ummah*: the orphans and *dhimmis* whom he urged not to wrong as they are under the protection of God and risk His punishment: "I urge you to adhere to honesty . . . fulfill covenants and do not wrong orphans or non-Muslims who have a treaty with the Muslims, for Allah will be the opponent of the one who wrongs them" (ibid: 122).

In the light of the recent killings of the Governor of the Punjab in Pakistan who was shot point blank about 28 times for speaking against the Blasphemy law, and the shooting to death of a Christian minister who was one of the only champions of Christian rights in the government, many are concerned that today's extremists and terrorists have pushed the image of Pakistan and Muslims to something that is a far cry from the urgings of the Quran. In an atmosphere where few Pakistani Muslims read or are aware of the above quotes, knowledge—both Islamic and Western social sciences—needs to be reintroduced urgently.

My visit to the seemingly well-educated, English-speaking elite Spongmai's house disturbed me deeply and made me think. Today's education, as it is, is not enough to enlighten minds. It has to be a different type of education, one in which other cultures and peoples are respected and genuine attempts are made towards deeper understanding and mutual respect. Some of these attitudes towards the West seem as out of touch as those toward Islam in the U.S. and U.K. But these misperceptions seem to step from a context of fear of what we don't know and misguided belief in inaccurate information. While there are, of course, many examples in both East and West of people who are open to other perspectives, we need to increase these numbers.

EDUCATION FOR A POST 9/11 WORLD

What type of education is needed then to encourage deeper understanding and mutual respect in a post 9/11 world? One which seeks to find common ground while respecting differences, one of the guiding principles of *Valuing Diversity*. In the first stage of the learning resource, we explore perceptions; through case studies we look at how we can value diversity, and we look at needs and fears, we look at stereotypes in literature and in the media, and we step into someone else's shoes (activity 9, page 22 of *Valuing Diversity*). Finally we explore interfaith dialogue through dialogue scenarios, communication cards and case studies of peacemakers.

In addition to being used in more than 2000 schools in the U.K., *Valuing Diversity* was also introduced at the International School of Islamabad (ISOI) which has an American curriculum and is comprised of students from over 30 different nationalities. One of the missions of ISOI ensures that each student strives to become a responsible global citizen. Three of the school's core values that impact the teaching of diversity and cultural sensitivity include: all people have intrinsic worth; all individuals are responsible for their own actions; and embracing diversity enriches the individual and society. ISOI high school teacher Andrea Fossum used *Valuing Diversity* in her high school World History class on WWII experiences. She reported on its power:

> The question of the Holocaust arose, and some of my Muslim students declared that Hitler and his Plan were "brilliant" and "legendary." That allowed us to discuss that the genocide of Jewish people was not the only part of the Nazi extermination program, and then assessed who among us would have "passed the test." Turned out, I was the only one. This also allowed for a discussion about other genocidal incidents throughout history and the ethical use of power over people.

I met with Ms. Fossum, the senior school teacher at the ISOI a couple of days after I had given the keynote speech on valuing diversity at the school's Cultural Diversity Day, where I presented the first copy to the head of the school. I suggested that a new curriculum was needed for schools internationally—one which emphasized and encouraged redressing stereotypes and caricatures of "Others" in literature and scholarly works and in which students would learn to question what they saw and heard on television and read in newspapers, an exercise I had become familiar with in my sociology classes.

The ISOI high-school teacher was enthusiastic about the idea, and wrote about her own insights: "Be honest with high school students. Acknowledge that hatred, bigotry and prejudice do exist. Discuss how stereotypes come to be. Laugh at the mundane ones (I'm part Irish so that's easy for me), and discuss why some comments can be innocuous while others can be inflammatory. Reinforce the idea that derogatory names are universally unacceptable—no one has the right to verbally deride a culture even if it's his or her own."

Another valuable point she suggested is: "Privately reflect upon your own prejudices because they do exist and can evolve throughout our lifetime. Understand how they came to be: Did your parents teach them to you? Did you have experiences with different ethnic or religious groups that formed these beliefs? Did the media or popular culture create these negative views? How do your prejudices affect what and how you teach certain material?"

I believe it is time for schools internationally to accept their responsibility for opening minds in our post 9/11 world. I would like to see a new curriculum in schools around the world, and hopefully in the women's university I am setting up; one which will include building blocks for interfaith and intercultural dialogue, including critical analysis of what students see and hear around them, whether in their home life or community, or the media, or scholarly works. Based on core values embodied in *Valuing Diversity*, students (and teachers) should be encouraged to:

a. Respect other people's freedom to express their beliefs and cultural ways;
b. Learn to understand what others believe and value and allow an expression of this in their own ways and on their own terms;
c. Learn to respect the convictions of other peoples' food, dress and patterns of behaviour and not behaving in offensive ways;
d. Prevent disagreement from escalating into conflict and violence;
e. Learn to listen to other people with sensitivity, honesty and kindness;
f. Respect the right of others to disagree with our point of view;
g. Avoid violent action and language;
h. Read about other cultures and peoples;
i. Overcome stereotypes of peoples and cultures in books, media and one's own personal beliefs through honest and scholarly discussions and interfaith and intercultural forums.

CONCLUSION

Don't be "color-blind." As teacher Andrea Fossum notes: "I was once engaged in a heated debate with a fellow teacher in a workshop who stated (rather naively I thought) that she loved all her kids and was truly color-blind. I thought this statement to be rather foolish because it negated the unique qualities of the students in her classroom and the fascinating cultural traditions and experiences of the students. Loving all our children equally is necessary for effective teaching, but stating that you are 'color-blind' reinforces the idea that sameness is the goal which then begs the question: what is the measure of sameness we're trying to achieve?"

Finally, after a rich experience as a teacher in various universities and schools, I have found that the only way to overcome current religious misconceptions is to eliminate stereotypes by making interfaith dialogue an intrinsic part of education systems in both the East and the West. In addition to making recommendations for what needs to be done, the *Valuing Diversity* teaching resource is an illustration of how we can open minds if we challenge students to understand "The Other." Thus, we hope that it becomes the model for what works. It is my hope that a similar curriculum and additional adult dialogue could be introduced worldwide to help people understand and value "The Other."

NOTES

1. See my book, *Sorrow and Joy Among Muslim Women* (CUP) 2006.
2. This is the Arabic word for God; e.g., Christians in Egypt had the word "Allah" or God written on the fronts of their churches.
3. *Desi* is a widely used South Asian term meaning local or indigenous—a "confused *desi*" is one who is often understood to copy the West blindly without using his or her mind or perspective.
4. Muslims add "peace be upon him" (pbuh) after the name of Prophet Muhammad in order to display respect and love and they add similar greetings of respect for other Prophets such as Jesus, Moses and others (peace be upon them all).

REFERENCES

Abdel-Fattah, Randa (2007). *Does My Head Look Big in This?* London: Orchard Books.
As-Sallabi, Ali Muhammad (2007). *The Biography of Uthman Ibn Affan—Dhun-Noorayn*. Houston, TX: Darussalam Publishers & Distributors.
Bauben, Jabal Muhammad (1996). *The Image of the Prophet Muhammad in the West: A Study of Muir, Margoliouth and Watt*. Leicester, UK: The Islamic Foundation.
Malinowski, Bronislaw (1929). *The Sexual Life of Savages*. Whitefish, MT: Kessinger Publishing (2005 reprint).
The New Encyclopaedia Britannica (1974). Chicago and London.
Valuing Diversity: Towards Mutual Respect and Understanding (2002, 2nd ed.). The Centre for the Study of Jewish-Christian Relations (CJCR), the Centre for the Study of Muslim-Jewish Relations (CMJR) and the Society for Dialogue and Action, Lucy Cavendish College, University of Cambridge.

ABOUT THE AUTHOR

Dr. Amineh Ahmed Hoti obtained her PhD from the University of Cambridge. She was the co-founder and first-ever director of a major study Centre at Cambridge where she outlined a Cambridge University on-site course and taught an array of students, including imams and rabbis. She organized several major conferences involving distinguished personalities such as HRH Prince Hassan of Jordan and the Archbishop of Canterbury, who launched a book for schools. She has given media interviews on both international television and in major national papers. She was a member of the body that advises the UK government on Religious Education (SACRE). She is the consultant editor of *Valuing Diversity: Towards Mutual Respect and Understanding*, which is an important learning resource for secondary school teachers and students from 11-17+. This book has been distributed to about 2000 UK and international schools, as well as schools in Pakistan and the United States. Dr Hoti's book, *Sorrow and Joy Among Muslim Women*, published by Cambridge University Press (2006), was nominated for the 2007 Kiriyama Prize. She is a fellow-commoner at Lucy Cavendish College, University of Cambridge, executive director of the Society for Dialogue and Action, an advisor to the Three Faiths Forum and patron of charities aiming for peace and world solutions, such as the UK Friends of the Bereaved Families Forum. Dr. Hoti has currently returned to Pakistan with her family with the aim of introducing top-quality, cutting-edge education to take steps towards helping the women and children of South Asia.

Chapter 16

The Passion of a Lifelong Australian Educator

Teaching Students First

Jeff Scanlan

It was 1968 when I graduated from Kelvin Grove Teachers' College in Brisbane. Back then, teacher training was done in a separate institution run by the state government to train teachers for state schools. In Australia, education is run by state governments and a teacher, in theory, can be posted to any public school anywhere in the state. As I was from Queensland, a state larger than Alaska or France, that meant that I could be sent to places more than a thousand miles from my home and family.

I am a fourth generation Queenslander. My family on all sides has lived in the south east of Queensland since migrating there in the 1800s from Germany, Ireland and England. My parents worked a farm on the side of a mountain with my grandparents. My primary school education involved early morning rising, catching my horse and riding the two and a half mile goat track to the one-teacher school in the valley. For high school I mostly stayed with friends in a nearby town or got a lift with someone working there. After graduating from high school it was off to the Kelvin Grove Teachers' College in Brisbane.

The general primary school teacher's course was only two years in the 1960s. After graduating as a public school teacher, I could be sent to Camooweal on the Northern Territory border, Thursday Island near Cape York in the extreme north of the state, the Gold Coast in the southeast or anywhere else in between.

The transfer system is one of the distinctive features of Australian education. No one ever argues that we abandon it. It gives security of employment and a career path to public school teachers, and the Education Department undertakes to move teachers from difficult locations after they have served a reasonable period of time there. Mostly they have been true to their word.

Because the one Education Department runs all public schools the disparities between schools are not as great as they might otherwise be. Schools with a strong and affluent parent community will be better resourced, but being in one state system does have a moderating effect.

PUTTING IDEALISM TO THE TEST

The 1960s when I was trained and began teaching were days of heady idealism. The Vietnam War was at its height, and in Australia as in the United States the protest movement was growing. We were very much aware of the civil rights struggles in the south of the US and in South Africa and believed that current inequities could not continue. I was not immune from that idealism and as a young teacher I believed that education could solve so many of the world's dilemmas. If only people could be educated, have work and be fed, then the world would be a happier place.

I was only 19 when I got my first teaching position. This first appointment was to the Gatton State School near my home town of Laidley, about 70 miles west of Brisbane in a farming community. I wrestled with the usual problems of not knowing how best to approach some lessons, struggling to complete everything that was expected of me, and even creating effective discipline . . . yes even back then!

After two years, and as was normally expected of career male teachers at the time, I was sent out from my comfortable home environment over 1000 miles away to the northwest of Queensland to the mining town of Mount Isa. After a year there, I was transferred to the multi-racial town of Normanton on the Gulf of Carpentaria, also in the northwest of the state.

In Normanton my idealism was put to the test. It is easy for one to be idealistic about racial equality and to look down on other countries for their instances of racism, but now I had to deal with the reality of it. The town was divided evenly between European Australians and Aborigines, and some things that I saw there were a cause for concern.

Aborigines have been in Australia for a long time. The most conservative estimates suggest at least 40,000 years. As with most indigenous peoples around the world they suffered quite extensively in their early encounters with European settlement. For most of Australia's history since the first settlement in 1788, they have been marginalized considerably to the extent that when the Australian constitution was established in 1901 they were not regarded as citizens.

Under Australia's constitution a change can only be made by the vote of a majority of voters and a majority of states in favor of the change. That has not made it easy for governments to effect changes. However, in 1967 90% of Australians voted for the change that henceforth Aborigines were to be regarded as citizens.

After such a result, indigenous issues were soon to become a focus of attention nationally. And in view of what we knew was happening in other parts of the world it was clearly becoming incumbent on Australians and their government to do something for the first Australians so that they could participate in society and the economy as equals with everyone else. It was in this context that in 1972 I took my posting to Normanton State School in Australia's outback.

I was surprised at what I found there. In spite of all that was being said about stopping racism, there were still some instances of segregation in Normanton. Aborigines were discouraged from drinking at certain bars and hotels. They were even assigned to different wards in the local state run hospital.

The teaching was not easy. The curriculum was probably more appropriate for European children in a suburban white-picket-fence environment than in a multi-racial town where so many indigenous children lived in the local camp poorly lit with little running water. The subject matter did not always relate well.

We had not yet heard of Vygotsky (1933), the Russian educationalist, and his notion of a zone of proximal development and the need to scaffold learners so they could better understand what we were trying to teach them. We became very frustrated when the children often just did not catch on to what we were teaching.

Many teachers just gave up in the face of the difficulties they encountered. They could not wait for the time when they could get back home, usually in the south east of Queensland.

I also struggled with attempts to introduce mathematical signs and symbols such as + and − and then × and others. And then there was the need to have them appreciate the alphabet and understand the purpose of writing generally. The indigenous children all found this very difficult.

And yet here were people who could teach the non-indigenous much about the bush and how to survive there. They could find water in the most remote of locations. They could find a meal where anyone else would starve.

They could track animals not only knowing what animal it was but whether it was lame or not. This was a skill that was often used to great effect to find lost children and anyone else who was missing. They did not lack intelligence. They just had difficulty understanding many of the things that were part of the European Australian culture.

It was time to think outside the square. Instead of trying to do math out of a book and on the chalkboard and with pencils and written numbers, I decided to use concrete materials. We sat on the floor—something that was not done very much in those days of formalism—and played with blocks of different color, making sets of different sizes and talking about what would happen if we combined a set of three and a set of four.

I started to think about words and writing too. I noticed that the local speech differed from formal college English that was expected of teachers. The verb 'to be' was mostly missing from their speech as were prepositions. I might think they should say, "I am going to town" but they would say, "I going town." The word for 'grandmother' was 'granny' and the word for 'grandfather' was 'granddad.' They would never use the formal English word for either of these words.

I could see that I needed a new approach to reading and writing. I decided to prepare my own reading books for my students. The books that I would prepare would be about what they themselves had experienced. This was very rare at the time though in more recent times classes often prepare their own story books. One that I prepared was "Hunting with Dad." It went like this.

I went hunting with Dad. Dad took a shotgun and a 22.
We saw a boar pig. Dad shot at it with the 22. He missed.
Then we saw some ducks on the swamp. Dad shot at them with the shotgun. We got a duck. We plucked the duck and took it home.

The students took to these books because they described experiences they could relate to and words that were familiar to them. This is the guiding principle today behind development of multicultural literature. All children deserve books in which they can see themselves and the world in which they live reflected.

On the weekends I got to know many of the parents and grandparents because of the church that I attended. Actually it was not a church so much as the local Aborigines Inland Mission where a missionary would work with and conduct services for the Aborigines. They were quite happy for me to attend there too.

It was at the mission station that I got to know quite a number of the Aboriginal people and there that I realized that many of the stereotypes of an "indolent" people were quite false. Many Aborigines did not abuse alcohol and many had quite large sums of money saved up from the hard work they did on the cattle properties around the town. All in all I learned to take Aborigines as I found them without any preconceived ideas as to what they were like.

After a difficult year the Queensland Department of Education decided that we had spent long enough there and we all needed to move on. We all transferred back to the "big smoke," which is an Australian term for a large city (*The Australian Slang Dictionary*, 1997–2011). I am not sure what the next group of teachers did, though I do know that the paradigm concerning approaches to indigenous education was changing. Cultural differences could no longer be ignored and some money for indigenous education was beginning to be spent. For my part I had learned that teaching the student as an individual with needs and understandings was the key to reaching that child.

I came back to Brisbane at the end of 1972 where I have worked as a teacher ever since, except for a brief time when I went back to the university to upgrade my qualifications. Also in 1972 a new government came into office in Australia with policies to improve both education and the treatment of indigenous people. Many government programs were set up to address the various issues of education and racial inequality.

Not every policy that was implemented was effective. Not all money spent was well spent. However there was now a national consciousness that something needed to be done both for education and indigenous Australians. New curriculum materials were introduced and, where practical, indigenous languages were used.

After my teaching at Normanton I did not encounter many indigenous students but there were always some. I am pleased to say these experiences were positive even though to this day problems still remain with education of indigenous students.

VALUING THE INDIVIDUAL

When I returned to study at the University of Queensland I looked for a place to stay, and as it happened I found myself in a house with a university lecturer in dentistry. He had not long graduated from the university himself and now he was back teaching there, doing his PhD in a related field.

One encounter with my flatmate I remember quite well. As I was getting to know him, in my youthful naivety I said that I did not think I would like spending my life treating mouths! He quickly responded, "You don't treat mouths. You treat people."

Of course! Wasn't that what I had already worked out for myself in relation to the teaching of indigenous students? You treat people as people first. If that was true of dentistry, was not that also true of teaching? Isn't that what I was doing for the indigenous children in Normanton? I was not teaching curriculum and subject matter as much as I was teaching students, children of a variety of backgrounds and needs who had a right to a good education suited to their culture.

In time I finished my university courses and returned to teaching in the later 70's in the outer suburbs of Brisbane. In 1980 I received some information on a conference that was to held at Sydney University. It was the third International English Teaching Conference and as I read the information flyer I decided that I could go. It was during vacation time and the only real cost would be the bus trip down from Queensland and the accommodation down there. The conference fee was nominal.

This conference was not only important for me personally but a watershed for the teaching of writing in Australia. The theme of the conference was "More writing in the 80's," but I was not prepared for the revolutionary ideas that were to be presented there. At the conference were many world-renowned experts on the teaching of writing, including Donald Graves, James Moffett and James Britton.

For someone who had always thought of writing as something that was taught by teaching the conventions of English, such as grammar, punctuation, paragraphing and spelling, what they had to say was quite radical. They said that teachers should encourage children to write what it was that they had within them and wanted to say. Fixing up the mistakes in the writing so that it followed the technical conventions of English was something that could be done later as the writing was edited and revised.

All this made sense to me. How often had I thought that what my students had written was so very interesting and expressive, but then I had to put my red pen through it. How often had I only discouraged students from writing because I thought the commas were not where they should be or the capital letters were not being used properly.

Not many years hence I saw this very theory proven in a very real way when I had to teach a first grade class. I had not taught children so young before and I did so in great fear. When it came to writing, another teacher told me to give them paper and just tell them to write. How that would work out I was not sure, but I did it anyway.

I need not have worried. My young five year olds had no problem picking up a pencil and writing. Sure, for many it was scribble patterns at first, but as the year progressed I began to see letters and words, and then sentences, being put down on the blank paper. A writing community was materializing before my very eyes. There are few greater joys in teaching than to see such evidence of children learning a skill that hitherto they had not had. And all of this was appearing before my very eyes.

There was a lesson there, I had no doubt. Not only did I need to think of teaching children first, before subject matter, but it was also necessary to recognize that within each student there were the resources and capacity for their own learning. Respecting and valuing them for what they were, as I did with indigenous students, was the way to go.

VALUING THE ROLE OF FAMILIES

In the late 1980s I began to teach in a school where I was to remain teaching for the next 17 years. Schools were now becoming conscious of their indigenous students and programs were initiated at this school to assist in the development of pride. As a result more and more students were acknowledging their indigenous heritage and some improvements in school culture were being made.

Over the past several decades, much money has been spent improving indigenous education. The support has been effective especially when schools make attempts to draw in families to assist. At the school where I taught until 2005, there was an excellent program for indigenous students. Specialist trainers were brought in to teach indigenous dances, which were then performed for the rest of the school and parents. Often indigenous students were taken away on camping trips and other enrichment excursions. At times they were allowed to bring a non-indigenous friend with them.

So well-integrated had the indigenous students become that I often had to think, when asked, if I had any non-European children in my class when in fact I did! One day at the school assembly I looked up at the school captains, or student leaders, who were conducting the proceedings, and noticed that all three of them were either Aborigine or Pacific Islanders. I had simply committed myself to teaching students first and curriculum second so that their ethnic origin did not matter.

Or did it? Well it did matter in a way! It mattered because if I was to teach children as individuals their family and cultural background were important. As it was often very much a part of them I considered it my duty to encourage children to be proud of their heritage. If they were indigenous they should be proud of the fact. If they were Pacific Islanders, and we have many of them in Australian schools and communities now, then I would encourage then to talk about that if they wanted to.

I learned so much from my Pacific Island students. From Roslyn I learned how important family was for them, as I listened to the way she described the times she had after dinner each night. Roslyn came from the large family and she had a cousin who was also in my class. Her family members were clearly devoted to one another. Roslyn's cousin, Stephanie, surprised me one day with something that I had never heard of before. She said that she was really Roslyn's sister but that her parents had adopted her because they could not have children themselves. In other words, Roslyn's parents voluntarily gave up their child to be raised by other members of the family because those relatives could not have children.

I also learned about family experiences from a young Aboriginal girl that I had one year. Her name was Sanna. She was delightful, lovely smile, lovely neat handwriting and could do some really lovely drawings.

One day we were talking about snakes and I asked her if she had ever eaten one. She said she often ate them because her father, being an Aborigine, was allowed to catch them to eat. Native animals in Australia are otherwise protected. She told me that he goes up the road near her place where there is some bush and knows just where they hide.

I asked her if she ate the skin of the snake. She replied, "That is the best part!" I had learned something and after all isn't a teacher meant to be a good learner as well?

There is still much to do for indigenous students in Australian schools. Since returning to Brisbane I have only been in contact with urban indigenous children. Many still live in the communities and settlements in the remote areas of Australia where many social problems persist. However some are integrating into Australian life and doing well.

As my understanding of teaching and pedagogy developed over the years, I began to understand one important aspect of teaching: Parents are very important. I have heard many teachers say that parents do not care about their children's education because they do not attend meetings at the school but my experience is that that is untrue. Parents do care and they do want to know what is going on. They may feel inadequate or their own experience of school was not a positive one, and thus they may feel uncomfortable at their child's school.

I remember one single mother who was discussing with me her son's progress at school. As she was about to walk away she said to me quietly that she was still frightened of teachers from when she was at school.

Really, I thought! How could that be? But I am afraid that it is the truth. Schools were not, and probably for some are still not, happy places.

I began to think more on the question of parents, no matter why it might be that they are reluctant to come to the school. First, I realized that children are important to parents. In fact, they are everything to them. They are their life and they would do whatever they could do, if they knew what it was, to improve their children's chances in life. Second, I realized that I needed to bridge the gap with those parents, and I found a way that I could do just that. I would make sure that I knew all the parents of the children in my class. And when there was something commendable about a child I would make sure that the parent knew about it.

One time I remember that by carefully dealing with a parent I was able to turn a situation around from hostility to constructive engagement. I was reading Mark Twain's *Tom Sawyer* to the class where there is a passage where it is written:

And thus he would die—out in the cold world, with no shelter over his homeless head, no friendly hand to wipe the deathdamps from his brow, no loving face to bend pityingly over him when the great agony came.

One little girl went home and reported what I had been reading to the class mentioning what was said about Tom Sawyer's melodramatic thoughts of death. The next day her mother came up to see me to complain about what I was reading.

I wondered how a parent could complain about the reading of a classic like Tom Sawyer? But then I thought, "I need to respect this lady, this mother. Here she is with an interest in her child's education. It is not for me to judge her negatively for this complaint."

As we talked it was clear there was more to this than I had realised. They had had a family member not too long ago commit suicide and that death was still very much in their thoughts. How often is it the case that when we feel aggrieved there is more to the situation than one might first think?

"I'm sorry," I said. "I guess I did not think that someone was going to have that reaction."

That mother seemed to accept my response. Doesn't the Bible say, "A soft answer turns away wrath"?

Some time later I had cause to interact with that mother again. We took the class on a camping trip for a few days, a quite common school activity in Australian schools. We do have summer camps, but in our summer we also have Christmas which is a family affair, and so there is not as high a demand for camping activities. Thus, schools often fill the void during other months with camps for up to a week during school time. The trips might be even longer to visit places such as our high country, the Snowy Mountains, or the national capital of Canberra.

On this trip, a young lady named Joanna caught my attention. We were in the mess hall having our dinner and I was in charge of the after-dinner clean up. It seems to me that children are children and never keen on household chores whether at home or away. But here was Joanna stacking the dishes and wiping down the tables as you would expect of a mature adult, not a child.

I was impressed. I was determined that I was going to relay to her mother how good she was at helping out because that is what I really believed. When I told her mother, her face brightened and she was clearly pleased with what I had to say. From that time on, I received a friendly greeting from them all when I would meet them at work or out shopping.

This is something that I have always done. I have never gone out of my way to look for commendable actions on the part of children in my charge. I have allowed them to happen before my eyes, and when I see something really good happening, I try to make sure that the parents know about it.

In recent years of course we have moved into the digital age. We have cell phones and email and this makes communication much more simple and effective. Some years ago I decided to hand out my email address and phone numbers to parents. I did not tell other teachers because I was sure that they would think that I was crazy.

I have been doing that now for over ten years and can honestly say that I have never been harassed or overburdened by frivolous and vexatious calls. On the contrary it has enabled parents to reach me and talk to me when there are problems. I say to parents that if there is anything that is bothering them, please just call and we can sort it out right then.

Email, similarly, is very effective. It allows for quick communication. Personally I prefer to be able to talk face to face with parents, but that is not always possible. Email affords an immediate opportunity to explain a situation and effect changes.

Parents are one of the best resources that you can have, and an even better resource at times can be grandparents. What I have found recently is that many grandparents are around my age and have similar experiences and memories to what I have. Children tend to think that everything before they were born is the olden days. I remember one student writing about the olden days before there were CDs!

Just recently, our governments decided that not enough history was being taught in our schools and it was suggested to me that I might start doing history in the lower schools. That was something that was going to be quite new for Australian children. Never before had we thought that history was a subject that should be taught in the lower school to children aged 5 to 8.

It was then that I thought that I could do an exercise that would not only help children to learn history but would open channels of communication between them and older family members. The exercise would be to find out how certain things were done in the past. These exercises included questions such as: "How do you kill and prepare a chicken for dinner?" "How do you use a crank telephone?" "How do you use a copper washer to wash your clothes?" "How did you start a car before electric starter motors were invented?"

The exercise proved quite fruitful. Children spoke with parents and grandparents concerning things that they no longer did but which were so much a part of the lives of people who have gone before us.

I am nearing the end of my teaching career now. I have a good retirement plan to keep through however many years of life I have left. I could retire now but I know that when I do there will be much that I will miss. Children energize you. I learned that years ago when I watched children perform for people at retirement homes.

In the many years that you teach and wonder if you are achieving anything, it is worth remembering that there is much more to teaching than just getting information into willing and unwilling minds. It is about the relationships with your students, and using the power of those relationships to broaden the world of those whom, for a brief time, you teach.

REFERENCES

The Australian Slang Dictionary (1997-2011). From Koala Net www.koalanet.com. au/ australian-slang.html.

Walshe, R.D. "Donald Graves in Australia: Children Want to Write." *PETA*: NSW. 1983.

Gattegno, C. Caleb. "Gattegno's Mathematical Approach to the Rods." From educationalsolutions.com/visible-a-tangible-math/mathematical-situations? menuId=79&ms=2.

Vygotsky, L. "Play and its Role in the Mental Development of the Child" (2002). www.marxists.org/archive/vygotsky/works/1933/play.htm.

ABOUT THE AUTHOR

Jeff Scanlan is a primary (elementary) school teacher at Wellington Point State School in Redland City which is an outer suburban community of Greater Brisbane in the state of Queensland, Australia. Jeff has bachelor's degrees in arts, divinity and education and two master's degrees in education. He is also a trained school counselor. He has taught with the Education Department of Queensland for all but three of the last 42 years. He has a passion for including the whole family in the schooling of young people which he believes makes for a fuller education. Jeff lives in Redland City and is married to Christine. They have five adult children and four grandchildren.

Chapter 17

Multicultural to Intercultural

Developing Interdependent Learners

Sean Grainger

When I started teaching seventeen years ago, little did I know that my first job would have so much influence on my perspective toward culture, and in particular the concept of cultural diversity. I took a position teaching first and second grade at Tall Cree, an Indian reservation in the far north of Alberta, Canada. The community I taught was remote; three hours of gravel roads after the pavement ended. I lived in a teacherage beside the school in the community that had no services, just houses, a school, a church and a band administration office. I and four other teachers were the only non-Aboriginal people living in the community of about two hundred residents.

In Canada we are proud of the multicultural mosaic of people that make up the population of our vast country. I grew up learning and understanding that multiculturalism was a good thing. I was used to living among people representing cultures from around the globe, so why was I so anxious about living and teaching on this Indian reservation in my home province? I chalked it up to nerves surrounding my first teaching job, but deep down I knew it was more than that. Despite growing up immersed in a multicultural society, and near many Aboriginal communities, I was nervous about actually living and interacting with these people.

I was about to realize that multiculturalism was not the positive conduit I thought it to be toward an understanding and culturally interdependent society. I was about to realize that a peaceful, understanding and culturally interdependent society depends on our willingness to engage each other, learn from each other and do everything we can to understand each other's perspective.

THE THING ABOUT CULTURE . . .

There is some irony in the word *culture*. German poet Hans Magnus Enzensberger stated interestingly that "culture is a little like dropping an Alka-Seltzer into a glass—you don't see it, but somehow it does something" (Enzensberger, 2010). It's a word that most people would claim to understand, but have some difficulty clearly defining. We represent culture from our personal perspective; we wear it on our sleeves. In so many ways our culture makes us unique, but it's also what defines us as part of a group; we are unique and homogenous at the same time. Perhaps the best description of culture I've heard is simply *how we do things around here*, each one of us as part of a group consisting of people and elements that are very similar.

The complex function of human diversity we call culture helps identify us as individuals, and as groups within a world that is growing and shrinking at the same time. It's easier than ever for people from every corner of the globe to mobilize and connect because contemporary technology has made physical and social mobility more efficient and accessible to us; the distance between us is shrinking. We are exposed to each other as a result like never before; our history, language, customs, religions and perspectives . . . our awareness of each other is expanding.

This new global reality presents both challenge and opportunity. We are challenged to coexist peacefully and purposefully in ever-closer proximity than we appear to be comfortable with. Attempts to create cultural uniformity addressing this challenge have repeatedly failed. If we can't all be the same, perhaps a shift in thinking that views our differences as assets instead of deficits would be the good medicine required to initiate a new paradigm. Refocusing our diversity this way is our cultural and moral opportunity on the path toward increased interdependence and peace. After all these years of coexisting socio-cultural harmony continues to elude us. We have to learn how to get along.

WHERE DO SCHOOLS FIT IN?

As opposed to simply reflecting the multicultural nature of society, the social learning places we call schools are uniquely aligned to exercise a moral priority (Fullan, 2003), to reframe it as one of cultural interdependence—an intercultural society. In society, and in schools, the ignorance and perhaps prejudice we display while coexisting in a multicultural environment percolates under a facade of tolerance and acceptance. *Multi* as a prefix simply means *having many*. *Inter* as a prefix means *amid, among, between, mutually, reciprocally, together, within* . . . words that connote interaction within a group. To tip an evolution toward engaging intercultural school environments that replace multicultural tolerance and acceptance with competent intercultural understanding of and respect toward others, schools need to create positive opportunities for multicultural kids to peacefully and purposefully share more than just space. They need to share personal and group cultural perspectives with each other.

Diverse schools that emphasize teaching all students how to be peaceful, purposeful, and hopeful have the capacity to produce young people who advocate for and demonstrate peace and hope in a larger social context; the effort is scalable.

We are hearing the call for change in our education system loud and clear from every angle, but how to contextualize that change is a big question. If we frame diversity as variance or divergence it becomes synonymous with change. It seems a natural assumption that diverse schools would support the process of educational change. Globally recognized Canadian education reform researcher Michael Fullan asserts that "as the main institution for fostering social cohesion in an increasingly diverse society, publicly funded schools must serve all children, not simply those with the loudest or most powerful advocates" (Fullan, 2003, p. 29). Fullan's words, *main institution for fostering social cohesion in an increasingly diverse society*, resonate with me. Schools have the capacity to be the mirror instead of the reflection. Instead of reflecting society, schools can shape the image of society by demonstrating a paradigm shift from multiculturalism to interculturalism. As intercultural learning laboratories, schools provide environments where intercultural perspectives can be practised and evaluated continuously.

A balance is struck in culturally diverse schools when students realize that being different isn't a quality reserved for others, but rather a state that describes each one of them. When students learn how to celebrate this balance in support and recognition of each other, the gap of ignorance between them narrows, and they begin to function as interdependent learners on their way to becoming well-adjusted, high-functioning peaceful global citizens of an intercultural society.

PERSPECTIVE—OUR CULTURAL LOOKING GLASS

The circumstances that surround every single conversation about culture are a sum total of the perceptions of those participating. If we are to peacefully and hopefully engage each other, we have to try to understand and empathize with each other's cultural perceptions. Twisting our cultural lens a bit focuses awareness of how self-identity is influenced by our perception of others, the world and everything within it. Culture is what we believe.

I used to teach at Venture Middle School, a specialized, segregated middle school program designed for kids whose behaviour and social-emotional problems were too severe for them to stay in a traditional classroom. My colleagues and I worked very hard to get to know these kids perceiving that there was more to the story about why they ended up with us than met the eye. In order to learn the stories behind our students' stories, we had to identify, as best we could, their cultural perspectives. David Nicholson was one of my teaching colleagues in the program. At the end of one particularly challenging day he said, "I think I'm starting to understand these kids; to them *we're* the strange ones." At the time I'm not sure we fully understood the profound impact this game-changing epiphany would have on our program.

We perceived that these students came from different worlds—what we understood as cultures of poverty, neglect, violence, abuse and a litany of other social and environmental cultural realities, cultures most of us weren't personally very familiar with. This reality radically affected their ability to conform to what we thought was a pretty effective intervention model.

In their perspective however, where our student's came from was what they understood to be *normal*, their reality. We were trying to address their social and emotional needs from our cultural perspective, not theirs. Enlightened by David's realization, we redesigned our program backwards based on what our students needed from their cultural perspective instead of what we thought we needed to see from ours. We listened to them, we cried with them and we became hopeful by taking action to help them adjust to a broader world offering different forms of support and care previously withheld in the environments they knew.

Shifting our focus from how we could *reform* our students so we could return them well-packaged to fit nicely in a homogenous mainstream classroom, to how we could better understand our students' cultural perceptions about what they needed from us was a major shift. We worked on building trusting relationships with our students by assuring them we would not judge them. As they became more at ease understanding we had no reform agenda, they began to engage us. We listened to their stories, and they became valuable interpersonal learning tools for us and them. We were becoming culturally interdependent. We began to understand that normal is just a setting on the clothes dryer, and that honouring the unique and personal elements of our students' cultural perspectives was key to creating a school where all felt a sense of belonging. It was then that we could begin helping them formulate a purpose behind their presence within our school program. We became solution-focused collaborators writing learning stories with our students instead of for them. It was an empowering shift for all of us.

Exposing how we perceive the world, and in turn becoming open to alternate points of view causes the lens we look through to gain a broader and clearer scope. Exercising opportunities to see the world through the eyes of others allows us to challenge our own perceptions, to reflect on our purpose and the manner in which we influence the world. The interpersonal tools we access to negotiate cultural understanding become sharper and more focused when we open ourselves up in this way.

When I started teaching my friends back home used to ask me what it was like to live and work on an Indian Reservation. I didn't have to think very hard about the answer. I was quickly realizing that living among the Woodland Cree people in my new home a mere seven hundred kilometres away from my old home was as different to me as I could imagine it would be living seven thousand kilometres away on the other side of the world in a foreign country. I became increasingly ashamed that I hadn't learned more about these people with whom I shared a home province. I didn't really know the first thing about them. I was humbled by their willingness to embrace me as they openly and naturally shared the rich and timeless nature of their traditional ways, language, spirituality and customs, elements that have undeniably influenced my perspective toward life, culture and teaching in profound ways. I am so grateful to have been blessed by this experience. I felt supported and important to my new community. As I became increasingly aware of the people surrounding me who were so different, their perspectives and beliefs influenced my perspectives and beliefs.

I was fully exposed while living and teaching as a minority within an Aboriginal community. Members of the community didn't make explicit efforts to teach me their traditional ways, they just went about living them. Realizing there was much to be learned from immersing myself in their day to day lives, I let go of my anxiety and started to become intercultural before I even had any real notion of the term, or its meaning.

The irony of my position living and teaching in that remote northern community became more apparent to me over time. I was hired by this group of tribal people to teach their children when in reality, simply by being there, I was learning more from them than they were from me. I began to wonder why the school that was re-shaping my cultural perspective couldn't evolve as an institution that shaped the broader perceptions of Aboriginal culture. I formed a belief that schools have the capacity to be natural conduits for teaching culture. We teach what we know. Schools that know culture have much to offer in leading society toward open and informed cultural perspectives.

PERSPECTIVE OF SCHOOLS—OUR CULTURAL MICROSCOPE

My observation is that schools typically take a reactive position in relation to the challenges of society. We adjust our practice according to what we perceive our communities and the larger society need from us. Whether schools should continue functioning in a reactive context toward social challenges is another big question. I think we can do better for our children by providing an example that teaches them to be proactive. The diverse nature and far-reaching social scope of public schools create powerful potential to influence socio-cultural attitudes. Schools should think bigger. Schools provide real-time, action oriented opportunities to explore the dynamics of culture. Instead of reacting to cultural realities affecting our school environments from outside our walls, we should be seizing the opportunity to lead a necessary paradigm shift in how we view our role within a diverse society. As institutions formed for the purpose of educating, schools are highly suited to the leadership challenge of teaching society how to be culturally proactive.

It's time for educators to take action on this reality and lead schools in becoming intercultural learning places that perceive cultural diversity as an asset, not a deficit. On behalf of society, schools would then be intercultural proving grounds; places where our communities look for direction and insight regarding the recognition that what we've viewed as our multicultural challenge is much better framed as our intercultural opportunity.

MY HOPEFUL (ACTIONABLE) FUTURE

Iconic Austrian psychologist Viktor Frankl once said that "Everyone has his own specific vocation or mission in life; everyone must carry out a concrete assignment that demands fulfillment. Therein he cannot be replaced, nor can his life be repeated; thus, everyone's task is unique as his specific opportunity to implement it." We are here on earth for a purpose. Many of us may not understand yet what that purpose is, but it's there for all of us. I believe purpose is the element that defines our hope. When we lose hope, we become purposeless.

Hopeful schools leverage intercultural synergy to improve the quality of their learning environments. They understand the imperative to prepare kids for the global realities of a changing world, and they surround the hope they have for their students with concrete conceptual teaching designed to explicitly prepare a new generation of culturally responsive global citizens. In this sense their hope becomes purposeful.

Mattie McCullough School, where I am a teacher and vice-principal, recently became a member of the United Nations Educational, Scientific and Cultural Organization's (UNESCO) Associated Schools Project Network (ASP Net). A major goal of ASP Net is to promote and support intercultural, collaborative learning connections among associated schools around the world. UNESCO frames learning within four pillars: learning to know;

learning to do; learning to be, and learning to live together (Canadian Commission for UNESCO). These pillars frame purposeful learning brilliantly, and align synergistically with a developmental model I created called the Hope Wheel.

I created the Hope Wheel during graduate school as part of my action research while working at Venture Middle School. I was struggling to visualize a paradigm that encompassed the intercultural perspective our program was shifting toward. I returned to the roots of my professional teaching choosing a medicine wheel model to represent my evolving point of view. My experience working and living among First Nations people exposed me to timeless wisdom surrounding learning philosophy. To First Nations people, learning is the essence of living; it's organic and natural, and for many, represented by the medicine wheel in one form or another.

Michael and Judy Bopp are co-founders of Four Worlds International, a human and community development organization with roots in indigenous peoples' development work in North America and well known for its ability to bridge between the cultures of communities and the culture of the agencies and professionals who attempt to serve them (Bopp, 2006). They explain that,

> *Medicine* in tribal tradition refers to any substance, process, teaching, song, story or symbol that helps to restore balance in human beings and their communities. The medicine wheel is an ancient symbol which represents an entire world view (a way of seeing and knowing) and the teachings that go with it. (Bopp, 2006, p. 22)

Borrowing from the timeless wisdom of the medicine wheel provides us with all we need to establish a simple, non-linear framework of intercultural purpose.

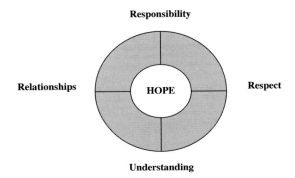

Figure 17.1. Hope Wheel

The Hope Wheel became a powerful guide for my colleagues and me as we navigated the varied cultural perspectives of our students. We placed our students on the Hope Wheel relative to their experiences in life, how they viewed them and the emotions created as a result. As we became aware of their social, emotional and cognitive states (what we framed as their cultural perspectives), we were able to work with them in purpose-driven contexts as they learned to advance themselves on the wheel in different domains of learning how to know, do, be and live with each other. We formed meaningful dialog around each student's variable position on the wheel, and used the graphic model as a template for personal growth.

NAVIGATING TOWARD CULTURAL COMPETENCY

In the context of creating culturally competent global citizens the Hope Wheel provides teachers a valuable visual representation of student development and progress. Hope is the elemental foundation supporting the process. Surrounding this hope are four concepts, each representing a concentric path toward cultural interdependence. The first path is *Respect*.

RESPECT

Respect is the place on the Hope Wheel where young people gaze with wonderment at the world surrounding them and begin to simply realize they are part of this world; they are *learning to be*. They begin to feel an implicit purpose to learn. They need answers to the question "why?" When we walk the path of discovery with students, we support finding the answers they seek; we establish value in learning . . . we help them define purpose. A template for interaction between themselves and others is established on the path of respect. Interacting with ideas and concepts in the domain of respect leads to the establishment of self identity, and orients kids toward the evolution from dependence to independence.

UNDERSTANDING

The domain of understanding is where kids *learn to know*. Skill acquisition, new knowledge and rationale for life-long learning are established within this domain. Students at this stage begin developing an independent nature as they take risks with learning and start to develop intrinsic motivation to discover. In the domain of understanding students sharpen their focus on the surrounding world; they look more critically at themselves and others in their quest to gain knowledge and make sense of things.

RELATIONSHIPS

When students move to the relationships phase of the wheel, they begin to understand the value of interdependency among people; they *learn to live with each other*. Kids who function competently at this stage seek extrinsic sources of support in their developing relationships, and they begin to understand that interdependency is about distributing strengths among a network of collaborative people working together to learn. In the domain of relationships students become more resilient by seeking the support of significant others. They learn how to think deeper and critically about ideas, and they establish self-imposed boundaries.

RESPONSIBILITY

Students who have traveled full-circle on the Hope Wheel enter the domain of responsibility where they *learn to do*. They display an implicit understanding of the imperative to serve self first so they can responsibly serve others. They understand what taking action means. They become caregivers for those traveling the hope paths behind them. In the domain of responsibility students display intrinsic knowledge and insight as a result of their experience, and they begin to feel confident enough as leaders to engage others, to support and nurture them. The Hope Wheel is grassroots theory applied to our personal and interpersonal perspectives. It's a model we can use to place ourselves and those around us on a continuum of human development. We enter the phase of respect when confronted by something totally new, but perhaps function confidently in the domain of responsibility in a different context as a result of our experiences and the knowledge we gained as a result. Where we fall on the Hope Wheel is a reflection of our developing cultural identity. Owing to the notion that self-awareness leads to self-confidence and the willingness to share our values and perspectives with others, the Hope Wheel is also a conduit for confident intercultural communication leading to increased cultural knowledge and responsiveness.

KNOWING SELF FIRST

The cultural perspective we hold is shaped by our experiences as influenced by our birthplace, our family, our spirituality and the zeitgeist within which we were born; it's the cultural reality lens we look through. Our cultural identity is learned beginning the moment we're born. Obvious physical characteristics and genetic traits define our culture in part from the second we're conceived. After we're born, the evolving cultural identity we form is largely influenced by our relationships and surroundings. Steve Van Bockern, coauthor of *Reclaiming Youth at Risk: Our Hope for the Future* (Brendtro, 2002), refers to this identity as our *cultural tail*. I had the pleasure of attending a retreat with Steve on the Morley Indian Reservation west of Calgary in 2002. He explained that we can't *cut off* our cultural tail; it's always there, behind us affecting our perspective, but also that great things are possible in everyone's future despite this tail that follows us. (Bockern, 2002) Whether good, bad or indifferent, our cultural tail tells the story of where we've come from; who we are in terms of how our environments affect us, but it doesn't have to predict where we're headed.

From a cultural perspective, in many ways I believe we begin our lives rather innocently. Like clay to the sculptor, we start as unformed material yearning to be moulded and shaped into a more tangible form—our growing cultural identity. Just as soon as we see the light of the world we begin forming perceptions and feelings about our culture and how we are different from others. We are the sum total of what we think we are. Adults must be responsible about noticing the cultural perspectives of children so we can help them form positive perceptions about their personal identities. This enables them to confidently build relationships and circles of support as they share their perspective with others.

One fall day during my first year teaching at Tall Cree Indian Reservation, I was reading a book to my first and second grade combined class just before the end of school. The book my student-of-the-day chose to read was one on the "American Indian." Without giving it much thought, I began reading the book to my class.

The mother of one of my students was our janitor, and she would typically start her day before ours ended by emptying the garbage cans in the classrooms to get a head-start on her evening cleaning duties. As she entered our class she said "hi" to her son, and he replied by saying excitedly, "Mom, we're reading a book about Indians!" I was immediately struck by his statement. As his mom chuckled a bit and made an inquisitive face toward us, she asked him, "Brandon, you know you're an Indian, right?" He gave her a puzzled look back and said, "Oh yeah."

My student was an Aboriginal person, an "Indian," as his mom described, but he hadn't given that fact much thought. At the tender age of six he simply existed, and although he had been raised to that point in his life within a very distinct and rich cultural environment, his personal, private view of the world hadn't been fully shaped or formed yet. He was functioning very happily in the domain of respect on the Hope Wheel; gazing with wonderment at the surrounding world and simply realizing he was part of it; he was *learning to be*, and his mom was helping him make sense of that.

It's so important that adults, and particularly parents, make the effort to speak explicitly about culture. Culture is an element described in part by a person's race. Birgitte Vittrup conducted research in 2006 around young children's judgement of others based on race (Bronson, 2009). She determined that kids as young as six months old judge others based on their skin colour, but also noted that families that talked about interracial friendship dramatically improved their kids' racial attitudes. Her assertion is that actually talking about race is the key to helping children become unintimidated by differences as they develop the social skills necessary for a diverse world (Bronson, 2009) and helping them form their own *private logic*.

As we grow our cultural identity continues to evolve; we develop what Alfred Adler describes as *private logic*. According to Adler, "private logic is the reasoning invented by an individual to stimulate and justify a style of life" (Wikipedia, 2010). Our environment and the people within it shape and form our private logic relative to cultural identity. Adler contrasts the concept of private logic with the idea that "common sense represents society's cumulative, consensual reasoning that recognizes the wisdom of mutual benefit" (Wikipedia, 2010). We perceive ourselves, others and the world around us, drawing conclusions about each as we live, learn and grow . . . this perspective becomes the essence of our cultural perspective, what we develop in the domain of understanding on the Hope Wheel. We can never implicitly understand other's perceptions, but we can be empathetic toward them. In simplest form, it's this empathy that encapsulates our degree of cultural responsiveness.

We're experts on our personal culture identity and frame it in infinite ways, but when it comes to defining, or better yet understanding the culture of others, we aren't nearly as contemplative. Adler's theory as applied to the context of culture appears to suggest that our cultural private logic is the point of view we take relative to our personal cultural identity, and that cultural common sense is the way we perceive the culture of others, and most importantly the wisdom that can be gained from that perspective; how we become culturally interdependent.

Culture is more than who we are, our skin colour, where we come from or our ethnic or religious values; it's the summation of all the elements of our lives that influence our thoughts, ideas, values and passions. The kind of school I want all kids to attend is one where thoughts, ideas, values and passions are nurtured and shared toward increased understanding of others. When we are exposed to the thoughts, ideas, values and passions of others, our eyes are opened to learning possibilities we may never had considered otherwise.

Contextualizing the Intercultural School-Engaging Perspectives

Culturally diverse schools are living laboratories demonstrating and exemplifying the virtues of interdependence. Effectual and purposeful communication within them allows kids to learn from each other as they evolve beyond the paradigm of multiculturalism and begin to function competently in the domain of relationships on the Hope Wheel.

Keeping in mind Adler's private logic theory, every individual student within a school possesses a personal cultural perspective; "I am, others are, the world is, therefore" . . . Of course all schools are multicultural as defined in this context, even if obvious elements of culture like skin colour, religion, language, dress, etc., are environmentally homogenous.

Intercultural schools go a giant step further to acknowledge the social, emotional and academic benefits of *cultural common sense*, the idea that if schools are multicultural by nature, why not leverage opportunities to illuminate the learning that emerges when so many different thoughts, ideas and passions are represented? Intercultural schools openly celebrate, share and utilize these thoughts, ideas and passions as learning tools. Engaging learning relationships develop in an intercultural school environment.

My friend Brian Plastow teaches social studies at École Lindsey Thurber Composite High School. He shares a story about improved learning resulting from the inclusion of kids possessing diverse cultural backgrounds within his class.

Two years ago in a tenth grade class I was teaching about some of the challenges presented by economic globalization; specifically the lesson was about child labor. We looked at some textbook examples, watched a video on children working in dangerous tanzanite mines in Tanzania, discussed several other examples and looked historically at child labor in England during the Industrial Revolution. The class in general was appalled by the conditions kids had to work in; how unsafe and unjust it was that these kids had to work instead of going to school. There was one student, however, who had emigrated from Afghanistan. He shared a point of view that exposed us to a completely different perspective. He explained that in developing economies some families can't afford the luxury of not having their children contribute economically to their family. Kids had to work. Without their labor the families would have absolutely no hope of getting out of their poverty and the hardship and oppression it caused. This student's contribution to the dialogue in class truly showed us how difficult this issue is to solve and showed us that it might be unfair for us in Alberta to judge people in completely different social circumstances. Thanks to these students from different backgrounds we truly get a global picture of the world. (Plastow, 2011)

So many differing perspectives within an intercultural school provide infinite opportunities for kids to analyze thought (their own and others), and nurture creativity by looking at things from different perspectives. The implicit purpose of intercultural schools is to create transparency between cultural perspectives as an integral teaching and learning tool. In my teaching I use Hope Wheel based talking circles as one way to do this.

Talking circles provide formal opportunities for kids in school to address each other respectfully utilizing the Zen concept that one should only speak when what is being said improves upon the silence. One talking circle I remember in particular moved us to a transparent place where we could empathize with a student who was all but written off by everyone.

This student whom I will call Bill barely attended school, but when he did his influence was felt by every staff member and student. The level of disdain he displayed for others was extreme. He was defiant and belligerent to the point where, to be honest, we were relieved when he wasn't there. One day we had a fight break out on the bus to school. During the fight, both combatants yelled horribly demeaning comments and racial slurs toward each other. Bill was on the bus that day, and although he wasn't involved in the fight directly, he was the catalyst.

Relative to the Hope Wheel, it was clear that neither party had displayed an ounce of respect for the other during this incident so, on their request, we agreed to initiate a talking circle dealing with that as our starting-point. In a talking circle only one person is allowed to speak at a time. All others must listen to the one who holds the icon (in this case a talking stick, simply a short stick ordained with the symbolic colours of our school banded around one end) until it is passed to the next person in the circle who may choose to speak or just pass the stick along.

The point of view of each participant was represented as the stick traveled around the circle and we began to understand the context of the fight. It started with Bill calling a boy a racial slur on the bus, and another laughing at his name-calling. Fearing the consequences of standing up to Bill directly, the victim of his name-calling punched the boy who laughed instead and the fight was on.

As the dialog around the incident developed, intense emotions began to emerge from many who had once been the victim of name-calling, some of it racially motivated, some just plain old bullying and teasing. As usual during the talking circle process Bill silently stared at the floor. A good half hour passed and we were winding up having heard unsolicited apologies from both fighting boys, when the stick came around to Bill on the final pass. Bill took the stick, looked up from the floor and we could see the stress on his face.

He looked right at his victim, stood up and said he was sorry. He told us that he knew what it felt like to be called names because he was called names every day. He explained how he was constantly looking out for his own personal safety in the neighbourhood; that he lived in constant fear, and that he knew what that felt like. Then he sat down and passed the stick along.

Nobody else spoke after that. Bill became transparent for us that day and we were able to get a glimpse of his private logic. We understood him better and he wasn't so scary anymore. I wouldn't say the kids became friendly with him, but they weren't afraid anymore, and for the most part he refrained from random intimidation and bullying of his classmates from that day on. When Bill offered a glimpse of his cultural perspective that day, he altered the dynamics of our program. The fact that he refrained from perpetuating his wrath of fear told me also that he took responsibility for his actions providing us with a less stressful environment to teach and learn within.

Seeing the world through the reality lens of others can be a humbling and enlightening experience, and in this case, a very restorative one too. We started by addressing the domain of respect that day, and through the process of our talking circle restored understanding, functional relationships and some relative responsibility to our environment.

A WILLINGNESS TO SHARE IS A VERY GOOD SIGN

We learn empathically when we are blessed with the opportunity to experience authentic elements of different cultures. Opening ourselves up to the lifestyles of others teaches us that we all have the same basic human needs, but culturally unique and interesting ways to satisfy them. Intercultural schools don't have to explicitly invite kids to share elements of their culture. They are implicitly open to how different kids satisfy their basic human needs in different cultural contexts. Visceral cultural elements permeate intercultural schools in ubiquitous ways.

We appreciated when a Pakistani boy in my class last year used to bring Pakistani sweets and pakoras for the class each time he went for dinner with his family to their favourite restaurant. Nobody asked him to do this; he just did it because he felt comfortable sharing these cultural elements with us, and the socio-cultural intent to honor us behind the gesture. We can learn about others by experiencing their customs first-hand; food, art, language, dress, music, sports . . . when we eat, see, do, hear and speak the customs of others, we are able to get a glimpse through their reality lenses, and we understand them just a little bit better. Kids who share personal cultural elements without needing a prompt or a contrived purpose are displaying the natural and organic unfolding of culture that must be a hallmark of truly intercultural schools.

When kids share their cultural backgrounds and stories, they spark the imaginations of those around them. Listeners form images in their minds about what they are hearing. Sir Ken Robinson says imagination is a precursor to creativity (Robinson, 2009) calling creativity "applied imagination" (Robinson, 2009, p. 67). He explains "you could be imaginative all day long without anyone noticing, but you would never say that someone was creative if that person never did anything. To be creative you actually have to do something" (Robinson, 2009, p. 67). Like hope, create is also an action word. Being mindful about the culture of others illuminates opportunities to build relationships, form altered or fresh perspectives, synthesize ideas or perhaps engage a learned skill in an act of creative self-discovery. Intercultural schools influence creativity through the routine and natural sharing of cultural elements and perspectives.

OTHER'S STORIES—CONNECTING THE BROADER COMMUNITY

In my community we are lucky to access the services of Jan Underwood at the Central Alberta Refugee Effort (CARE). CARE supports the efforts of immigrants and refugees to overcome barriers and participate fully in Canadian life as valued members of the Central Alberta community. CARE is very involved supporting the work of central Alberta schools to embrace cultural diversity and offer a welcoming school environment to all students.

On one occasion Jan brought a guest with her to our school, MonyBany Dau, a Sudanese refugee who is now living locally with his family. We had been speaking about racism with our grade five classes and felt MonyBany's visit would add some authentic value to our message. He shared part of his story as he spoke about belonging in profound ways. As a child soldier at age nine, he saw things that our students could never have imagined. He explained that war in his homeland resulted from conflict between different people, and that through his experiences he developed an understanding that diversity is the natural order of human existence, and that we should celebrate it, not fight over it. He taught us that each finger on our hands is different, but they all come together for a shared purpose (Dau, 2009). This bit of wisdom resonated with many of the kids who hung on his words that day. One girl commented that every time she felt like excluding someone from her *group*, she would look at her own hand to remind her of MonyBany's words.

The opportunity to hear MonyBany speak had a lasting effect on our fifth graders. The vivid stories he shared provided so much more insight and transparency than reading them in a textbook or via the Internet would have. Connecting with CARE serves to expand our students' scope of reality and helps put some of the daily school issues they confront in perspective. I have great respect for the responsible effort CARE makes to connect our intercultural school to the broader intercultural community.

OUR OWN STORIES—CONNECTING INSIDE THE SCHOOL

As much as it benefits students to hear personal stories from responsible community members, an intercultural school also provides many great opportunities for them to hear each other's stories. The effort kids make who are willing to share their stories is often very personally meaningful and provides them with a golden opportunity to be responsible as story tellers with their own important message. Those that are emotionally willing to tell their stories benefit from the opportunity to express why they are who they are, why they do what they do and act the way they act. It can be a cathartic experience to share intimate details about ourselves seeking acceptance and understanding. Bill could attest to that as indicated by his willingness to share with us that day in the talking circle.

If we aren't willing to engage this culture of sharing, our stories aren't told and opportunities to support healing and acceptance of what cannot be changed are lost. Opportunities to celebrate our skills and experiences, to teach empathy, and perhaps sympathy as well, are also lost. Perceptually (culturally) speaking, students don't have to be from the other side of the world to benefit from the opportunity to share their personal stories. Disadvantaged kids; disabled kids; kids from non-traditional families; kids who have excelled . . . all children have a perspective and those willing will benefit from sharing it. I have always said that self esteem is defined in two simple steps: we require opportunities to become good at something, anything, and then more importantly, we require opportunities to share what we're good at with others. We know ourselves better than anyone else does, and sharing this expertise with others is a very responsible and esteem-building experience.

Our student's cultural views of themselves, others, the world and any perspective or action that develops as a result, are formed by their experiences, the story already written. Making a point to learn these stories positions educators well to help students continue writing their stories in the present and ultimately helps prepare them for the stories they intend to write in the future.

MAKING "CULTURE" YOUR SCHOOL CULTURE

An intercultural school perspective is not something you simply *add-on* to the school that previously existed so you get the school you had before with a bunch of culture added to it. *Culture* can become your school culture. It involves an incremental process of continual learning and improvement. It requires a deliberate effort to notice differences, focus on them, think deeply about them and finally, to engage them in meaningful ways. The perpetual goal is to establish a learning environment that positively reflects meaningful and purposeful interaction among students and staff, and to never stop learning about others, and ourselves as a result.

One-shot *festival* style showcases of culture don't fit the bill if we're striving toward making culture an omnipresent aspect of our *school culture*. Interculturalism isn't working if it's reduced to a one-day event where kids display their culture—food, traditional clothing, art, music, etc.—all to be forgotten until the next time.

An authentically intercultural school is one where the diverse nature of the student body is pervasive; one where students are encouraged to represent their culture during discussions in the classrooms, hallways, cafeteria and sports fields. It's the kind of school environment where teachers appreciate the diverse cultural perspectives of all children, and plan their daily routines to include them. Natural and open interaction between people representing unique cultural perspectives is omnipresent in a school where culture is valued. Every aspect of administering the school program would consider how culture was going to fold in at the outset as opposed to an afterthought.

The slow-to-evolve industrial model of educating young people to create uniformity in society isn't getting us anywhere. All of us—parents, teachers, school administrators, and other responsible adults looking out for kids in contemporary society—need to carefully consider how poorly uniformly structured schools fit our purpose to create vibrant intercultural teaching and learning environments as leading institutions within our diverse society.

To help prepare our children for the realities of their future, and to function more productively within the realities of the present, educators must embrace the diversity of our world and do everything they can to help kids connect with and learn from each other. The path to enlightenment is learning, and getting a glimpse of how others view the world is an opportunity to grow understanding that we should not deny. The peace and hope we need to sustain our world depends on our ability to engage and understand each other. Let us all take responsibility for this effort.

REFERENCES

Canadian Commission for UNESCO. (n.d.). www.unesco.ca/en/interdisciplinary/aspnet/default.aspx.

Central Alberta Refugee Effort. (n.d.). www.intentr.com/immigrantctr/.

Bockern, S. V. (2002). October 3, S. Grainger Interviewer.

Bopp, J. B. (2006). *Recreating the World: A Practical Guide to Building Sustainable Communities*. Calgary: Four Worlds Press.

Brendtro, B. V. (2002). *Reclaiming Youth at Risk: Our Hope for the Future*. Bloomington: National Education Service.

Bronson, Merryman. 1. (2009). See Baby Discriminate. Newsweek.com: www.newsweek.com/2009/09/04/see-baby-discriminate.html.

Dau, M. (2009). September 23, S. Grainger Interviewer.

Enzensberger, H. M. (2010). Xplore Inc BrainyQuote.com: www.brainyquote.com/quotes/authors/h/hans_magnus_enzensberger.html.

Frankl, V. E. (n.d.). Xplore Inc. BrainyQuote.com: www.brainyquote.com/quotes/authors/v/viktor_e_frankl.html.

Fullan, M. (2003). *The Moral Imperative of School Leadership*. Thousand Oaks: Corwin Press.

Plastow, B. (2011). February 13. S. Grainger, Interviewer.

Robinson, K. (2009). *The Element: How Finding Your Passion Changes Everything* New York: Viking.

Wikipedia (2010, October 12). *Classical Adlerian psychology*. Retrieved December 1, 2010, from Wikipedia, The Free Encyclopedia: en.wikipedia.org/wiki/Classical_Adlerian_psychology.

ABOUT THE AUTHOR

Sean Grainger is a teacher and school administrator in Alberta, Canada. He holds a Bachelor's Degree as an elementary generalist teacher, and a Master's Degree (Presidential Honours) in Leadership focusing on school counselling. Sean is in his seventeenth year of teaching, having worked with kids from first grade to high school on a broad educational spectrum. Sean believes there is always a better way, and that change is not an outcome; it's a process. He speaks from his personal perspective on the topics of resiliency and change, and also on behalf of the Alberta Teacher's Association Corps of Professional Development Instructors on a wide variety of educational topics and issues. He is a sitting member of the Alberta Teacher's Association's provincial Diversity, Equity and Human Rights Committee. Sean writes on his blog, KARE Givers at www.seangrainger.com. Sean lives with his wonderful wife Bina, and two children, Avery and Wyatt.

Index

About the Editor and Contributors

Shriya Adhikary is a student at Wheeling Jesuit University, double majoring in international studies and communications. Shirya immigrated to the United States from Nepal with her family in 1998, and since then has lived in Omaha, Chicago, and in Annandale, Virginia. She is the current news editor of her college newspaper and hopes to pursue a career in the field of international correspondence. Shirya is a firm believer in overcoming "impossibilities" and the idea that laughter is the best medicine.

Dr. Jioanna Carjuzaa is an associate professor of education at Montana State University-Bozeman. She holds a Ph.D. in multicultural, social and bilingual foundations of education from the University of Colorado-Boulder. She has over twenty years teaching experience as a multicultural teacher educator, diversity trainer, and English for academic purposes instructor. At MSU she teaches multiple sections of multicultural education in addition to offering graduate courses in social justice in education, indigenous research methodologies, American Indian studies for teachers, and Teaching EFL/ESL. Of Greek heritage, Jioanna is well aware of the challenges culturally and linguistically diverse students face when competing with native English speakers in demanding content courses. Jioanna is grateful to serve as the co-advisor to American Indian Council and has had the very enjoyable opportunity to team teach Powwow Leadership and Powwow Fundraising with Jim Burns numerous times. In addition, Jioanna serves as the facilitator for Indian Education for All professional development opportunities for MSU faculty, staff, and students. She resides in Montana with her husband Gilles and their two keeshonds, Lance and Arthur.

Debra Fulcher is an educational consultant for the Office for Children where she co-coordinates the School Readiness Teams in Fairfax County at eight elementary schools. As co-coordinator, Debra is involved in the creation of the collaborative model, as well as facilitating and documenting the work of the teams. Debra serves as the local coordinator for the Virginia Star Quality Initiative in the Fairfax Coalition. Debra is a part-time faculty member in the Gradate School of Education at George Mason University where she teaches early literacy and assessment and supervises interns working toward a Master's of Education and/or licensure in Pk-3. She serves as an advisor to early childhood education and special education graduate students. Debra worked for more than 30 years in Fairfax County Public Schools as an early childhood teacher and administrator. She served as the coordinator of the Early Childhood and Family Services department where she served as the director of Early Head Start in addition to developing early childhood curriculum, assessments and staff development for teachers and schools. Debra and her husband, Terry, live in Herndon where they raised their daughter, Lindsay and continue to remain active in the community.

Waliha Gani is a student at James Madison University, majoring in international affairs with a minor in Middle Eastern communities and migrations. Waliha is the current president of James Madison University's Muslim Student Association. Born in Rawalpindi, Pakistan, Waliha came to the United States at the age of eight in 1999, and she and her family have resided in Northern Virginia for the past 10 years. Waliha's ultimate goal in life is "To serve others."

Jesse Bethke Gomez is president of *Comunidades Latinas Unidas En Servicio* (CLUES), a leading provider of behavioral health and human services for Minnesota's Latino population and among the Top 25 Hispanic non-profit agencies in America (*Hispanic Business Magazine* 2007). Jesse's professional experience includes clinical system redesign for healthcare, business consultancy for international business, government, education, non-profit and private companies, advanced executive leadership development, international relations, health and human service administration, and fundraising, where he has raised over $50,000,000. Jesse is among the "100 Most Influential Healthcare Leaders in Minnesota" (MN Physicians Publication Sept, 2008), and the first Minnesota recipient of the Reconocimiento Ohtli Recognition from the country of Mexico (2006). He is a national Kellogg Fellow, an alumnus from the University of North Carolina–Chapel Hill as an Emerging Leader in Public Health, an alumnus from the Minnesota Executive Program for Advance Strategic Leadership from the Carlson School of Management,

University of Minnesota, and a Presidential Scholar Recipient from Elizabeth Dole, then president of the American National Red Cross. Jesse trained with international leaders Tor Dahl, chairman emeritus of the World Confederation of the Productivity Sciences, and Dr. Edwards Deming. He holds a Masters of Management and Administration degree from Metropolitan State University, where he was Alumnus of the Year in 2008, and a Bachelor of Arts degree from the University of Minnesota. He serves on the board of trustees of the University of Minnesota Amplatz Children's Hospital and has served on numerous boards of directors, including The Minneapolis Foundation and Blue Plus of Blue Cross and Blue Shield of Minnesota. Jesse also has composed and arranged a music score for orchestra entitled "Mi Vida Amor!" Jesse lives with his wife Raquel in Woodbury, Minnesota.

Sean Grainger is a teacher and school administrator in Alberta, Canada. He holds a Bachelor's Degree as an elementary generalist teacher, and a Master's Degree (Presidential Honours) in Leadership focusing on school counselling. Sean is in his seventeenth year of teaching, having worked with kids from first grade to high school on a broad educational spectrum. Sean believes there is always a better way, and that change is not an outcome; it's a process. He speaks from his personal perspective on the topics of resiliency and change, and also on behalf of the Alberta Teacher's Association Corps of Professional Development Instructors on a wide variety of educational topics and issues. He is a sitting member of the Alberta Teacher's Association's provincial Diversity, Equity and Human Rights Committee. Sean writes on his blog, KARE Givers at www.seangrainger.com. Sean lives with his wonderful wife Bina, and two children, Avery and Wyatt.

Young-chan Han immigrated to the United States from South Korea as a child with her family in 1973. Her career in education began in 1999 as an international student and family outreach specialist for the Howard County Public School System in Maryland. There, she worked closely with over 3000 immigrant families and refugees, developed a parent leadership institute for immigrant parents, and created services and programs benefiting immigrant students and families. In November 2007, Young-chan expanded her local focus to the state level where she currently works as a family involvement specialist for the Maryland State Department of Education providing leadership, coordination and assistance to local school systems and schools on programs, projects, and activities that promote family engagement in schools. In her spare time, Young-chan serves as the president on the board of directors for a local non-profit, FIRN (Foreign-born Information Referral Network), teaches kindergarten class and serves as a children's ministry advisor for her church. She lives with her husband of more than 25 years and three children in Columbia, Maryland.

Ashley Harris is the senior instructional coach at YES Prep Public Schools in Houston, Texas. Her primary responsibilities include developing novice teachers through one-on-one coaching and creating and facilitating sessions on instructional strategies. As the senior coach, Harris is also responsible for providing professional development opportunities for the other Instructional Coaches. Harris began her career as an assistant buyer at a major retailer in the D.C. area but quickly realized her heart was in education. After two years in the private sector, she returned to Houston and joined Teach For America. She taught in the Houston Independent School District for four years before joining YES Prep as an instructional coach in 2007. Harris graduated from The University of Texas at Austin in 2001 with a B.A. in Plan II Honors and a B.S. in Marketing. She holds a master's degree in curriculum and instruction from The University of Houston. She lives in Houston, Texas, with her husband and three children.

Dr. Amineh Ahmed Hoti obtained her PhD from the University of Cambridge. She was the co-founder and first-ever director of a major study Centre at Cambridge where she outlined a Cambridge University on-site course and taught an array of students, including imams and rabbis. She organized several major conferences involving distinguished personalities such as HRH Prince Hassan of Jordan and the Archbishop of Canterbury, who launched a book for schools. She has given media interviews on both international television and in major national papers. She was a member of the body that advises the UK government on Religious Education (SACRE). She is the consultant editor of *Valuing Diversity: Towards Mutual Respect and Understanding*, which is an important learning resource for secondary school teachers and students from 11-17+. This book has been distributed to about 2000 UK and international schools, as well as schools in Pakistan and the United States. Dr Hoti's book, *Sorrow and Joy Among Muslim Women*, published by Cambridge University Press (2006), was nominated for the 2007 Kiriyama Prize. She is a fellow-commoner at Lucy Cavendish College, University of Cambridge, executive director of the Society for Dialogue and Action, an advisor to the Three Faiths Forum and patron of charities aiming for peace and world solutions, such as the UK Friends of the Bereaved Families Forum. Dr. Hoti has currently returned to Pakistan with her family with the aim of introducing top-quality, cutting-edge education to take steps towards helping the women and children of South Asia.

Karyn Keenan is a second grade teacher at Passages Charter School in Chicago, Illinois. She has taught students from more than fifteen countries. Her passion is helping each of her students tell their unique stories. Karyn earned her B.A. in Elementary Education from DePauw University, as well as her certificate to teach English Language Learners through National Louis University. As a SMART Exemplary Educator, Karyn works to improve instruction through the use of an interactive whiteboard. Raised in Wilmington, Delaware, Karyn now lives in Chicago where sunny summer days at the beach outweigh the long winters.

Nardos E. King is the principal of Mount Vernon High School in Fairfax County, Virginia. In October 2007, she was honored as First-Year Principal of the Year in Fairfax County Public Schools. Nardos' career at Mount Vernon High School began in January of 1996 as the Finance Technician, then serving as an instructional assistant, teacher, administrative intern and sub-school principal until her appointment as principal in July 2006. She graduated from Virginia State with a B.S. in Business Information Systems. She holds a Master of Arts Degree in Special Education from George Washington University and a Masters of Education Degree in Educational Leadership from George Mason University. Nardos is currently working on her Doctorate Degree at Virginia Tech. Nardos and her husband Stan, a Lieutenant Colonel in the Army, are the proud parents of Chad and Tracy, both pursuing college degrees. She enjoys spending time with her family and friends, her book club and participating in community service through her sorority, Delta Sigma Theta, Inc.

Eileen Gale Kugler is a global speaker and consultant strengthening diverse schools, worksites, and communities. She breaks through dangerous *myth-perceptions* and shares strategies for building on the unique opportunities that diversity brings. Eileen is author of the award-winning *Debunking the Middle Class Myth: Why Diverse Schools are Good for All Kids*, which was called "a community and civic blueprint for the 21st Century." Eileen's articles and commentaries appear in wide-ranging publications, including *USA Today* and the *Washington Post, Educational Leadership, Phi Delta Kappan* and *Education Week*. She has been quoted in hundreds of publications and has been a broadcast guest on national and regional media. Her family's volunteer work in South Africa, including creating a 25,000-book library for a rural school, was featured in *The Washington Post* and on Voice of America television. Eileen lives with her husband Larry in Fairfax County, Virginia, where their two children grew up.

Sara Kugler is a reading teacher with Bailey's Elementary School for the Arts and Sciences in Fairfax County, Virginia. Prior to that, she was a literacy staff developer at the Reading and Writing Project at Teachers College, Columbia University, leading workshops on balanced literacy and critical literacy throughout New York City public schools as well as in Florida, Illinois, California, Minnesota, and Gothenburg, Sweden. She has taught in multiple elementary schools in Fairfax Country, Virginia, and in Brooklyn, New York, co-leading one school's Diversity Committee. Sara has also volunteered as a literacy staff developer in rural South Africa. She earned her master's degree in Reading and Writing Education from Teachers College, Columbia University. Sara lives with her husband and daughter in Fairfax County, Virginia.

Graciela Rosas is an ESL, biliteracy, and Spanish teacher at Pacific Beach Middle School, part of San Diego Unified School District. Ms. Rosas has earned an M.A. in education and a B.A. in political science, and is enrolled in the Administrative Credential program at San Diego State University. She has both a Multiple Subject and Single Subject Credential and has taught Kindergarten through eleventh grade. She has been an educator since 2006. Most importantly, she is a Mexican-American who was also a language learner, and she has found her calling and passion for helping struggling long-term English language learner students. She lives in San Diego with her son, Erizen, and her two dogs.

Jeff Scanlan is a primary (elementary) school teacher at Wellington Point State School in Redland City which is an outer suburban community of Greater Brisbane in the state of Queensland, Australia. Jeff has bachelor's degrees in arts, divinity and education and two master's degrees in education. He is also a trained school counselor. He has taught with the Education Department of Queensland for all but three of the last 42 years. He has a passion for including the whole family in the schooling of young people which he believes makes for a fuller education. Jeff lives in Redland City and is married to Christine. They have five adult children and four grandchildren.

Howie Schaffer is a vice president at Cook Ross Inc. He is a respected speaker, trainer, and facilitator on cutting-edge topics in diversity, inclusion, and cultural competency. For more than a decade, Howie served as the public outreach director at Public Education Network (PEN) in Washington, DC. He created and edited the award-winning PEN Weekly NewsBlast. Howie has an undergraduate degree in communications from Cornell University and a graduate degree in philosophy of education from Teacher's College at Columbia University. He is a proud husband and the father of two dazzling sons.

Roni Silverstein is principal of Fallsmead Elementary School in Montgomery County Public Schools (MCPS), Maryland. She recently returned to school-based leadership after serving as the director of elementary leadership development for MCPS, coaching and designing professional development for over 275 aspiring MCPS administrators. In that role, she developed the spiraling curricula for assistant principals that include race and equity, professional growth systems and evaluations, and Baldrige processes. Prior to joining the central office, Roni served as principal of Clopper Mill Elementary School in Germantown, Maryland, for four years. During her more than thirty years of education experience, she has also served as special education coordinator and teacher. Her professional experiences include developing and conducting needs assessments and designing and delivering targeted staff development to teachers, assistant principals, elementary and secondary principals, directors and central services administrators. In addition, Roni has redesigned and taught the data-driven decision making course for MCPS administrators, presented "Are You Data Rich and Analysis Poor?" at the National Staff Development Conference, and presented at the U.S. Department of Education Office of English Language Acquisition (OELA) Summit V, "Turn Data into Knowledge, Knowledge into Action." Roni and her husband Robert live in Montgomery County where they raised their three children.

Andrea Sobel, Ed.D. is an educational consultant and co-director of National Educational Consulting Services, LLC. Andrea consults with Office for Children where she co-coordinates the School Readiness Teams in eight school communities in Fairfax, Virginia, Andrea is involved in the creation of the collaborative model, as well as facilitating and documenting the work of the teams. Andrea is a part-time faculty member in the Graduate School of Education at George Mason University where she teaches curriculum, assessment and family courses for early childhood and early childhood special education candidates. She coordinates the field-based university support for the *Teach for America* early childhood cohort through George Mason. Andrea serves as a "master trainer" for the state of Virginia's Quality Initiative. She trains raters and mentors around the state in the quality improvement system. Finally, Andrea continues to provide professional development training in the Washington DC metro area that supports the creation of high-quality programs with an emphasis on enhancing diverse learning communities and promoting strong, effective family-school partnerships. Andrea currently lives in Annandale, Virginia, with her husband Mike, where they raised their two children, Gina and Eric.

Stacie Stanley is an elementary school principal in a suburban school district just outside of St. Paul, Minnesota. Stacie has earned an M.A. in Education, a postgraduate certificate in K-12 administration and recently is working on her dissertation to complete her doctorate degree. She has served in a variety of education roles including that of teacher, math specialist, curriculum and staff development specialist, and integration and equity program director. She also serves as an adjunct faculty member at Hamline University. Stacie's African-American heritage fuels her fervor for educational equity. She currently lives in the Twin Cities with her husband and college-age children.